TRUE GHOST STORIES

DR. FRANCIS EDWARDS
A child's friendship with the ghost of her Great-Grandfather

TRUE GHOST STORIES

Marchioness Townshend of Raynham
&
Maude M. C. ffoulkes

KONECKY&KONECKY

Konecky & Konecky
72 Ayers Point Rd.
Old Saybrook, CT 06475

10 digit ISBN: 1-56852-745-4
13 digit ISBN: 978-1-56852-745-1

TO ALL THOSE WHO HAVE
FALLEN FOR THE LURE OF
THE SUPERNATURAL

ACKNOWLEDGMENT

THE Marchioness Townshend of Raynham and Maude M. C. ffoulkes beg to thank the following for their courtesy in allowing them to make use of certain matter contained in this volume :
The Rev. Archdeacon St. John D. Seymour, B.D., Litt.D., Miss Estelle Stead, Messrs. George Allen, the Editor of the *Daily Mail*, the Editor of the *Wide World Magazine*, the Society for Psychical Research, and Messrs. Hurst and Blackett. Also to H. Eyre, Esq., Manager at Messrs. Jerome's, Bovay Place, Holloway, for his personal attention in making the photographic reproductions used as illustrations.
Mrs. ffoulkes wishes especially to acknowledge the kindness of the Directors of Chiswick Products, Ltd., who allowed her access to Boston House, and to Maurice Kelly, Esq., for his interest and assistance.

COLLABORATORS' NOTE

These true Ghost Stories of All Nations comprise only the best authentic psychic manifestations. The majority of them have never been published, and are first hand personal experiences. They are told somewhat in narrative form, as being more picturesque and interesting, whilst leaving the *facts untouched* by imagination, or embellishing them with any description of ultra "pen" painting.

> I merely mean to say what Johnson said,
>   That in the course of some six thousand years,
> All nations have believed that from the dead,
>   A visitant at intervals appears ;
> And, what is strangest, upon this strange head,
>   Is that, whatever bar the reason rears
> 'Gainst such belief, there's something stronger still
>   In its behalf, let those deny, who will.
>   BYRON.

CONTENTS

PAGE

ACKNOWLEDGEMENT vii

COLLABORATORS' NOTE viii

LIST OF ILLUSTRATIONS xiii

INTRODUCTION xv
By Dr. Nandor Fodor, LL.D.

THE GHOSTS OF RAYNHAM HALL 19
By Gwladys Townshend of Raynham

THE STORY OF SARAH FLETCHER AND EDWARD CRAKE . 27
By Maude M. C. ffoulkes

THE HAUNTINGS AT ASH MANOR, ASH GREEN, NEAR
GUILDFORD 41
By Maude M. C. ffoulkes

DANGEROUS HILL 59
By Gwladys Townshend of Raynham

TO FETCH HIM AWAY 67
By Maude M. C. ffoulkes

GRAVE NO. —, KENSAL GREEN 77
By Maude M. C. ffoulkes

A CHILD'S FRIENDSHIP WITH THE GHOST OF HER
GREAT-GRANDFATHER 83
*By Dr. Francis Edwards, M.D.Brux, M.R.C.P.
Lond., M.R.C.S.Eng.*

THE LOVER AND THE BEAM 89
By Anne, Lady Selsdon

THE CASTLE WITH SEVEN STAIRCASES . . . 97
By Anne, Lady Selsdon

PAGE

TWO GHOSTS I HAVE SEEN 101
By Winifred Graham

MRS. GRAHAM'S GHOST STORY 105

THE GHOST OF LADY BOSTON AT CHISWICK AND SOME
OTHER HAUNTED HOUSES 109
By Maude M. C. ffoulkes

THE GHOSTLY MONKS AT BILSINGTON PRIORY . . 117
By Mrs. Joseph Conrad

THE RETURN OF RUPERT BROOKE 121
By Dr. A. I. Copeland

SOME TRUE ITALIAN GHOST STORIES 123
By Signor Arno Monducci
Miss Mary Boyle's Experience

A HAUNTED COTTAGE IN MAYFAIR 133
By Maude M. C. ffoulkes

THE CAPTAIN'S RETURN 141
By Mr. T. Macfadden

SOME GHOST STORIES FROM INDIA 145

TWO IRISH GHOST STORIES 155
By courtesy of the Rev. Archdeacon St. John D.
Seymour, B.D., Litt.D.

TWO GHOST STORIES FROM AMERICA 169
By Maude M. C. ffoulkes and Miss Estelle Stead

SOME CLERICAL GHOST STORIES 181
By courtesy of Miss Estelle Stead

JASMIN 191
Contributed by Mr. Aslett Baldwin, F.R.C.S.,
and narrated by Gwladys Townshend of Raynham

THREE GHOST STORIES 199
By H.H. Princess Marina Chavchavadze

THE GHOST AT HUNSTANTON HALL 211
By Gwladys Townshend of Raynham

CONTENTS

PAGE

WHERE DID SHE COME FROM ? 217
   By Sir Ernest Bennett, M.P.

THE MAN IN THE IRON CAGE 223
   Lady Pennyman's Experience at Lille

TRUE STORIES OF ANIMAL GHOSTS 231
   By Miss Thessel Cochrane and Maude M. C. ffoulkes

THE SWEET SPIRIT OF GORDON KNIGHT . . . 247
   By Miss Estelle Stead

TWO GHOST STORIES OF ST. ALBANS 253
   By Mrs. Butt

QUAKER'S BURYING-GROUND 259
   By Miss Grace Webb

THREE GHOST STORIES 263
   By The Hon. Mrs. Greville Nugent

MY TWO MEETINGS WITH THE GHOST OF A DEAD
MAN ON THE FOLKESTONE ROAD 271
   By Maude M. C. ffoulkes

THE FARRIER OF SABLON 279
   Vouched for by the Duc de St. Simon

LIST OF ILLUSTRATIONS

Dr. Francis Edwards . . . . *Frontispiece*

PAGE

Raynham Hall 22

Where the brown lady walks at Raynham Hall . 23

The haunted picture-gallery, Raynham Hall . . 23

Sarah Fletcher 32

The grave of the Reverend Edward Crake in
Tevington churchyard 33

The graves of the Reverend Edward Crake, his
wife, and only son 33

Ash Manor, near Guildford 48

Mr. C. F. Miller, who saw the ghost several times . 48

The ghostly materialization at Ash Manor . . 48

Dame Armine Le Strange 49

Nicholas Le Strange (the jolly gentleman) . . 49

St. Albans, Hampton-on-Thames . . . 106

The haunted magnolia tree at St. Albans . . 106

Boston House, Chiswick 107

Bilsington Priory 117

The Old Vicarage, Grantchester 118

The exterior of the late Rupert Brooke's sitting-
room at the Old Vicarage 118

The ruined tower of Cannacio, showing the opening
through which the ghostly hounds come and go 126

The haunted cottage 127

The late Mrs. Brownlow and the Maltese dog who
"returned" 232

Villish Mona Veen 232

Fairy Flax 232

The late Alfred Louis 233

INTRODUCTION

By Dr. Nandor Fodor, LL.D.

(Head of the International Institute for Psychical Research)

THE reader will find some very remarkable ghost stories in this collection by the Marchioness Townshend of Raynham and Maude ffoulkes. From the evidential point of view, "To Fetch Him Away" appeals to me most. The old servant may have embellished and dramatized the elements of the story, but the essential details stand out clear and are very well attested. "Meeting cases" (the dead calling for the dying) are, of course, well known in psychical research. They form the most puzzling class of psychic manifestations and offer the best presumption for continued existence of the dead. For the dying, as a rule, the existence is one of surprise and joy. In no cases have I seen the sinister touch which the persistent calling of little Alfred and William on cruel John Craven shows.

Fresh thrills even to the most inured creep-addicts will be found in "Grave No. —— Kensal Green", and in "The Lover and the Beam". The stories are convincingly told and illustrate the two main types of ghostly manifestations : the mechanical and the intellectual. The first type indicates the persistent survival of great mental agonies and their periodical projection as a kind of film on an etheric screen. The acceptance of such emotional detritus absolves from the consideration of survival. The second type implies direct discarnate action : the return of the dead, their appearance in the body, or in a vision caused by their thoughts or dreams.

That the dead should dream is a strange idea. Still stranger that they should suffer from nightmares and that we should be able to see these nightmares in scenic presentation. We know that dreams are pictorial. Perhaps, thoughts are also things. And it may be comforting to know that when a murder is daily re-enacted in the haunted house, the unfortunate victim only exists in the murderer's dream. This leads straight back to Wonderland, where Alice hesitates to wake up the King of Hearts because she only exists in his dream, and out she would go as soon as he woke.

It is by following the same idea that spiritualists claim to cure haunted houses. By the help of a medium and spirits communicating through him, they try to wake up the dead. When the dead wake the nightmare goes and the house is cleared. Unfortunately, in practice, the problem is not so simple as it sounds in theory. But it is important to know that in some cases, at least, the effort is followed by success.

I often wonder what the other side of the picture of haunting is in Ghost Land? Is it the dead alone that can disturb the living, or can the living similarly disturb the dead?

Suppose a murder was committed in a house and the house is afterwards pulled down. Spiritualists will claim that a mental counterpart of the house survives. (Ghosts often enter through walled-in doors.) If the murderer, while yet on this earth, is seized with remorse and self-torture, will his state of mind produce a haunted house in the spirit world?

I am not submitting this query in a spirit of fun. If there is a spiritual world, it is quite possible that our influence on it is far greater than we suspect. The living see sometimes phantoms of the dead. Are we sure that the dead do not see our apparitions when we are in a great mental agony? Isn't the claim that inspiration comes from the spirit world a little onesided? May not our brilliant minds unknowingly inspire hosts of less developed spirits? In other words, if there are two worlds, aren't they in constant interaction? Perhaps the motive behind the overwhelming interest which, as we are told in Spiritualism, spirit guides, teachers, and groups of higher spirits take in our advancement, is one of mutual elevation ; perhaps it is necessary to strike a balance between the two worlds, to thin the barrier both for their own good and ours.

Such flights of fancy may not be out of place in a book on ghosts, the contents of which are certain to give an unusual stimulus to the reader's imagination.

LONDON,
August 1, 1936.

TRUE GHOST STORIES

THE GHOSTS OF RAYNHAM HALL

SOME AUTHENTIC STORIES OF SUPERNATURAL OCCURRENCES IN NORFOLK

By Gwladys Townshend of Raynham

I HAVE said in my recently published volume of *Recollections*, that whilst accepting Dr. Johnson's opinion of ghostly returns, as "all argument is against it, but all belief is for it", I must confess that I believe in ghosts, and I have lived for many years in a definitely haunted house.

Raynham Hall, known throughout Norfolk as the Great House, the home of the Townshends for successive generations, is haunted not only by the historic Brown Lady (mentioned in all important literature on the subject of the supernatural) but also by a tragic Duke and the harmless phantoms of animals and children.

Place aux Dames—so I will take my readers with me to Raynham, and introduce them to Dorothy Walpole, better known as the Brown Lady.

Dorothy Walpole, the sister of Sir Robert Walpole, married the second Viscount Townshend, but the marriage was an unhappy one, and Dorothy's sole interests in life were centred in her children, who remained at Raynham in charge of their grandmother, their mother for some reason having been deprived of any share in their upbringing.

The Viscountess is said to have been a charming, frivolous creature, with a pardonable love of pretty clothes, judging from a lengthy bill for chiffons which is kept amongst our family papers. Her husband may have resented her extravagance, but he did not advertise the fact, and,

as no breath of scandal was associated with her name, I
suppose one may assume that, in colloquial terms, Lord and
Lady Townshend "didn't hit it off".

An amazing story has always persisted, and still persists,
in connection with Dorothy Walpole, who, according to
tradition, was starved to death at Raynham Hall. In the
seventeenth century, enforced starvation in surroundings
like those of Raynham Hall would have been impossible,
unless Lady Townshend had staged a hunger strike of such
magnitude that she died from it ; and, with such an important brother as Sir Robert Walpole living close by she
could not have been "removed" in this manner. Had
Dorothy Walpole lived when knights were bold, and
oubliettes, and torture dungeons part of the daily round,
starvation would not only have been possible, but highly
probable.

I have accepted the story of starvation as being sym-
bolical of Dorothy Walpole's tragedy of starved affections,
which always represents such a terrible death-in-life. However, the unhappy wife and mother has now become the
Family Ghost, and, as the Brown Lady, she chiefly confines
her appearances to the principal staircase and some of the
corridors at Raynham Hall.

One of the best authenticated stories of her appearance
was in 1849, when a large house-party met at Raynham as
the guests of Lord Charles Townshend, who then owned
the Great House—amongst them, Major and Mrs. Loftus,
near relatives of the Townshends.

Major Loftus, who had no use for the early-to-bed
régime, preferred to interpret early as a.m. and not p.m.,
sharing Tom Moore's belief that "the very best way to
lengthen the day, is to steal a bit from the night, me dear",
and one particular dawn, when he was making his way
upstairs after an all-night sitting, the friend who was with
him drew his attention to a lady wearing a brown silk dress,
standing on the landing.

Ladies in early Victorian days were not in the habit of
waiting up in the small hours, except to give their husbands
curtain lectures, and as Major Loftus did not "belong" to

this lady, he was naturally puzzled as to her identity; but when he hailed her, the Lady in the Brown Silk Dress vanished !

The next night, Major Loftus sat up to watch for the mysterious lady, who in due course made her appearance; and the Major, who was familiar with the geography of the Great House, determined to waylay her, cut off her retreat, and come face to face with her in a side passage. His plan succeeded—and he encountered a handsome woman, dressed in brown—but, to his horror, two empty sockets represented the place where the eyes should have been.

The Major, who was able to see the ghost quite plainly by means of the lamp he was carrying, was so much impressed that, before meeting the house-party at breakfast, he made an excellent sketch of the Brown Lady and passed it round in corroboration of his adventure, which inspired the guests to sit up night after night, facing the haunted staircase, hoping to see the ghost, who obstinately refused to show herself.

Unfortunately, when the story of the Brown Lady was thoroughly assimilated in the servants' hall, the entire staff gave notice; and although Lord Charles Townshend declared the ghost had appeared to him more than once in his bedroom, and the servant exodus having destroyed for the moment the amenities of life, he became suspicious that the Brown Lady was in the nature of some distasteful practical joke. He determined to find out things for himself, and he replaced his missing servants by a capable staff of detectives, who remained at Raynham for months on end without obtaining the smallest clue, either to the ghost or to the instigator of the suspected trickery, the case of the Brown Lady proving as elusive as any modern unsolved police mystery.

The Brown Lady continues to haunt Raynham, and she was seen quite recently by my brother-in-law's (Mr. James Durham) sister, Mrs. Cyril Fitzroy, and her daughter, who, not being unduly troubled with flights of imagination, are reliable witnesses as to the actual existence of the family ghost. Her last but one appearance was to no less a person than my son George, when, as a small boy, he and Walter Rothermell, a little American friend, met a lady on the staircase who not only frightened, but puzzled them, because, as George said, they could see the stairs *through* her.

Captain Marryat, known to an earlier generation as a writer of adventure stories, was not so kindly or "artistically" disposed towards the Brown Lady as Major Loftus had been, so, when she appeared in the semi-twilight of one of the corridors at Raynham, he discharged his pistol full in her face, whereupon she vanished, and the bullet found its billet in the door behind her.

During the remainder of his visit Captain Marryat always slept with loaded pistols under his pillow.

About twelve years ago, when Sir Henry Birkin (better known as "Tim" Birkin) rented the shooting at Raynham, he sat up especially to wait for the Brown Lady, and, like Captain Marryat, he was disposed to shoot at sight. But he waited in vain, although the dog who shared "Tim's" watch on the stairs showed signs of terror and uneasiness in the small hours.*

The Monmouth Room at Raynham (so called on account of the ill-fated Duke of Monmouth having slept there when he stayed at the Great House with his royal father) is haunted by the ghost of the Duke, who appears not as a Rosenkavalier, but as a Red Cavalier, and he once enacted the role of a ghostly "Scout", as he certainly did one good deed on this especial night.

At one of my house-parties the Monmouth Room was occupied by the loveliest débutante of her year, who begged to sleep there, as she wanted, beyond all things, to meet the Red Cavalier. The phantom of the Duke did *not* materialize, so I suppose that ghosts are amongst those

---

* On June 3, 1918, the Rev. W. P. M. M'Lean, Rector of West Raynham, wrote to the Rev. Charles L. Tweedale, Vicar of Weston, Otley:

"I remember fourteen or fifteen years ago, a guest staying at the Hall told me that he was convinced that he saw this Brown Lady one evening, and I have heard that the children of the people in the Hall—years ago—asked who the brown lady was who came into their room frequently."

RAYNHAM HALL

THE HAUNTED PICTURE GALLERY,
RAYNHAM HALL.

Where the Brown Lady walks at Raynham Hall.
Inset : The ghostly children

who can't be "druv", and in consequence the "lovely" drew a blank.

The next person to sleep in the Monmouth Room, two days after the "deb's" departure, was a connection of the Townshends, a spinster of uncertain age, destined by Fate to lead one of those small smothered lives devoid of romance and its possibilities.

Nevertheless, it fell to her lot to experience one glamorous night, when she suddenly awoke to see the Red Cavalier standing at the foot of her bed, smiling in a most encouraging manner. She told us afterwards that she was not in the least frightened, only happily interested ; and when, as befitted a courtier, the Duke paid her the homage due to a Princess of the Blood, and bowed himself out into the shadows of the opposite wall, he became the happiest memory of a drab lifetime.

It was a *beau geste*, worthy of the son of the Merry Monarch, who, if he never said anything wise, at least was consistently charming to women.

There are two ghosts of children at Raynham ; one of them haunts a room known as the Stone Parlour, and she was first seen (although I believe often previously heard) by Miss Baumer, my German governess, who I asked to act as hostess one day during my Mayoralty at King's Lynn (where I was due to open a bazaar), and receive Lady Norah Bentinck, her two little children, and the Dowager Countess of Gainsborough, who were coming on a visit to Raynham.

The visitors were welcomed by Miss Baumer, who presently said to Lady Norah : "I thought you were only bringing *two* children, but I see there are *three*. Is the other child sleeping with Biddy, and, by-the-by, wherever has she got to ?"

"*What* other child ?" asked Lady Norah. "There are only Biddy and Henry ; I don't know what you mean by *three* children."

Miss Baumer explained that when Lady Norah and the children got out of the car, a little girl wearing (so she described it) a "picture" frock, went with them up the

steps leading to the entrance, and ran through the hall into
the Stone Parlour.

"It was impossible for me to be mistaken," she added.
She always insisted that Biddy and Henry must have been
accompanied by the Townshend child, who still loves the
Stone Parlour for the sake of its earthly associations ; and
I wonder whether the ghostly spaniel which haunts Raynham belonged to these phantoms from the past ? It would
be joyous to think that Raynham was still a garrison of
smiling children, and that for evermore the tune of little
feet will be heard along the floors trodden by so many generations of the Townshends.

The ghostly spaniel is not seen, although it makes its
presence felt. One late afternoon in October 1935, Maude
ffoulkes, who was staying with me, went up to her room
by one of the doors opening on to a small vestibule leading
to the principal staircase.

Directly Mrs. ffoulkes closed the door, she heard the
pitter-patter of feet beside her, but thinking it was my
son's dog Rex, she took no notice, and, as the staircase was
unlit, she could not see anything definite. However, when
she stooped to pat "Rex", she discovered there was *no* dog,
and, taking her courage in both hands, she ran back into
the Marble Hall, where she saw Rex and his friend Rip
sleeping in front of the fire.

I may add that Maude ffoulkes had never heard about
the ghostly spaniel, so her evidence is entirely unprejudiced,
but she confessed that after this she was always a little
nervous of what she might meet on the staircase associated
with so many "returns" from the Invisible World.

Apart from the appearance of the Brown Lady, the death
of a Townshend is heralded by various portents usually
associated with historic houses.

Shortly before my mother-in-law, the Dowager Marchioness, became seriously ill at her house at Gloucester, I
gave a party at Raynham, and Miss Baumer, who had been
helping with the arrangements, noticed a tall fair woman,
wearing a flowing pink dress, coming out of my bedroom,
holding her handkerchief to her eyes,

Seeing her evident distress, kind Miss Baumer hastened
to ask me whether any guest had arrived after dinner, and
if there had been any contretemps—hence these tears. I
told her no . . . and we decided that what she had seen
must be in the nature of a warning.

This proved correct ; the Dowager died before many
weeks had passed, and my sister-in-law, Lady Agnes
Durham, tells me that previous to the death of her father,
the fifth Marquis, when Raynham Hall happened to be let,
the tenants were awakened by hearing the footsteps of many
people passing up and down the staircase, and when they
proceeded to investigate, waves of blackness alone flowed
past them, and there was not a sign or sound of anything
or anybody. The same thing happened on the following
night, and next morning, news arrived that Lord Townshend had died in Paris about the time when the disturbances
occurred.

Some kind of sympathy must exist between the Townshend family and the world of ghosts, as when Lord George
Osborne, the second son of the then Duchess of Leeds
(née Lady Charlotte Townshend), was killed at Oxford in
1831, Mrs. George Portal, Lady Anne Townshend's niece,
saw George Osborne pass through the room where she was
sitting. Mrs. Portal spoke to him, but he did not answer, and
the servants declared that neither Lord George, nor anyone
answering to his description, had entered the house. But on
the morrow word came of the fatal accident which Lord
George had met with at the moment when he had been
seen by Mrs. Portal.

In the royal bedroom at Raynham, not far from the
saloon where the picture of the lovely Duchess of Leeds
gives additional beauty to her surroundings, it is quite
usual to find the heavy chairs, set overnight well against
the wall, arranged next morning round the large card-
table. Perhaps some of the gamblers who lost fortunes at
Raynham are permitted to indulge—not in a quiet rubber,
but in a more exciting game of chance.

The ghostly card-players remind me of other occurrences, when strange noises are heard on *the* landing, and

whisperings and the swish of skirts testify that the picture gallery is alive with the "Quality" who ruffled it in the days when the splendour of the Great House was undiminished.

The Hon. Mrs. Yorke Bevan, who often comes to Raynham, and occupies the room above mine, once told me that she was sure some of the servants held secret "revels" in the vicinity of her room. "I think you should speak to them," said she; "such things ought not to go on; I hear noises coming from the room next to mine quite late at night."

The room adjacent is a bathroom, giving immediately on to the roof, and, once on the roof, there is no other way in, or out, so it was evident that ghosts, and not servants, were responsible for disturbing Mrs. Bevan's slumbers.

An infinitely more peaceful psychic manifestation is associated with the little oratory which I instituted at Raynham in memory of Townshend. It has always been customary to burn incense on the anniversary of our return to the Great House, but we were once absent when the anniversary came round. However, at twilight, the sweetness of incense breathed a benediction over the Great House, pervading every nook and corner so noticeably that the housekeeper came running to see who had done this thing. However, the charcoal did not glow, and the spices remained lifeless—and she returned to her room no wiser than when she came, but always followed, she said, by the perfume of the non-existent incense.

THE STORY OF SARAH FLETCHER AND EDWARD CRAKE—SOMETIME VICAR OF JEVINGTON

Told by Maude M. C. ffoulkes

THE tragedy of Sarah Fletcher, one of the best authenticated English ghost stories, will appeal to romanticists who, in these days of modernity, possess the courage to acknowledge that they are still in love with love.

The beginning and the end are two graves; the dead beneath are as the poles apart, one of them sleeps in Dorchester Abbey Church, the other in a village God's acre hidden away in the grey-green breast of the South Downs. The country Vicar and the "Unfortunate Young Lady" never met in life, and their sentimental association represents the spiritual side of a romance which brought comfort to a gentle ghost, to whom rest and happiness were denied.

In the summer of 1913 I rented a cottage on a backwater of the Thames, not far from Dorchester, and one idle afternoon I went into the ancient Abbey Church. As I walked down the centre aisle my attention was riveted by a plain slab, with this amazing inscription :

> Reader !
> If thou hast a heart famed for Tenderness and Pity, Contemplate this Spot, In which are deposited the Remains of a Young Lady, whose artless Beauty, innocence of Mind, and gentle manners, once obtained her the Love and Esteem of all who knew her. But when nerves were too delicately spun to bear the rude Shakes and Jostlings which we meet with in this transitory World, Nature gave way; She sunk and died, a Martyr to Excessive Sensibility.

MRS. SARAH FLETCHER,

wife of Captain Fletcher, departed this life
at the Village of Clifton on the 7th of June
1799 in the 29th year of her age.

May her soul meet that Peace, in Heaven, which this earth
denied her.

Spellbound is the exact expression which describes my state of mind as I looked at this pathetic gravestone shorn of the turf and flowers which do so much to beautify mortality.

Who was Sarah Fletcher? What was her story?—and, as if in answer to my question, the dust of a hundred years blew against my face.

"Are you interested in our mysterious epitaph?"—and turning in the direction of the voice, I saw someone who might easily have been the living counterpart of the Black Bishop of Polchester Cathedral. "My name is Poyntz," said the Black Bishop, "and I am the Vicar of Dorchester; I wonder whether you would care to hear how Sarah Fletcher died?"

"As the epitaph says—a Martyr to Excessive Sensibility?"

"Yes, and no . . . Sarah Fletcher took her own life; but let's sit down, and I will tell you the whole story."

So, sitting in one of the ancient pews, with the afternoon sunlight sending arrows of light from the jewelled windows across the church, I listened to the ageless tragedy of a broken heart.

"In the last years of the eighteenth century," said Mr. Poyntz, "Sarah Fletcher, and her husband, Captain Fletcher (one of the Fletchers of Saltoun), lived at Clifton Hampden —not far from here. Captain Fletcher was in the Navy, and, following the popular traditions of the sea, he was not only inconstant but unfaithful. He actually proposed marriage to a wealthy heiress living some distance away, and he was on the point of committing bigamy when Mrs. Fletcher, warned at the last moment, had only just time to reach the church and stop the ceremony.

"It is not difficult to imagine the scene which followed.
. . . Captain Fletcher literally ran away, made for London,
and sailed for the East Indies, the unwedded bride returned
home with her parents, and Sarah Fletcher went back to
Clifton Hampden and hanged herself in her bedroom,
fastening her pocket-handkerchief to a piece of cord
which she fixed to the curtain-rod of her bedstead. A pitiful
story, isn't it ?"

"Yes—a *very* pitiful story—where did she live ? I
am so 'drawn' to Sarah Fletcher, it's just as if I'd always
known her. I felt this when I saw her grave."

"The house has always had the reputation of being
haunted," said Mr. Poyntz, "but, as it is now some kind of
an institution, perhaps poor Sarah's ghost no longer revisits
it. However, I will ask the owner of the property to allow
you to look over the place, and, at the same time, he may
be able to give you further particulars about Sarah Fletcher."

During the rest of that day, and most of the ensuing ones,
I was obsessed with Sarah Fletcher. . . . I asked myself
what had become of the innermost flame that burns when
all else is ashes—surely it existed somewhere today ?
I *knew* I had not heard the end of the story, even when the
Black Bishop told me that we were up against a dead wall,
as the owner of the house disapproved of my supernatural
yearnings, and refused to help me to discover new facts
about the forgotten tragedy. What could I do in the face
of such seigniorial opposition ? Mr. Poyntz was frankly
angry at what he called "churlishness"—then, an idea
struck him, and he exclaimed :

"The very thing ! Why didn't it strike me before ? I
had completely forgotten Edward Crake !" He explained
that a friend of his, the Rev. Edward Crake, now Vicar of
Jevington, near Eastbourne, had lived for many years in
Sarah Fletcher's house when it was a private school for
boys, kept by his parents. "I'll write to him at once," said
my friend, "and he can get in touch with you in London ;
in the meantime use a little tact, and try to get a glimpse
of the house for yourself."

I took Mr. Poyntz's advice, but I was disappointed

when I first saw the solid uninteresting Georgian mansion, three storeys in height, with a flat leaded roof, from whence previous occupiers had looked down upon the country through a network of trees.

Once admitted—the sense of familiarity with the dead became intensified, and, as I waited for someone to take me to the Matron, I distinctly saw a woman wearing a black cloak looking at me in the shadows of a passageway, whose white face and anguished eyes were crowned with a tangle of auburn curls intertwined with coloured ribbon . . . then "it" disappeared—and, feeling a thorough fraud, I interviewed the Matron as one solely interested in the welfare of girls—not ghosts. But although I put forth various "feelers", I could get no information about the supernatural.

"Yes . . . there *were* noises—but there were always noises in old houses."

"Wasn't there some story about the place ?"

Yes, she seemed to remember *something*. "However"—brightly—"I have so much to do that local gossip doesn't possess any interest for me."

After the front door closed behind me, I stood in the old carriage-way down which Sarah Fletcher had driven in haste on the morning when she discovered her husband's wickedness, and down which she was carried to her last resting-place in Dorchester Abbey Church. It was a strangely deserted environment, although today youth pulsated inside the house of so many sorrows. All around me was the bitter scent of evergreens, and no flowers flaunted their beauty against the burning blue of an August sky—but here existed one of those psychic mysteries that neither science nor religion are able to explain.

I described my impressions to Mr. Poyntz. "Do you believe in ghosts ?" I said.

"My answer shall be that of Madame du Deffand, 'No—but I am afraid of them'. However, Edward Crake is unshaken in the reality of his supernatural experiences—and what *he* does not know about Sarah Fletcher is not worth knowing."

A week afterwards I gave up the tenancy of my cottage and bade good-bye to the genial Black Bishop. Little did I think when he wished me well, and blessed me in my undertakings, that I should not meet him again on this side of Eternity—even then he was in the first stages of mortal illness. He was a very gallant gentleman, full of understanding, and his little world was the sadder because of his passing.

Back in London, I possessed my soul in patience for news from Jevington. Mr. Crake suggested lunch at the Berkeley, "afterwards we can discuss the matter which interests us both so deeply". In this way I discovered the truth, and nothing but the truth, about Sarah Fletcher, and heard the story of the romance between the quick and the dead.

On the surface, my new friend was the typical country parson, a quiet, unassuming man, possessed of a certain personality, although he was the last person whom one would have suspected of indulging in flights of sentimental imagination. I was to find out, however, that Mr. Crake did not *imagine* things, and he merely described what he had seen and felt to be true. As we sat in the drawing-room of my queer little swallow's-nest home, which in the past had already seen strange happenings, I listened to the Vicar's story.

"My father was a schoolmaster," said Mr. Crake, "and when I was ten years old, his school outgrew the accommodation of the house in which we lived. So a friend, the non-resident lessee of a large house some eight miles away, made him an offer of this at the surprisingly low rental of twenty pounds a year.

"Owing to its eerie reputation the property had been neglected for years : the gardens were a wilderness, the stables and outbuildings in a ruinous condition, and the approach was a damp, muddy lane, often flooded in winter. The house in itself was sound, its walls were very thick, and my father took possession, in the face of assertions on every side that we should not stop there more than six months.

"Seven years passed, and I had arrived at the impressionable age of seventeen. . . . I was a healthy, normal boy, and, as my father had strictly forbidden any gossip likely to prejudice the school, I knew nothing about the tragedy of Sarah Fletcher until the night when she made her presence known, and—let me frankly confess it—I fell in love with her. I have been blest in my marriage, Mrs. ffoulkes, no man more so, but the memory of the other remains in the secret chamber of my heart . . . where it will exist till I die—just as Sarah's personality will never leave the place where she lived out her life. Hasn't someone said that Tragedy is always a more tragic thing when it is brought upon oneself by one's own act—how true it has been in this particular instance !

"One moonlight night I lay awake in my bedroom, which opened out of a large room known as the 'Lower Room', when I heard steps, which awakened subconscious recollections, descending the stairs. The door opened, and the unseen walker entered—hesitated, and went out—I lay curious and speculative, until the sound of the church clock striking three set the air vibrating—but, as I heard nothing more, I turned over and went to sleep.

"The next night the same thing happened : I felt there must be something uncommon about these footsteps, so on the following night I determined to lie in bed with my door open and see for myself *what* or *who* came down the stairs. I had not long to wait—the footsteps of *someone wearing high-heeled shoes* came into the room towards my bed . . . then retreated. I sprang up, and ran into the long corridor—as bright as day in white radiance of the moon.

"Then—*she* was made manifest, and I saw Sarah Fletcher standing by one of the long windows. She seemed tremendously alive. There was nothing "dead' about her; her eyes were full of tears, she had come from the edge of the world, and from soundless space, to seek my love and pity."

"I wonder if she looked as she did when I saw her ?" I said.

Mr. Crake turned sharply. "Have *you* seen Sarah Fletcher ?"

SARAH FLETCHER
From a drawing by Mrs. Margaret Moffatt
The story of Sarah Fletcher and Edward Crake

THE GRAVE OF THE REVEREND EDWARD CRAKE IN
TEVINGTON CHURCHYARD
(*Above*) THE GRAVES OF THE REVEREND EDWARD CRAKE,
HIS WIFE, AND ONLY SON

The story of Sarah Fletcher and Edward Crake

I nodded. . . . "What did she look like ?" I asked.

"She wore a black silk cloak, fashionable at that period for protecting ladies dresses from the dust of the roads . . . she was hatless, and her hair was twined about with a purple-red ribbon, most probably as on the morning when she rushed across the countryside, broken-hearted and desperate. I was not in the least frightened. I wanted to help her, to befriend her—then all at once a patch of moonlight alone marked the place where she had stood.

"The next day, when I cautiously communicated my experience to one of the assistant masters, I found I had stumbled on everybody's secret—that, at a quarter to three each morning, restless footsteps wandered from the room in which Sarah Fletcher hanged herself to the bedroom in which I slept, but for some reason or other I had never been aware of them.

"My friend said that, once, as he was going upstairs, he met the steps coming down, and felt a cold wind pass him (a quite understandable phenomena, cold being an invariable feature of psychic manifestations), whilst my younger brother, no longer tongue-tied, related that he, like many others, had heard the phantom footsteps, but it had been tacitly agreed never to discuss them, because (more important than anything else) it would stir up trouble and 'make my father furious'.

"Curiosity, once aroused, is usually insatiable. I began to make inquiries in the village about Sarah Fletcher, and I was fortunate enough to meet with an old man named James, then between ninety and a hundred years of age, who remembered her 'artless beauty', and who told me details of her unhappy life. A search in an Oxford library yielded the information published in Jackson's *Oxford Journal* for Saturday June 15, 1799, which will interest you." And Mr. Crake gave me a paper on which was written in his neat, clerical handwriting :

On Saturday last, an inquest was taken at Clifton, in this county, before R. Buckland, Gent., one of His Majesty's Coroners, on the body of Mrs. Sarah Fletcher. The lady put an end to her existence by hanging herself with her pocket-handkerchief, which she fastened to a piece of small cord, and affixed it to the curtain-rod of the bedroom in which she usually slept. After a full investigation of the previous conduct of the deceased, and the derangement of her mind appearing very evident, as well as from many other circumstances, the jury without hesitation, found a verdict—Lunacy. The husband of this unfortunate lady is an officer in the Navy, and is now on his passage to the Indies.

"The truth was hushed up ?" I said.

"Yes, there was a conspiracy of silence—the body was buried in consecrated ground. Captain Fletcher was well away, the other woman and her family would naturally take the line of least resistance—but, nobody reckoned with the earth-bound spirit irresistibly drawn back from the other side to haunt the scene of her destroyed illusions and her wasted affection.

"Having at last obtained some key to the mystery," continued Mr. Crake, "I asked my friend to sit up with me all night in his little room, which, it so happened, had been partitioned off from the bedroom once occupied by Sarah Fletcher, and strange to say, our vigil took place on the very anniversary of the fatal day—or, rather, night.

"The evening dragged heavily; we read, played draughts, but all was quiet until the June dawn made itself dimly seen through the window-curtains. . . . It was a quarter to three, and as we sat looking at our watches, we heard footsteps behind the thin partition . . the footsteps went down a little passage, and then passed our door.

"We both jumped up and looked out. The passage was fairly well lighted and I distinctly heard the unseen wanderer from the beyond going along it as we followed a few paces behind. The steps reached the staircase and began to descend the stairs : we looked over the balustrade, but at that juncture my friend's courage gave out, and I went down the flight of stairs alone.

"Midway was a landing, and a succession of short stairs, ending in front of a window ; on the right hand was the door of a lower room. Between the dawn on the one hand, and the moon on the other, I saw Her again. This time she smiled at me, and her face had lost something of its tragic intensity; she turned the handle of the door—opened it, and I ran towards her . . . she was so 'real' that I could not believe I was in the presence of someone dead in the body for many years. 'Speak to me,' I begged, *'please, please*, speak to me'. . . . But the door closed in my face, and when I pushed it open—the room was empty, except for a few boys sleeping quietly, unconscious of the phantom which had passed by.

"I now knew my romance was beyond human agency, but its beauty and sadness appealed to my heart and to my imagination, and it constituted a bitter-sweet happiness. Sometimes I *saw* Sarah Fletcher, but I always sensed her 'nearness'. At times I felt I had only to turn my head to find her beside me, whilst the footsteps continued night after night.

"Occasionally a visitor staying with us would say to my father, 'You were very late last night, Mr. Crake.'

" 'No—I went to bed before twelve,' said my father.

" 'Well, I heard footsteps just before three o'clock, so I thought you must have had a late sitting.'

"Of course I said nothing . . . I *knew* whose footsteps they were! No man ever wore Sarah's little high-heeled shoes!

"Strangely enough, within a year the footsteps ceased . . . the atmosphere was more peaceful, and for ten years nothing untoward occurred. I suppose the lovely ghost knew that she was no longer destitute of sympathy, although she did not materialize as often as in the early days, but to me, Sarah Fletcher represented, and still represents, the Undying Romance of Youth. These ten years saw many changes. My father and mother had retired. My brother, now married, was Headmaster of the old school and I had been ordained, and was now Chaplain of a large school. Everything was apparently uneventful in our lives, when just before one Christmas holiday I received a letter from my brother asking me to come home.

" 'Do you remember the ghostly occurrences of ten years ago ? [he wrote]. They are worse than ever, and we want you to investigate them.'

"I returned to Clifton Hampden, wondering why Sarah Fletcher had suddenly become 'active'; did she wish to recall me—was she desirous for some sympathetic intercourse with one who pitied and loved her? I asked myself these questions a hundred times, but when I talked things over with my brother, I found that the present manifestations, whilst keeping to the same hour, were by no means confined to it. Some of the pupils declared that a woman occasionally came into their dormitory, and my sister, who was sharing Sarah's bedroom with a cousin, was awakened by finding her in hysterics, brought about by a 'presence' which had stood by her bedside—and disappeared. Our cousin knew nothing of the story, neither did the nurse who was sent for at my sister-in-law's confinement, and given the 'haunted' room, as being nearest to that of the invalid.

" 'Is it possible for me to have another room?' the nurse inquired, on the morning after her arrival.

" 'Why . . . aren't you comfortable?' asked my brother.

" 'Oh . . . never mind, it really doesn't matter, I'll try it again,' said the nurse, but the next day she declared she positively *must* sleep elsewhere, as every night someone came and threw himself, or herself, down on a non-existent bed and, when nurse struck a light, *no one was there*.

"All very disconcerting, wasn't it? For a day or two, I heard and sensed nothing, until one bitterly cold night when I was awakened by a succession of noises; of doors opening and footsteps in the passages; after these, frantic knockings sounded upon the ceiling beneath my room, and my bell rang so violently that each instant it and the wire threatened to part company.

"I put on a dressing-gown, and hurried down to my sister's bedroom.

" 'Poor L . . . is terrified,' said my other sister, who slept with her. 'Do go and see what the noises mean . . . are there burglars? Remember, except for the servants in the other wing, we three are alone in the house.'

" 'There are no burglars,' I assured them, 'but I'll go through the house to satisfy you.'

"It was a weird experience, for although I loved the unseen woman who now walked close beside me, I felt there were other evil entities at work, and I knew enough about such matters to understand that evil possession is often attended by horror and danger.

"Nevertheless, I examined every room in the house. By the way, have you ever noticed how *different* rooms seem at night, just as if they are given over to other people ? And at last I saw her again in the darkness and the oppressive stillness which saturated my soul. This time romance came to me by candlelight, and with my eyes held to hers, I saw once more the sweet perfection of Sarah Fletcher's beauty, and realized the pathos of a broken life. Here, at any rate, was no dark spirit of evil—and the abnormal extension of vision and perception granted me had been vouchsafed solely for Sarah Fletcher's good and my own happiness.

"I went back to my sisters and bade them trust in God, as nothing could harm them. But after I left them, I was awakened by a deafening crash outside my room, repeated three times.

"An idea inspired me. I was a priest . . . why not use the ancient form commanding spirits to depart in the name of the Father, Son, and Holy Ghost ? I did so, and quiet descended on the house of tragedy for the remainder of the night.

"My attempts at exorcism did not produce lasting results. From that night, until my relations left the house, it was the scene of many psychic disturbances, and once, when my brother was in London, my sister-in-law was awakened by sounds as if furniture removers were shifting furniture preparatory to removing it . . . she even heard bedsteads being taken down, and the iron laths placed on the floor. Terrified, she roused a visitor sleeping in an adjoining room, who had listened in astonishment to the uproar, wondering why the household was apparently occupied with moving preparations in the middle of the night !

"This occurrence was prophetic ; within a year, fever broke out in Clifton Hampden, and it extended to the school. So my brother, wearied alike of illness and the terrors by night, moved the school, lock, stock, and barrel, to a town on the south coast."

"Was this the end of your romance ?" I said.

Mr. Crake smiled. "Actually, yes—definitely, no—since such a memory is unforgettable. As a scientific and absolutely true experience, I think it is unique, and I have placed the majority of the more prosaic facts on record with the Society for Psychical Research. The sentimental side I kept to myself, but your interest and appreciation have led me to tell you the part which Sarah Fletcher has played in my life. All the *facts* have been corroborated, and the assistant master who sat up with me on June 7, 1854, has furthermore stated officially that one night he saw a cloud-like shapeless mass when the muffled footsteps reached his bed, and he never forgot the feeling of horror which it aroused."

"Who lived in the house after your brother left ?"

"A succession of tenants occupied portions, and when two Balliol College men went to see it in 1885 it was divided into a couple of cottages. The door at the foot of the stairs was permanently closed, and the ante-room ceiling had been removed to give place to a new staircase. Our old cook and her husband lived in one part of the house, and I used to go there every year on a sentimental pilgrimage, but latterly I've discontinued doing so. After all," said the quiet little clergyman, "what do distance or places signify to the secret dreamer ? To quote H. G. Wells : 'This life too is a dream. Dreams within dreams, dreams containing dreams, until we come at last, maybe, to the Dreamer of all Dreams, the Being, who is all beings.'"

We bade each other *au revoir*, with the hope that any friendship created in mutual sympathy would be lasting. But hopes, like promises, are unreliable. We never met again—trouble overtook me, and temporarily overwhelmed me. Then came the upheaval of war ; the Vicar of Jevington died in the following year.

The Rev. Edward Crake's body lies in Jevington churchyard beside those of his wife and his only son. He had been Vicar of the parish for twenty-eight years, and, standing by his grave last March, I realized that there are indeed more things in heaven and earth than are dreamt of in our philosophy, and that one half of the world does not know how the other half lives !

It was a windless, sunless day, but the breath of spring was in the air; hosts of daffodils waved their green spears in cottage gardens and in the free stretches of meadowland patches of violets stained the hedgerows like spilt wine.

Jevington churchyard, so typical of this pastoral countryside, is as still as the Downs which enfold it. But it responds to the touch of the changing seasons—the sun shines, and the rain weeps for the dead, and the moon enshrouds them in silver. The "Artless Beauty" has no such kindly benediction. Heedless feet pass and repass daily over her head, and she sleeps in a tomb within a monument raised by pious hands to the glory of the God who alone understands the heart's bitterness and the frailties of His children.

The story of Sarah Fletcher, and the romance which she inspired, have remained hitherto unwritten, but I believe that in a beneficent and beautiful paradise she and the vicar have met again, and that his prayer and intercession have obtained for the beloved ghost "the peace which this earth denied her".

[Mrs. ffoulkes desires to acknowledge the courtesy of the Society for Psychical Research in allowing her to reproduce the original plan of the haunted house at the time of the Crakes' residence there, and also in permitting her to use the documentary evidence in their possession, which corroborates the late Rev. E. E. Crake's personal communications to her in 1913.]

THE HAUNTINGS AT ASH MANOR, ASH GREEN, near GUILDFORD

By Maude M. C. ffoulkes

THE facts are contributed by the owner of Ash Manor, Maurice Kelly, Esq., and corroborated by the statement of Mr. F. C. Miller of what occurred during his employment there in December 1935.

The story of Dr. Nandor Fodor and Maude ffoulkes' vigil at Ash on the night of July 19, 1936, when the latter saw the ghost at 4.30 a.m. near the Oast House, is exact in every detail.

The photographs of the haunted landing and of Mr. F. C. Miller are especially interesting in view of Mr. Miller's evidence. The photograph of Mr. Miller was taken standing on the trunk of a tree bridging part of an old quarry in the country—haunted by the ghosts of two men, who fought on this precarious footing and fell into the quarry below, where their skeletons were recently discovered.

I first had the pleasure of meeting Mr. Maurice Kelly in March 1936, and our acquaintance began on business lines, when I went to the wonderful offices in the Strand associated with the multiple interests of the well-known firm of which he is a member.

One thing usually leads up to another, and after I had told Mr. Kelly I was collaborating with the Marchioness Townshend in a volume of true ghost stories, he smiled and said :

"Do you *really* believe in ghosts ?"

"Absolutely. I don't think one can doubt their existence."

"Well, then, it may interest you to know I live in a haunted house, and until I saw what occurs there for *myself*, I should never have imagined that I could possibly believe in the supernatural. You'd never guess, from my appearance, profession, or environment, that I had really seen a ghost ?"

As Mr. Kelly sat facing me in his private office, he represented the best type of the intellectual business man—indeed, he might easily have passed for an Oxford don. He also gave me the impression of weighing his words well before speaking; but as the refined, clever face was that of a thinker whose brain reasoned, and did not dream, I was convinced he had spoken the truth when he said that he had seen a ghost and lived in a haunted house.

When Mr. Kelly bought the property in 1934, the owner did not give him the slightest hint that anything unusual existed, although, each time he inspected the house, he commented on the fact that the large bedroom at the extreme left of the Manor was always kept locked. However, he accepted the explanation that servants had previously slept there, and after they left, the unoccupied room had become a dump for unwanted furniture.

Mr. Kelly fell for the lovely place, with its wealth of old oak and its historical associations as a fortified monastery, built, so it is supposed, on the site of a Druidical temple. After the completion of the sale, he heard rumours that it would be difficult to get servants to come to, or to stop at, the Manor, but this was a foregone conclusion as it lies well away from dance-halls, cinemas, and shops. So, hoping that he and his wife would eventually meet with contented working domesticity, the Kellys came to live at Ash Manor in June 1934.

No wonder that this fired my imagination, although I listened to the story in the most prosaic surroundings. . . . The roaring sea of London life surrounded me, but the quiet voice of the speaker harmonized so well with his grave face, and his simple directness over facts which would have been easy to exaggerate or to embroider, convinced me of his good faith. I also heard how two professed "ghost layers" had come to Ash, and how the hauntings had increased, and not decreased, after their visit. Then Mr. Kelly said :

"The best thing will be for you to spend a week-end with us, and sample the supernatural for yourself. In the meantime I will send you a photograph taken at midnight on the haunted landing ; my own story of what I have seen at Ash ; and the 'deposition' of the ghost layers."

Our interesting interview happened in March, but a series of unexpected worries prevented my going to Ash. At the end of June, Mr. Kelly sent me his "statement", with that of the ghost layers, and invited me and Dr. Nandor Fodor to an all-night sitting at the end of July.

Here is Mr. Kelly's own story :

Ash Manor House,
Ash Green, Surrey.

The Manor House of Ash dates back to A.D. 1279. I first came to live there on June 28th, 1934. At that time I was not aware that there was any possibility of its being haunted, nor had any such thing ever occurred to me.

Nothing unusual occurred until early in November of that year, when there were quite unaccountable noises of tramping footsteps in the roof overhead, but we did not take much notice of that.

On the night of November 18th (a Sunday) I was suddenly awakened by three violent bangs on my door—I am a very heavy sleeper and not easily awakened. I thought that it was probably my wife (who sleeps at the other end of the house), so I got up and walked down to her room. There was nothing to be seen (and I wasn't even thinking of a ghost at that time), but my wife assured me that she had never even stirred from her bed, far less knocked at my door. I didn't think anything more of it, and went back to bed. Nothing more happened.

The next night exactly the same thing happened, except that there were *two* knocks instead of three. Again I saw nothing, and my wife assured me that she had not knocked. The next night (Tuesday) it happened again, but with *one* knock instead of two.

Again I went along to my wife's room and she assured
me that she had never moved. Laughingly I said to her:
"Well, if it is a ghost, he is going to be unlucky tomorrow
night, for I shall be away." (I was away the following night,
and until the Sunday (November 25th)). On that night I
went to bed as usual, but I felt somehow that all was not
well. The room was unnaturally cold, and there was something unpleasant about it. I decided therefore to remain
awake, and see what I could see.

I stayed awake until 3 a.m., and nothing happened at
all, so I went to sleep. (I should mention here that I left my
bedroom door open on this occasion.)

A short while after (I now know it to be at 3.35), I was
awakened by a violent banging on the door. I sat up in bed,
and saw standing in the door the figure of a little oldish
man, dressed in a green smock, very muddy breeches and
gaiters, and a slouch hat on his head, with a handkerchief
round his neck. He was not in the least transparent or
ghost-like, but appeared to be solid flesh and blood. That
being so, it never occurred to me that he was a ghost, but
I thought that a servant had carelessly left a door open, and
a tramp had walked in. I asked him who he was and what he
was doing there. There was no reply. I repeated my
question: again there was no reply. Then I got out of bed
and went for him, and ran *right through him* as I went to catch
hold of his shoulders. After that I think I fainted, for I do
not remember much more, but I eventually reached my
wife's bedroom. I did not tell her what I had seen—I was
too upset—but she saw that something had happened, and
went back along the passage to get some brandy for me.
When she arrived outside my bedroom door, she also saw
him standing there. She, too, thought he was a real man,
either a tramp or someone playing a practical joke, and she
hit at him with her clenched fist. The only result was that
her fist went right through him, and she barked it against
the wall.

I had *not yet* told her what I had seen, and the next
morning she described to me what she had seen, and it
exactly coincided.

I should perhaps have added that, when she got close up to him, it was possible to see that his throat was cut from ear to ear.

Since then he has been seen in, or near, the same place on various occasions by different people, but he never attempts to make any movement, or to do any harm. It sounds, I know, an extraordinary and unlikely story, but those are the facts to which I and others can testify.

On the advice of a member of the Council of the Society for Psychical Research, I had down two men who claim to be able to "lay ghosts". I attach a copy of their report on the subject, but would say that I do not place any faith in it, nor do I accept it all. Partly because, though I have searched every available record, I cannot trace anyone of the name mentioned, and also because they claimed, and still claim, that they have disposed of the matter, which is quite untrue, as it is still seen at intervals, and has been seen as recently as within the last fortnight.

MAURICE KELLY.

26.6.36.

I wonder whether the deposition of the gentlemen who tried to lay the ghost was written during a trance condition? According to Mr. Kelly, no record exists in the locality of any persons by the name of Henry Knowles, or Rose Cross, and if such a murder had taken place, it would surely have been remembered in the countryside, and handed down from father to son to successive generations, much in the same way that the murder of the sailor on the Devil's Punch Bowl has become a tradition of the Portsmouth Road.

Here is the deposition :

DEPOSITION OF THE GHOST LAYERS

The man's name is Henry Knowles. In this room (Miss Kelly's) slept a girl in the year 1819. She was a milkmaid. An itinerant cobbler and mender of harness (Henry Knowles) paid visits each three months to the farms in the

district, staying between two, three, and ten days, according
to the amount of work he found to do. Here he fell in love
with the milkmaid. She promised herself to Knowles. At
his next visit after the promise the girl told him that she
had not cared for him, but that she had just amused herself,
she, in the time that had elapsed, having herself fallen in
love with a gardener who had but lately come to this place.

Knowles left, and that night slept in a common lodging-
house at Guildford. There, after drinking a deal, he went to
bed cursing the girl, Rose Cross, and, ere sleeping, thoughts
of murder were in his heart. 'Twixt thoughts of murder and
the drink, he took his cobbler's knife and did end his incar-
nation by stabbing himself in the throat. Being almost out
of his body at the time, quickly did he leave his body, and
took the thoughts of vengeance with him.

He comes to the house each three months, always with
the idea of wreaking his vengeance on Rose Cross. When
seen, which betimes he hath been, it would be noted that
he were listening so as to make sure that they who slept in
the other rooms were asleep.

He always came in at the back entrance, which was
indicated by Mr. N.

One morning last July, Mr. Kelly rang me up and asked
me if I cared to come to Ash with Dr. Fodor on July 23.
"Did I care ?" I certainly *did*, and I knew I could count on
Dr. Fodor. But, remembering Mrs. Kelly's recent bad
health, I insisted there should be no "fuss", no preparing
a bedroom for me to rest in next morning. I'd just bring a
small attaché-case with first-aids to face repairs necessary
after a sleepless night. I'd change and "tub" when I got
back to town.

Sunday, July 23, must have been, to misquote Tenny-
son, the rainiest Sunday in all the rainiest year. Dr. Fodor
wished to reach Ash as late as possible, in order, so he said,
not to fill in the afternoon with small talk inimical to the
supernatural. At six o'clock, when I retrieved Dr. Fodor at
his flat, it was raining heavens hard, but we stowed him
away in the car, with various cameras, and suit-cases, more

or less comfortably, and started out on another (for me) great adventure. As yet, I had never had such an experience, but the old friend (through whose kindness Dr. Fodor and I were able to do the journey by car) was not at all surprised when I told him my destination was a haunted house. After going with me and Algernon Blackwood in the dead of night to wait for the eclipse of the sun in the heights above Clitheroe, and meeting Pan *en route*, nothing surprised him. He assumed that people who wrote books were "odd", and left it at that.

It still continued to rain. In places the road looked like the swimming pools which are advertised so largely out of London, cars couched Ariel-like under the trees, and motor-cyclists sought sanctuary beneath tarpaulins. Road-houses and childishly christened cafés were anything but inviting or gay—I wondered whether the serried lines of ideal homes were as damp as they looked, and, sad to confess it, I sighed for the unspoilt country of yesteryear.

At Guildford the rain ceased, and the long glistening road streaked upwards like a wet snake. As we ascended, fields and woods gradually spread themselves like a green map below us—in places rising earth mists met the mists of twilight—the breath of the rain was everywhere.

Presently we turned down a narrow side road, apparently going downhill all the way, occasionally meeting little groups returning from evening service. But when we inquired our way from some of the Church "returns", we were told that they hadn't any notion of the whereabouts of the Manor. Others somewhat unduly emphasized their ignorance. It is curious that country people, who usually know all there is to know about other people's private lives, are never able to tell you where they live.

All unknowingly, we were only five minutes' distant from the Manor, and we found out from a solitary hiker that if we turned in through a white gate lower down, we should find ourselves at the Manor.

A drive led through pasture meadows, and we came upon the ancient house, looking, in the semi-twilight, something like a crouching animal—we glimpsed a moat,

whilst a large oast-house of mellow rose-red bricks
lay on our right, separated from the garden by a low
wall.

Outside the entrance we were welcomed by Mr. Kelly,
who took us into what was once the monks' refectory
—now a lounge. A fire of logs burned on an open
hearth, and a pretty, fair-haired girl introduced herself as
Patricia Kelly. Behind her was Mrs. Kelly, the loveliest
woman I have ever seen. More than usually tall, her small
head with its blue-black hair framed an oval face as creamy
as a magnolia petal, and her unrelieved black gown served
as a sombre sheath for the weapon of her beauty. Her only
touch of colour was a little coronel of jade; she was the
last person one would have dreamed of finding in this hidden
place, tenanted by the strange terror that walked in darkness. One instinctively associated her with southern skies
and a *vie mouvementée*.

Mrs. Kelly is a niece of Maximilien Harden : her intelli-
gence equals her beauty. . . . There was no question of
"strangeness"—you felt you had known her mentally all
your life. At times she was reminiscent of Melusine, at
others her personality missed centuries, and she stood for
what Josephine Beauharnais might have been in the hey-
day of her charm.

I left Dr. Fodor and Mr. and Mrs. Kelly talking over
the best places for the special flashlight cameras, whilst
Patricia Kelly and I went into the gardens, "before it gets
too dark to see the water-lilies". And Patricia explained
that in one place where the ground rose slightly, a draw-
bridge had formerly existed, and at some time or other
one side of the moat had been filled in. But sufficient water
remained, she said, to make punting pleasant, and I was
introduced to the cluster of water-lilies waiting to open and
greet the night. "There are numbers of goldfish in the moat.
Father had it stocked with them, and in the daytime they
look just like flecks of moving gold."

I stopped outside the Oast House—there was something unusual about it, something watchful, people might
easily have met here and planned things—but *what*? I

ASH MANOR, NEAR GUILDFORD

(*Above*) MR. C. F. MILLER, WHO SAW THE GHOST SEVERAL TIMES

(*Above*) THE GHOSTLY MATER-IALIZATION AT ASH MANOR

DAME ARMINE LE STRANGE

NICHOLAS LE STRANGE (THE JOLLY GENTLEMAN)

The Ghost at Hunstanton Hall (See p. 211)

hastily retreated from the company of my sub-conscious self—I mustn't become fanciful.

As we went in to supper Mr. Kelly whispered: "Remember, not a word about ghosts before the staff—they think you are film people, who have come to get some close-ups of an old English manor house by night."

A little later business began in earnest. We first went upstairs and explored the oak-beamed passages, in places so low that your head touched the ceiling, and where unexpected steps made pitfalls for unwary feet. I saw doors opening with ancient bobbin latches, and a staircase which features in most books on historical houses in that part of England. Last, but not least, we wondered at the construction of the immense chimney, almost as big as a house, part of which is built outside, and part inside, the room where Mr. Kelly first saw the ghost.

This room has "atmosphere"—the heavy atmosphere of a secret. Dr. Fodor suggested the chimney might provide the key to the hauntings, as the man with his throat cut usually appeared here. He advised holding a séance. There was also a large open cupboard, where the darkness closed on you like a trap.

"This is the room which was always locked when I first saw over the house," said Mr. Kelly.

It was a well-worth-while experience, even from the artistic aspect, as the passages and rooms were full of strange moving shadows, possibly our own, but how easy it was to believe them otherwise!

Dr. Fodor arranged to take a flashlight photograph every half hour after midnight, and we went downstairs to discuss the hauntings.

Mr. and Mrs. Kelly were firm in their belief that the ghost existed—both of them had seen it, not once, but often, and Mrs. Kelly said how much she wished that it would leave them in peaceful possession of their home. She went on to describe the heavy footsteps which came from a now *floorless* room at the top of the house, a room where in ancient days the Manor servants had slept on bundles of straw.

"Only last week," she said, "I was lying awake, reading in bed, when our dog Ross, who was asleep in the room, woke up, looked at the door, and began to growl and whine. The door opened, and I heard footsteps *thumping* across to the far corner, when they went upwards, and I distinctly heard them overhead. I couldn't make this out : there wasn't the vestige of a stairway in that particular corner. But next morning I sent for a builder whose father and grandfather had worked at the Manor, and he told me that a ladder-way had once existed in my room, but it had been removed some years previously, and the trapdoor in the ceiling to which it gave access closed."

"This has only happened once," continued Mrs. Kelly. "But the other evening, as I was coming down the passage, I suddenly felt confronted with the invisible presence of such concentrated Evil, that I fell on my knees and prayed to be delivered from it."

"Do your children know anything about the hauntings ?" asked Dr. Fodor.

"It's impossible to prevent it," said Mr. Kelly. "Patricia hears the noises, and knows that something uncanny exists, but Michael, who is at Winchester, is away from home so much that he doesn't suspect anything. It is very difficult to keep servants, as they hear all sorts of stories in the village. Those we have now have only been here a week—perhaps they'll give notice tomorrow, they've already complained of the 'noises'."

After Patricia went to bed our host and hostess suggested making black coffee, and Dr. Fodor and I were left alone. It was then that we heard a succession of heavy thuds overhead, which had no connection with Miss Kelly's bedroom, or the kitchen end of the house.

We told Mr. Kelly. "At any rate," he said, "you've heard a little of what often goes on for nights on end. But what are you two going to do ? I am off to bed—the 8.23 a.m. train to town won't wait for me . . . but perhaps Dr. Fodor would like to take a little rest—the haunted bedroom is at his disposal—and there's a choice of bedrooms for you."

"I'm going to sit down here," I said. "I told you I

intended to see this through . . . anyway, I am going back to town at seven o'clock."

"You don't mean to stop by *yourself*!" exclaimed Mr. Kelly.

"Why ever not ? I'm not frightened."

"I shall stay with her for a couple of hours," said Mrs. Kelly. "I never sleep. Besides, I want to talk to Mrs. ffoulkes."

Dr. Fodor (who decided to return to town by train) and Mr. Kelly bade us good night, and Mrs. Kelly and I sat in the now dimly lit room and talked, as people do who meet on congenial ground and who know and appreciate the colour of life, the lure of the unusual, the hatred of the cage which existence so often represents; who have a mutual appreciation of books, the dislike of remaining in the rut—and who possess the thousand and one things which contribute to create the (often fatal to happiness) artistic temperament.

At three o'clock I insisted upon my delightful new friend going to bed. "I'm perfectly happy," I said. "It will soon be morning."

Left alone, I must confess to a momentary feeling of nervousness. The divan on which I was sitting faced two dark passages at the other end of the long room. At any instant "*It*" might come down one of them. "Well—let it come," I said to myself. "It doesn't seem to want to *hurt* anyone."

But nothing appeared. I made up the fire, listened for strange sounds, and read.

Presently the dawn drew near. The house was as silent as the grave, but I waited another half hour before drawing the curtains aside. I wanted to see the garden, and breathe the fine air of morning. I looked at my watch . . . it was exactly half past four.

I opened the window and leaned out. I was almost on a level with a bed of sleeping flowers breathing faint sighs of perfume : the turf glistened with the tears of the night—and the row of tall orange lilies growing by the low wall seemed like flower sentinels on duty to protect the garden.

I was looking directly across at the Oast House, still as secretive as it had been in the evening—*normal*—but secretive. Suddenly I was aware that a man was standing by the door. I could not see his face—but I paid no particular attention to him, as I supposed it was someone employed on a nearby farm, waiting for one of his mates. I watched the man walk round to the back of the Oast House, and I did not see him again.

But—as it will be seen from Mr. Miller's statement—I had actually, and all unknowingly, seen the *Ghost*.

. . . . .

At seven o'clock my friend appeared with his car, and took me back to London, laden with all kinds of interesting memories and the promise of better acquaintance in the future with the haunted Manor House.

On Tuesday morning I received a packet from Mr. Kelly, delivered by hand. This contained the negative of the photograph taken by Mr. Miller when he was employed at Ash Manor last January, with a detailed account of his experiences there. As a reliable and independent witness it is impossible to doubt the truth of what he saw and heard, and I reproduce his statement exactly as I received it.

When I came to the part in which he describes his meeting with the ghost outside the Oast House, I *knew* that I must have seen the same thing . . . so that although I missed the fear, and thrill of an encounter with the supernatural, I had the consolation of knowing I had sat up to some good purpose, and that my sub-conscious feeling about the Oast House was fully justified.

"4 Halliford Road,
"Sunbury-on-Thames,
"Middlesex.
"July 19th, 1936.

"To Maude ffoulkes.
"Dear Madam,
"I trust you will find sufficient information and notes, etc., to help you in your investigation. I have given

you the whole story as it occurred to me. Therefore you are entitled to use it as you wish. With regard to the negative, there are stains on it due to deterioration and dampness, but the actual image is still in good preservation.

"Yours respectfully,
"F. C. MILLER."

"4 Halliford Road,
"Sunbury-on-Thames,
"Middlesex.
"19.7.36.

"To Maude ffoulkes.
"Dear Madam,
"I am pleased to say I am now in a position to give you a full and detailed account of my experiences in connection with the Ash Manor House ghost, and it is as follows :

"In December of last year, 1935, it was the wish of Mr. and Mrs. Kelly for my wife to go down there and give a little assistance for the Christmas, she having been in their service during the time they lived in Sunbury. Circumstances were so complicated with us that one could not go without the other, so the arrangements were made for us both to go. On the 22nd of December we were driven down in Mr. Kelly's car. I may say that 'part work' I was doing was attending to fires, lamps, and getting in wood, also attending to ducks out in the grounds. My first experience was the second night after we arrived. As I went out to the Oast House, I saw a person standing in the doorway. I turned my head and looked across the kitchen garden, but when I turned my head again in the direction I was going he had gone. I did not see him inside, but I naturally thought that he had gone out through another door, and that he was probably a man employed by Mr. Kelly for the garden, but I learnt afterwards that there was no gardener.

"The next experience was, I think, a few nights after Christmas, and all were away in London, except for my wife, a child, the dog Ross, and myself. At about 11 o'clock in the evening Ross was asleep in the lounge near the fire. I was helping the wife in the kitchen. Suddenly Ross started barking viciously, and tore out of the lounge door and up the drive. Thinking that someone was trying to make an entry I at once followed. Taking one of Mr. Kelly's guns for protection in case of trouble, I reached the garage, and the dog turned and went back into the house as if scared. I at once stood still and listened in the darkness. Hearing nothing, I turned to go back to the house, when to my surprise a man stood quite ten feet away, slightly bent forward, as if creeping towards me, with a terrible determined look, and with eyes that I shall not forget in a hurry. I brought my gun to the ready and challenged him, at the same time watching for a hand to move with a weapon in it, but not a word did I get, neither did he move.

"I again challenged him, this time saying, 'If you don't speak I'll empty this magazine into your body.' Again no answer. I thought of my wife and the child in the house. Then I remembered I had seen this man before. I had also a feeling of great responsibility, and in any case I had to come out of this alive. So I fired, but immediately I did so a bluish light seemed to burst in front of me. This may have been imagination through fear and suspense; however, there was no dead man. My gun was gone from my hands, and my cap from my head. I put my hands to my head, for I thought I had lost my senses. I then groped about for the gun, which must have been four or five yards away from where I stood. I left my cap until the next morning, and found it down by the garage door.

. "I walked back into the house that night as cold as though I had been on a block of ice. I felt I dare not mention this to my wife. Could I tell Mr. Kelly when he came home ? No, I dared not, he would probably tell me I was mad, or that I had been drinking, and there was no room for such men as me in his house. So I set to work to discover what I could do to trace this thing, that now I knew only too well was a Spirit. When Mr. Kelly came home, he happened to come into my bedroom one evening and asked me if I felt comfortable here, and did I sleep well ? That was only to be expected from such decent people, as my wife and I knew them to be, and I knew only too well that one answer to such a question should have been in the ordinary case sufficiently satisfying, for he had confidence in us, and was treating us more like two of his own family. But that same question was asked me again in the kitchen one evening by Mr. Kelly. It then dawned on me that he seemed very anxious to know, so I could not refrain from asking him point blank in these words : 'Now, sir, why do you ask ? Have you any inspiration that we are *not* happy and comfortable ?' The answer came : 'No, only that we want you to be comfortable.'

"But the expression on his face told me more than any words he could have said that there was something more behind this than I knew. So come what may, I was determined to speak, and in these words I said : 'Look here, sir, you are going to tell me that I am mad, or that I have been drinking, but this place is uncanny. I have seen very weird things lately.' It was then that I got his reply : 'Oh, then you *have* seen it !' But how thankful I felt when I found I had spoken to one who really knew. Fear left me. I was determined now to meet this Spirit again, and to get it to speak, because I felt that if any harm could befall me it would have happened that night I had shot at it.

"It was one night in January at the beginning of the New Year when I lay in my bed reading a book on photography, that I heard three distinct knocks. I looked at my clock; it was 12.25. I got out of bed, put on a few clothes, and crept very silently along the corridor, expecting to find a light shining through the bullseye glass in Mrs. Kelly's bedroom door, as I knew she often would read all night. But all was in pitch darkness. I crept down the narrow stairs and into the lounge, and looked out of the window on to the lawn, but not a thing was to be seen. I did not see a moon, although it was a fairly clear night—it came to my mind then that the dog never barked, he must have heard. I crept back, but this time up the broad staircase leading to Mr. Kelly's bedroom, determined to find out where those knocks came from, and half expecting to find some sort of clue. Yes, I was right, for there in the corner of the recess, outside Mr. Kelly's room, stood this now terrible Ghostly Spirit. That I need have no fear was evident, for it paid no attention to me; it did not even look at me, but stared, as if through Mr. Kelly's room, leaning against the wall with the right arm extended, and in a position as if to knock or push the door open.

"I was satisfied now, I could see it was producing its own light. There was a long gash across the throat, a handkerchief round the neck, on it was blood which looked to me quite fresh. There was a kind of skull cap on the head, and what appeared to be a dirty green smock, but I had seen enough. I thought of my camera, so I crept back to my bedroom, put a plate in the slide, and made my way silently back to the corridor, only to be met by disappointment, for it had vanished. It was no use calling Mr. Kelly now; besides, I knew he was sleeping sound. I would not mention this to Mr. Kelly in the morning, for I felt, and knew, what a fool I had been to have delayed the time, when I could have taken quick action and obtained results satisfactory to all. I knew that this would not be the last chance, so I set to work on a scheme to be in readiness for the next appearance.

"It was some days after when Mr. Kelly approached me on the subject, and asked me if I thought it was possible to get a photograph of it. I assured him that it was. So we arranged for a Saturday night, so that he could get a fairly good rest on the Sunday, should it take us into the small hours of the morning—which it did, for we watched and waited, and prepared a powerful electric light to make the exposure as short and sure as possible, but it seemed that it was not to be, for it never appeared, at least not to our vision. I knew that I was no more disappointed than Mr. Kelly, and he suggested taking a photograph of the corner in which it was always seen. The negative enclosed is the actual result of that particular exposure.

"Now I cannot offer any explanation for these most peculiar results, but I must point out the plain facts, and that is, that they are *not* thumb marks. I mention this because it came to my knowledge that this was the remark of a person, unknown to me, who saw the print. Mr. Kelly may have been ignorant of the remarks, but even if he was not, he is satisfied that they were wrong, because he had witnessed the whole process of development after the exposure, and again, other negatives taken at the same time showed nothing in that form at all.

"Any scientist into whose hands this negative should come will be able to see that there has been no faking. In the first place, the plates were bought by Mr. Kelly himself, one out of a dozen Anti-Wellington (the proper term Wellington Anti-screen 450 H. & D.). Now, if a thumb or finger were to be pressed on the plate during development there would possibly be a slight impression left on the emulsion, but *no* printing quality. If the thumb or finger were dipped in a strong fluid, such as acid, it would seriously mark the negative and so *obliterate* the background. If fog was present, caused by a hole in the bellows of the camera, it would look quite *flat* on the background. So if the print from this negative is looked at, it will be noticed that there is a *distinct* atmosphere between that marking and the background, making it stand out away from the wall. Here I must leave it to those who are more able than myself to carry out further experiments.

"I should like to end this account by saying that, unlike all the rest of the people in that house, I was in a position to get into all kinds of places in the grounds and in the house at such different times of the day and night, that I had discovered perhaps more in those ten weeks than Mr. Kelly or his family had done in one year.

"What Mr. Kelly thinks of those ponies that would come scampering up the drive, sometimes in the evening, and other times early morning before six o'clock, I do not know, but why was it that they did not run out of the gate and into the road? It was nearer and more direct from where they were, and a horse will mostly take the shortest course. They were frightened, and they showed it. Well, let us come back to the old moat, cross the lawn, and sit in a little garden chair on the corner of the house under Mr. Kelly's window. Keep your eye on the moat between the rustic bridge and the big ash tree in the corner, you will then get the clue to it. No, it is not the big white owls; fly round as they do, those ponies have no fear of them; only when those ponies are in that far corner field this happens, and then the time is so variable that it means possibly an all-night vigil.

"It was the voice of Mr. Kelly that shouted from his bedroom window to those horses who were already stampeded on to the lawn that morning before six o'clock. Yes, Mr. Kelly, I was up *very, very* early that morning, and it was not the first time, and after all, a nice cup of tea and a warm fire soon got the chill out of my body, and I felt as fit as ever. Now, unless the International Society for Psychical Research are prepared to carry out investigations on these lines, and over long periods, they will never discover one half of the happenings at Ash Manor House.

(signed) "F. C. MILLER,
"4 Halliford Road,
"Sunbury-on-Thames,
"Middlesex.
"July 19th, 1936."

Mr. Miller's statement concludes this true ghost story. There may be a sequel—who knows?—which will clear up the mystery of the sad and restless "return", and in bringing peace to the wandering spirit, it may also bring peace to all those who live at Ash Manor.

DANGEROUS HILL

Contributed by Gwladys Townshend of Raynham

THIS is a true story of a ghost and a disregarded warning. For obvious reasons I cannot give the name of the house, as it is usually to let furnished, and identification either of it or of the Dangerous Hill might be asking for all kinds of trouble. The House and the Hill exist today : you pass them on the way to the South Coast if you like to make a detour down a road off the beaten track of swimming-pools and petrol-pumps ; and you will have a glimpse of the English countryside as yet unspoilt.

The delightful environment is within an easy run from London ; in summer the scent of the pines, mingled with the tang of the heather and the sweetness of gorse, rises like incense in the dancing haze ; wild flowers star the earth with beauty : at first sight the house appears to be a sanctuary set in a garden of dreams, but, unlike most out-of-the-way houses, it represents the last word in modern comfort.

The house came into the hands of the West End agent as something of a surprise : perfect in every detail, furnished in exquisite taste, it bore no relation whatever to the usual furnished house ; it was an executor's investment, and the final transactions were in the hands of well-known lawyers.

My acquaintance with Dangerous Hill began about two years ago, with one of the Bright Young People, somewhat resembling the type described by Lorna Rea, who, when speaking of their parents say, "I sometimes think we make a mistake in trying to be nice to them, eating their ghastly dinners, and letting ourselves be dragged out to theatres by them. We're weak, we ought to make a stand against it."

Tanit, who tolerates me as a harmless survival of a

prehistoric age, and occasionally condescends to confide in me, told me that she was engaged to a nice boy, who I had known since he was an infant, whose mother was one of my school friends.

The girl Tanit, a lovely production of art and nature, is the embodiment of a pagan nymph of the woods and groves ; her brilliant hair, in some lights bronze, in others copper, flames round a heart-shaped, dissatisfied little face ; her grey-green eyes have looked on most things, and have tired of them. She is frankly *desenchantée*, but she is straight and delicate in line ; at times she is wholly nymph, but occasionally she reminds one of the loveliest film stars.

"I'm terribly glad," I said. "W—— is such a good sort, and as you'll have everything you want, I suppose you are satisfied ?"

"Yes," said Tanit, "W—— and I are very happy, and we've planned something quite unusual. No honeymoon : we are going to take a furnished house, and go straight there for a few months to see how we like it; if we find we don't get on, we can finish, and sub-let the house.

"You see," she explained, "it's not like marrying under the conditions girls of your time put up with. It's safety first today, and if at first you aren't happy, try again with someone else."

"Where are you going, my pretty maid, for this legalized trial of mutual 'suitability' ?"

" 'Mums' has heard of a terribly attractive furnished house, fifty miles from London ; we can run up for dances and cinemas, and have no end of a time playing tennis, tearing about the country-side, bathing by moonlight, and dancing on the lawn. I couldn't *live* in the country, but it has its points, and I'm terribly fond of flowers. Besides, most important of all, the dogs will adore it."

"Have you ever heard that 'short retirement often urges swift return' ?"

She looked at me suspiciously. "No. Anyhow, we are motoring down on Monday to see it. Mums can undertake all the sensible things, and see that there are enough cupboards, and we shall look round for the gay bits—there's a bathing-pool (the crowd will fall for that) . . . no end of fun, and no chance of being dull. Never a spare moment to ourselves."

"Under these pleasant conditions, you and W—— will get to know each other thoroughly," I said dryly.

Tanit, her beloved, and my old friend, duly went to inspect the house. The way of their return had been already decreed.

W——, the inconsequent Fortunate Youth, without a care in the world, in love with life and love, was brought home dead ; Tanit passed long weeks in a hospital, and when she was told what had happened, she remembered how they had lived for the moment, and found tragedy.

Later in the year, at Raynham, I heard part of the story of Dangerous Hill from "Mums", but the true explanation came from Tanit. "Mums" described the start on that fatal morning, and how W——'s latest speed car lived up to its reputation, and took the very steep hill marked "Dangerous" as gracefully and easily as a swallow's flight.

The house is at the top of the hill, with half a mile of tree-bordered drive leading to it, and "Mums" said the house looked "Spanish" when they saw it gleaming white in the sunlight. The grounds had been admirably kept up, spring was everywhere . . . daffodils danced in the orchard grass, and pink and white blossom foamed on the trees.

The caretaker, previously advised by the agent, was ready with keys and maps of the estate.

The house seemed "lived in", as if someone might come in at any moment, even the telephone was installed. Tanit actually allowed herself to enthuse, and the boy and girl raced upstairs and downstairs, full of excitement that it would soon be theirs, although they had no use whatever for domestic details.

"But, darlings," expostulated "Mums", "we must be sure that the kitchen and offices are in perfect order." This appeal made not the slightest impression.

Surely servants saw to that kind of thing, for what other use were cooks created, except to sample stoves, and cook food on them ? Just like "Mums" to fuss ; all elderly people ought to be put to sleep before they became senile. However, Tanit and W——, if casual, and on the surface heartless, were occasionally affectionate, and they left "Mums" to explore the kitchen premises undisturbed, whilst they went into the sunshine to meet the spring.

The girl described the gardens as "marvellous". The previous owner was someone with a taste for the antique : there were statues ; Tanit remembered one of Pan piping to Echo ; satyrs peeped from the cool darkness of a thicket, and, in the Italian Garden, fountains sent up jets of trembling spray.

The boy and girl presently discovered the Water Garden, where, in a few days, masses of iris would be seen in all their purple splendour. They sauntered along flagged paths, looked at rock terraces down which miniature cascades raced, and found a wide stone seat facing the glorious view across the green valley. Here they sat to plan their enchanted spring and summer on the summit of Dangerous Hill.

I will tell Tanit's story of what happened next as nearly as possible in her own words.

"We had been sitting there about a quarter of an hour, and then *She* came. We didn't notice her coming, which was strange, as the paths were flagged, and you could have heard a pin drop, it was so still.

"Have you ever seen a ghost, Aunt Gwladys ?"

"Yes—I certainly have."

"Because *She* must have been a ghost, although naturally we didn't think so at the time. All we saw was a tall woman in deep mourning, quite attractive, and terribly sad, who spoke in a sort of far-off voice.

"She said, 'What brings you here ?'

"W—— explained we were thinking of taking the house. 'It's just what we want.'

" '*The others thought so too.*'

" 'We are going to be married,' W—— said. 'We're both sick of the beaten track, we've been everywhere, done everything—cruising, motoring, winter sports.'

"The woman nodded. 'I understand. And you are very much in love ?'

"We felt a little awkward. Why be sentimental? 'We get on terribly well, we hope we shall be happy.'

They were *going* to be happy.

" 'The others loved each other very dearly. They were about your age—but the Hill did not allow them to be happy.'

" '*What* hill?' And we began to think our woman was very odd. *What hill* did she mean?

" 'I bought the house,' she said, 'although I was told that the site and the Hill belonged to ancient forces which resent intruders—but it was so beautiful I would not listen. *You must listen. Don't come here*, go back to London, forget this place. Remember the other two.'

" 'Who were the other two? Do you live here?'

"She said she didn't live far away. All at once we heard a bell tolling somewhere. I shivered. 'What a depressing sound! We must be close to a church,' W—— whispered.

" 'Can't you hear the passing-bell? Be warned,' said the woman.

"W—— was getting really angry, but the woman smiled a curious twisted sort of smile, and then she was gone! Disappeared as quickly as she came, and I remembered that though there was bright sunlight everywhere, the woman was *shadowless*. I had kept on wondering what was odd; now I *knew*.

"The air felt suddenly cold. W—— was still peeving. 'I don't like this, it's queer. What did she mean by forces? What forces? Let's go.'

"The bell kept tolling as we hurried into the house.

"We found 'Mums' up to her eyes in notes and queries. 'Shan't be ready for three-quarters of an hour,' she announced. 'We can easily have a late lunch at Reigate.'

" 'Who's the lady in mourning we met in the Water Garden?' asked W—— of the caretaker who stood by.

"He didn't rightly know; someone from the village, he supposed, and that's all we could get out of *him*.

"W—— was a bit nervy, and so was I. 'I don't like this place,' he said. 'Get back to the main road.'

" 'Mums' said she would join us later.

"As I got into the car, I am sure I heard someone laugh. . . . Seen from the top, the Hill looked very steep, and there was a nasty curve which I hadn't noticed before . . . a board was staring us in the face :

DANGEROUS HILL

"W—— stood up in the car—he was irritable and nervy.

" 'Damn you, Dangerous Hill !' he shouted. 'I don't care for you, or for any old forces ; we shall live here as long as we like. You can't stop us.'

"We streaked down the Hill. I heard voices in the air, and the distant bell tolling again.

"At the bottom a lorry came out of a concealed turning. We crashed with a sickening sort of grinding noise—the car turned over—*that's all.* The next thing I remember was the hospital. W—— was killed instantly. 'Mums' has told you what he looked like—he was dreadfully disfigured. It was terrible." Her grey-green eyes filled with tears. "I try not to forget he would have hated to be wept over. I believe he was a *sacrifice.*"

"A sacrifice ?"

"Yes, to the Things which own Dangerous Hill. I wouldn't say this to anyone but you . . . but it's true. The ghost in the garden was right—nobody must live in the house; if they do—Dangerous Hill steps in, and finishes things."

I said, "There's more to come."

"Yes—the others were like us—engaged. The boy was an only son. His mother was the woman in the garden : after the car smash on Dangerous Hill, when he and the girl were killed, she died of a broken heart.

"It must have been her ghost, and she tried to warn us that the Hill demanded a sacrifice.

" 'Mums' heard afterwards that they are buried close to Dangerous Hill. That may account for the passing-bell we heard. Well, I am going for a breath of fresh air, and don't think me an awful fool for believing in ghosts."

I said : "Take consolation. Remember these lovely lines :

"They shall not grow old, as we who are left grow old ;
Age shall not wither them, nor the years condemn.
At the going down of the sun, and in the morning,
We will remember them."

TO FETCH HIM AWAY

A True Family Ghost Story Connected with My Grandfather's Passing

By Maude M. C. ffoulkes (Maude M. C. Craven)

It may be considered the worst possible taste to allow any family skeleton under a hundred years old to emerge from its cupboard and make its dry bones live again. In this instance the skeleton represents a true ghost story ; the principal actors in the tragedy have been dead many years : with the exception of myself, and some distant cousins, the family exists no longer.

Once upon a time—to begin in the good old-fashioned way—John Chester Craven, a civil engineer, and his young wife, Jane, were living in Leeds, when railways were more or less in their infancy. John Chester Craven, who had served his apprenticeship under Robert Stephenson, was fast making headway, and, being a hard-headed Yorkshireman, he understood what the development of the iron road would signify in the future.

The Cravens had two sons, Alfred and William, and a daughter Eliza—the other children came on the scene later, and do not enter into this story.

I am William's only child. My grandfather-to-be was entirely devoid of sentiment, and, if he possessed hidden depths, nobody had the courage to plumb them—perhaps he did not even realize their existence. His gods were money and railroads, and to these deities he dedicated his brains and his life's work. For the rest, he had "the small, smothered life" of an early Victorian husband in a manufacturing town. . . . Outside his profession he had no interests.

Jane Craven's affections were centered in her eldest

son, and it is strange how often unemotional parents beget emotional and imaginative children. Alfred and William were both. . . . The elder, according to the meagre information given me in after years by my grandmother, was a handsome, sensitive lad with a charming disposition ; William, mercurial and outspoken, promised to be as clever as his father, and his character as a boy and man may be summed up in the damning expression, "Nobody's enemy but his own".

My grandparents married at the unripe age of nineteen, and they were still young when Alfred, William, and Eliza had reached the ages of ten, eight, and seven. Their mother loved them as a mother, but their father regarded his family solely in the light of obedience to a command from God to increase and multiply, and no doubt he hoped that his sons would be successful followers in his calculated and intelligent footsteps.

I always think of the dour man of thirty or thereabouts, with the keen grey eyes, whose black eyebrows almost met across his nose, as the prototype of Charles Laughton's *Mr. Barrett of Wimpole Street*, and, like Mr. Barrett, John Craven possessed an ungovernable temper. His rage was cyclonic; but, as he was quite aware of the danger which these attacks represented, he usually kept himself well in hand. Unfortunately, one day, when he had been engrossed for hours in the conception of a new locomotive, the designs were innocently destroyed by Alfred Craven whilst his father was away "down at the works".

When the little boy realized what he had done, he flew to his mother, and the mother and son, with William posted outside the front door, like Sister Anne, to see if anyone was coming, awaited John Craven's return. Presently, William, with Puck-like glee, announced that his father was in sight. "You'll not let him beat me, Mother," faltered Alfred.

"Eh, love," said his mother, "I'll not let thee be beaten. Stay quiet."

And the trio stayed so quiet that John Craven asked what ailed them as he went upstairs to work.

Presently the little group in the living-room heard a chair violently overturned—the bedroom door was thrown open, and slammed to with a wrenching crash that threatened its hinges, and John Craven, taking the stairs three at a time, demanded to know who had destroyed his designs.

There was a tense silence. "Speak up, damn you!" said the angry man. "Who did it?"

Alfred emerged from behind the sanctuary of his mother's rocking-chair, and raised candid, tear-drenched eyes. "Please, sir," he whispered (for in those days little boys addressed their fathers as "sir), "*I* tore up the drawings by accident. Mother wanted some kindling paper—the drawings lay on the floor, I thought you had flung them down as useless—and . . . I'm very sorry, sir; please pardon me."

His mother said, "Forgive the lad, John, he's but a child."

This affectionate interference made matters worse.

"Forgive?" John Craven repeated scornfully. "I'll teach him to meddle with my drawings."

To Alfred he said : "Take off your coat and waistcoat . . . now your shirt."

"What are you going to do?" cried Jane Craven.

Her husband silenced her with one of those terrible looks which, even when he was an old man, were able to reduce his adult family to silence. He went into the kitchen, and returned with a new piece of thin rope, which whistled through the air as he tried its strength.

"You are not to use that on Alfred," said his wife, placing herself between father and son.

John Craven took his wife by her shoulders, put her outside in the hall, and locked the living-room door.

He then thrashed Alfred, William watching open-eyed in a corner.

After Alfred's shrill shrieks had become moans, and his moans sobs, John Craven unlocked the door.

"Take him to his bed. He's learnt his lesson," he told his wife.

"My lamb, my lamb, don't weep—thy mother loves thee

—thy back will soon mend," whispered the poor mother, lapsing into the soft Quaker speech of her girlhood. And when Alfred lay in his bed, sobbing and trembling, she sat beside him and comforted him.

In the morning Alfred's bed was empty ; he had run away. William, questioned, only remembered seeing his brother going quietly out of the room.

All trace of Alfred was lost. Those were the days when fugitives of any description had a good chance of escape. On the sixth morning after Alfred's disappearance, word came that he lay dying at a small country inn twelve miles from Leeds. . . .

I cannot say how this news was received : my grandmother was the most unemotional and unsmiling woman I have ever seen ; so I suppose this phase dates from the evening when she stood by her son's dead body and listened to what the people of the inn had to tell. Alfred had died an hour before her arrival.

The little she heard was horror. Alfred's combined fear of the rope, and his father, determined him to run away— he knew not whither—and it mattered not—so long as he put distance between himself and his home.

His back was covered with weals, his nerves were wrecked,

> Like one, that on a lonesome road
> Doth walk in fear and dread,
> And having once turned round, walks on
> And turns no more his head ;
> Because he knows a frightful fiend,
> Doth close behind him tread.

Alfred told the innkeeper's wife, into whose motherly arms he finally stumbled, that he had eaten nothing save a few blackberries and a turnip or two filched at dawn from a lonely field : he slept in coppices, and cooled his tired feet in friendly streams. "After I saw your inn, I couldn't run away any farther. Don't tell my father—but can I see my mother ? And now, please, may I go to sleep ?"

The hospitable Yorkshire folk tended Alfred—with

whispered comments and conjectures: they bathed him, fed him, and after he had told them who he was, and where he lived, he sank from earthly sleep into a deeper and more restful slumber, from which he awoke to smile in a kinder world.

Jane Craven took the body back to Leeds in a covered wagon, and sat beside it. I have heard that she caused a pane of glass to be inserted in the coffin-lid, immediately over the dead boy's face, as yet untouched by corruption—and at times, on this Via Dolorosa, she looked at the quiet features from which fear was lifted for ever.

Alfred was buried in the grey Roundhay Cemetery at Leeds; from that day, until the day of her death, over fifty years later, his mother wore his miniature in a brooch—and, as a fatherless child of five, I remember asking her, "Who is that little boy?"

The slow years passed. The Cravens had settled at Brighton, where John Chester Craven's name was known not only as that of a remarkably clever engineer, but also in connection with his work on the L. B. & S. C. Railway. He had made a small fortune, and built a hideous barn-like house, where he continued the drab domesticities of many years. His son William was dead, slipping easily and unexpectedly into eternity one February evening, at the age of thirty-five, after experiencing some of the joys, and all the disillusions, of life's crowded hour.

And now the husband and father lay dying in the crimson rep-draped four-poster which he had shared with his wife at Leeds, and, although so seriously ill, he was still the tyrant, the sound of whose latchkey in the front door set the household a-fluttering lest the cook might be a minute late with dinner.

Like Charles II, my grandfather took an unconscionable time in dying, and whilst his complicated complaint afforded his family an endless topic of conversation, it must have been wearisome waiting for the sick man, drowning in the vast white sea of the feather bed.

At times he listened to the ticking of the watch

presented to him after he had made the Darlington Railway, now hanging in a golden blob from the purple velvet and beaded watchpocket, immediately over his night-capped head. Sometimes he would command White, his wife's personal maid (who was always in attendance in the sick room), to read aloud his favourite psalm, and White, by religion a strict Baptist, with a belief in the gaudy Terrors of a flaming Hell, was obliged, willy nilly, to drone out a description of cool green pastures, where a Kindly Shepherd led his sheep beside the still waters.

One afternoon, when I was a girl of seventeen, I was introduced into this milieu of protracted death. Hitherto, owing to the antagonism of my mother towards her hus-band's family, I had not seen much of my grandparents since my father's passing. But, as the shadow of death temporarily obliterates family quarrels, I had been allowed to see Grandpapa for the last time.

"Good afternoon, Grandpapa," I said, advancing to the bedside.

Two hostile eyes scrutinized me unfavouraby. "You are Maude, are you not ?"

"Yes, Grandpapa."

He raised himself with difficulty on his elbow, and pointed an accusing finger at me.

"William's girl—don't look at me with your father's eyes—I don't want you here. *Go away*, and tell William and Alfred I forbid them to wait for me. I never saw such impudence."

White closed the Bible. "Better not stay, miss, you only excites the master"—and the old servant, who had nursed me as a baby, bade me come with her into the large dressing-room opening immediately off the bedroom. "Shan't be long, sir," she said to her patient; "there's the hand-bell close beside you if you wants me."

I said, "Whatever did Grandpapa mean when he said Uncle Alfred and Papa weren't to wait ?"

"Sh-sh-sh, miss," reproved White; "there are things you *may* ask, and things you may *not*."

I was an impatient girl. "Don't be silly, White, they are both dead. Grandpapa is wandering."

White pursed her lips. "Better if he did 'wander'."

"Tell me now," I begged.

"The Master's time is drawing near," said White. "I can't, and I won't, tell you anything until after he's gone; then, maybe, when you hear what's happened night after night in this very room, you'll take things more seriously. I wonder what the mistress thinks about it? She's a rare one not to talk, but, depend upon it, she *knows*."

I looked round the dressing-room, the ugly mahogany furniture shining like a horse chestnut, the "display" dressing-table, and the long lace curtains discreetly draping the tall windows overlooking the drive. Nothing could *possibly* upset the smugness of a house like this!

In due time Grandpapa died, and when I next came to Brighton, White kept her promise.

"It's the horriblest thing that's ever happened in this house, but it must not cross your lips, miss, until there's none of us old people living. Listen, Miss Maude, *your Grandpapa was fetched away* by that poor boy he mishandled so shamefully years ago. It's gospel truth, and Mr. William came along to be company for his brother, though why *he* should mix himself up in it, beats me!

"Three months ago, every evening, towards eight o'clock, the Master began to get fidgety. 'White,' says he, 'is Mrs. Craven in the dressing-room? I hear someone moving about.'

" 'No,' I tells him, reproving. 'At this hour, as well you know, the ladies is sitting in the morning-room.'

"Well, Master would have it that two people were in the dressing-room. At first we put it down to 'fancies', but one evening when I came upstairs from my supper, I found Master carrying on like a raving lunatic, with the dressing-room door standing wide open.

" 'It's them!' shouted Master. 'Alfred and William are waiting for me. They came to the bedside, and Alfred asked me if I remembered beating him, and William said, did I

know that I had acted dishonestly to his widow and child'
(meaning you, miss). 'But Mrs. William was always
Madam Hoighty-Toighty,' says Master, 'and my actions
don't concern William—he's dead these many years. Lock
the door, White—keep Alfred out. I don't like the look of
him. Then sit down and read me the twenty-third psalm.'

"In walks the Mistress. 'I've seen Alfred and William,'
Master tells her. 'Both of 'em say I've got to go with
them.'

"The Mistress looks at him. '*Strange*, most strange.'
Then she says to me : 'You see how it is, White ; don't
mention this downstairs.' And she stood staring at Master.
'I *wonder*,' she whispered, 'I *wonder* if it is the justice of
God.'

"Well, miss, this sort of thing went on regular ever
since that night ; we tried giving Master sleeping draughts,
but 'tweren't no good, and he always declared that his sons
were waiting to fetch him away.

"The night before Master died, he called me, and says,
quite natural-like, 'White, I am going to die tomorrow
night. . . . But I'm quite prepared,' says Master. 'I want to
see the green pastures and the still waters. I'm a very tired
old man.'

"I hadn't the heart to tell him different, but I don't think
Master has got to them green pastures yet. A hard man he
was, but well-thought-of by the Vicar and the Town
Council. I dare say if he'd lived he would have been mayor
of Brighton.

"The next night Master was worse, and the Mistress,
Miss Craven, and Mrs. Hallett, didn't so much as take
their clothes off. Doctor said he was sinking fast, and
he was very restless, and didn't know anybody. Around
one in the morning everything was quiet, when all of a
sudden we were startled out of our wits by a loud sort of
cry under the windows, for all the world like a 'Hallo !'—
ending in a scream.

"The ladies heard it.

" 'Cats,' says the Mistress to Mrs. Hallett.

" 'An owl,' says Mrs. Hallett, looking at Miss Craven.

" 'Some drunken man,' snaps Miss Craven crossly.

"That very moment the call came again, but Master didn't take no notice. Past it, he was. Then, bless me, if it didn't come once more, louder, and more ghastly than ever.

" 'White,' says the Mistress, 'look out of the dressing-room window, and frighten those cats away.'

"I went into the dressing-room . . . but if I'd known who was waiting below, wild horses wouldn't have dragged me to the window, much less made me open it.

"There were the two of 'em, miss. Mr. William, as natural as life, and with him a little boy, the spit of the likeness in Mistress' brooch—a quiet little fellow, all eyes— looked as if he had been crying. They were staring up at the house, and the little boy was carrying some sort of a skipping-rope. I pushed down the window and ran back, shaking like a leaf.

" 'Well, White,' says the Mistress, shutting her eyes like you, miss, when you're none too pleased, 'I hope you've frightened away the cats.'

" ' 'Twas no cats,' I began. 'It was——' and I stopped, because Mistress opened her eyes, and looked straight at me. Then she went over to the bed, just in time to see Master die.

"That's all, miss, and it's the truth. I couldn't have dreamt it, for if ever I saw anyone clearly, I saw Mr. Alfred and Mr. William as clearly as I see you. I don't know why they were allowed to come back and plague Master, when he found such comfort in the twenty-third psalm, and had had plenty of time to repent of being such a nigger-driver with the railwaymen, but there's no doubt about it, Miss Maude, Mr. Alfred and Mr. William fetched their father away."

GRAVE NO. ——, KENSAL GREEN

(The facts of this story were vouched for by the late Hon. Alec Carlisle, who told them to Maude M. C. ffoulkes)

THE man who experienced this "return" was a materialist; he was self-made, rich, and a carefree publisher whose reputation gave him the entrée both into the Literary and the Smart Set. He admired brains and the cash value they represented, but he preferred to talk to Titles; good-looking in the somewhat florid style associated with the Prince Regent, he existed solely for himself. He possessed no known ties—legal or otherwise.

L. (let us mention him as an initial only) collected few friends, but numerous acquaintances. These he wined, lunched, and dined, at one or another of his clubs, or else at a restaurant where the salt of the earth forgather; he knew to a nicety the degrees of the social scale, and what status is demanded by Claridge's, the Ritz, and the Berkeley. His name never featured as a guest at Bohemian or theatrical gatherings. During his lifetime he walked in the Row every Sunday, and so regular was this habit that one is tempted to wonder what kind of a "contra." is offered these superb individuals in Another World.

L. disliked the idea of death, as signifying social extinction with (in all probability) a protracted *"lever du rideau"* of the sick-bed. . . . Above all else, he detested funerals. Thus, in a thoroughly disgruntled mood, he forced himself one afternoon to follow a member of the "Savage", when his turn came to be introduced to the family mausoleum.

It was a dreening day in late October—the air felt like a wet sponge, sodden leaves squelched and squirmed underfoot, the cemetery chapel was cold. Altogether a d——

unpleasant outing, and you could certainly bank on the aftermath of a chill.

When the last rites were over, the mourners, looking like a number of melancholy damp crows, exchanged trivial commonplaces on the deceased, and then separated —the family to discuss the will—the acquaintances to ʼremember the dead man in the particular aspect in which they had known him. L. thought of him as a kindred spirit, and a friend who never became the kind described as "familiar".

How much he would have disliked this journey on such a day ! L., who was thoroughly uncomfortable, wondered why the clay soil of the cemetery manifested a clinging partiality for his boots, and sauntered slowly away to find his car. By some freak of fate he missed his direction.

He found himself at last in an older part of the crowded cemetery, where the dead sleep under lighter and less ornate coverlets than those bedded in the villa-like residences with spacious sleeping accommodation. An air of faded gentility clings to this forgotten corner—the graves are private, but mediocre, and here L. came up against a past known only to himself and a handful of discreet intimates with convenient and elastic memories to suit all occasions.

This past, like most pasts, was in the nature of a cross. On it was a name—the name of a woman who had dwelt in L.'s Secret Orchard during his pre-publishing days. For years she had loved him in her own simple worshipping way, but, unable to "climb", with no working brains, and no money to speak of, she had gradually dropped out. L. had heard of Elsie's death with the indifference born of selfishness—he had not even sent a wreath, since the address was in the suburban neighbourhood facetiously described as "The Clerk's Dormitory", and he simply could not claim any kind of acquaintance with it. Imagine the Bond Street florist's expression—the irritating words, "Let me repeat the address, sir," and the surprised comments, "Well I never, et cetera. Fancy him knowing anybody there" following his pompous exit.

He had tolerated and neglected Elsie as it suited him ;

she had merely stood for the beginning of the crescendo cavalcade of amourettes, all of which had been powerless to hold him. Regal in his sensualities, he was always regal in his swift dismissals.

L. was conscious of a feeling of mental nausea at the sight of Elsie's grave. Why on earth had the woman chosen Kensal Green, when the Clerk's Dormitory possessed various local cemeteries in the offing? Then he remembered a nondescript aunt living at Kensal Rise who had probably paid for the burial.

The grave was weed-grown and bare of memorials, save a grimy bulbous glass-case covering a blowsy wreath of china flowers. The cross was weather-stained—soot-stained with the tears of London rain—the lettering needed re-leading. . . . He imagined Elsie lying alone in wet clay and deeper darkness—nasty sticky clay, like that which he tried to clean off his boots by rubbing them against the marble surrounds.

All at once L. took a sudden decision. He would find out the cost of doing up Elsie's grave. Someone might stumble on it as he had done, someone who knew the story and the name of the Invisible Mistress. He wrote down the number of the grave in a sumptuous pocket-book, and then made his way towards the main entrance.

Here L. found his car, and was soon delivered from the thraldom of mean streets, to breathe freely in Mayfair. Once in his flat, he shook the clay of Kensal Green off his feet, rang up the office—and allowed himself to relax.

He felt strangely tired. *Shivered.* "Hope I've not caught cold," he thought anxiously. Bowden, the butler with the Rabelaisian mind, and the exterior of a Benevolent Bishop, noiselessly drew the heavy velvet curtains. "Still raining, Bowden?"

"Yes, sir, and a suspicion of fog. Were you dining alone, sir, or had you an engagement?"

L. had no engagement ; he would dine alone. Make an early night of it. Bowden watched his master out of the tail of his eye. "Something's properly upset the Old Man," he thought, lapsing into the vernacular, and he was right.

L. *was* upset ; the Cross now represented the Fly in the
Amber and the crumpled rose-leaf, as well as the skeleton
in his well-ordered cupboard. Elsie, living, would have
constituted a glaring error of good taste—dead, her untidy
cross was no less offensive. He recalled her memory :
her fear of offending him, her childishness, her sentimentalities, how thrilled she was when he first began to spend
occasional week-ends in the Stately Homes of England,
sponsored by a Duchess with literary tendencies, who
imagined herself the Inspiration of the Publisher who was
beginning to be talked about.

"How lovely," Elsie would say ; "I'm sure you were the
best-looking man there, and, do try and remember what the
ladies wore." Then he would smile his superior smile, and
tell her not to be foolish.

This was twenty years ago. In twenty years he had
achieved Greatness. His "Lists" were a galaxy of Brains and
Names ; the Plain Janes and Elsies of his adolescence and
early manhood had paved the road to more subtly refined
adventures.

It suddenly occurred to L. that all worldly affairs end in
a cemetery. He meditated on this aspect of life during his
solitary dinner ; he remembered Elsie's cheap cross, streaked
with damp, slanting a little as if it were tired—set in a sog-
ging mass of clay—and he realized that unless he married
and begat children he would be lonely in his passing. He
also thought, with a touch of cynicism, that, as most cemeteries are more or less out of bounds, they provide a safe
excuse for the living to neglect the memory of the dead.
And yet some of the people in Elsie's world would queue
up for hours for a spectacular First Night. The workings of
suburban minds were certainly interesting.

Dinner over, L. went back to the library. Bowden,
with cat-like softness of tread, presently brought the
tantalus and siphon, the cigars and cigarettes.

L. simply couldn't face the remainder of the evening
alone. All this, he reflected, was owing to being weak enough
to see the last of poor W. G. . . . but never again would he
venture forth in the cause of sentiment. He'd ring up

"Tubby" (his stockbroker), and see if he'd come round for an hour. He lifted the receiver. . . . What the h—— *was* Tubby's number ? Why, he spoke to the fellow every day. Ah, he'd got it.

"Give me —— Kensal Green," he said, and then realized he was ringing up *the number of Elsie's grave*.

L. told Alec Carlisle, the sole recipient of this ghostly confidence, that he could not move, or even replace the receiver. He felt compelled to *wait*.

A voice, at first muffled, then gradually becoming clearer, said:

"Yes ; who's calling ?"

L. gave his name. The person at the other end uttered a little gasp of delighted surprise. And L., with his blood turning to water, recognized the voice of *Elsie*.

"Why, it's never you, darling! Do you want me ? Of course I'll come." (Just as she had always answered his one-time calls.)

L. wanted to say, *No, no, no,* but speech was frozen. "I won't be long," continued the voice ; "but I was very far away, darling, when you rang up."

Panic fear seized L. He dropped the receiver. "I can't stop here," he thought, and then he knew that he must await his visitor. When would she come ? What would she look like ? Surely she couldn't appear in her earth-stained shroud, with the seal of corruption on her face ? Damn it all, he wasn't afraid of any woman living, much less a dead one. *Let her come*—even if she brings all the clay of Kensal Green with her, he thought desperately. He poured himself a stiff brandy and sat down.

The flat was very still. Bowden and his fellow servants had gone to bed. A hoot from an occasional taxi set the superior air of Mount Street a-quiver, the Tompion clock in the hall ticked and chimed time away, sometimes a stray cinder fell on the tiled hearth. How long would Elsie be ?

As if in answer to his unspoken question, the front door opened noiselessly, then closed.

Footsteps which dragged a little, as if their owner's

limbs had recently been cramped, came slowly down the passage, heralded by a current of icy air. . . . There were three soft knocks on the library door. . . .

L. did not meet the visitor. He fainted—and lay unconscious until early next morning, when Bowden discovered him.

"And, believe me, or believe me not," said Bowden, when discussing L.'s unaccountable seizure, "bits of wet clay were sticking to the carpet, and some was on his dinner-jacket. Beats me how it got there. As for the hall mat ; it was all mussed up. Why can't people wipe their feet, like Christians, without 'aving to be taught to use the scraper beforehand ?"

L. recovered. He ought to have become a changed man, or a changed life. He was neither. He conducted his successful business as usual, and died, a few years ago, when the Season was at its height. After this ghostly experience he developed two marked peculiarities. He would neither ring up nor take a personal call, and he only attended Memorial Services—never funerals. Also, when an enthusiastic amateur gardener at a country house party spoke of a clay soil being good for rose-growing, L. gave him a glance which would have withered the hardiest last rose of summer.

THE STORY OF A CHILD'S FRIENDSHIP WITH THE GHOST OF HER GREAT-GRANDFATHER

Contributed by Dr. Francis Edwards, M.D. Brux. (la plus grande distinction, 1896), M.R.C.P. Lond., 1893, M.R.C.S. Eng., 1893 (Guy's and Brussels).

THE name of Dr. Francis Edwards is included in those of the famous alienists in Europe, but as he does not wish me to enlarge upon his career, I shall content myself with saying that Francis Edwards is the most human and understanding of created beings, and, like many others, I owe him a debt of gratitude which can never be repaid.

When I wrote to Dr. Edwards and asked him if he knew a true ghost story suitable for inclusion in this volume, he replied that he *did*, and would gladly relate all the circumstances connected with it. "It's too complicated to write," he said.

I met Dr. Edwards—and, here is the story :

During the period when I was acting as Medical Superintendent at Camberwell House [said Dr. Edwards], an old gentleman used to come at intervals to visit a patient (I fancy some distant connection), and I often had a chat with him ; he was quite an interesting individual, and, as you know how much the unusual appeals to me, I was not surprised when one day he asked me if I believed in ghosts.

"I certainly do," I replied. "It is impossible to deny their existence."

"Because," said he, "I once witnessed an extraordinary supernatural occurrence in my own home. I placed it on record at the time, and this I will send you. You will notice that I have included the most trivial details, but I have done so in order to support the truth of my statements. I have never shown the document to anyone : I'm morbidly sensitive at the possibility of being laughed at, and even if you relegate me as just over the borderline between sanity and insanity, you will not fail to be interested in what I have set down."

I *was* interested, and later a lengthy manuscript of two hundred pages arrived. As my acquaintance said, all details had been most painstakingly noted, and, shorn of unnecessary redundancies, this is what happened a few years ago, in an old "Terrace" house at Bath.

This particular family had lived at Bath for generations, but the Mr. R. I knew was blest, or curst, with the spirit of adventure, and this restless blood urged him to go to Australia during the Gold Rush of 1850. "I was born," he said, "when my father was over sixty years of age, so he was a very old man when I left home, and I had not been long in Australia before he died, leaving me, amongst other property, our house at Bath.

· "I had no inclination to return, and, as I intended to lead my life on broader and more unconventional lines, I instructed our lawyer to see that the house was kept in good order, and a responsible caretaker installed. I had inherited many family possessions which it would have been foolish to allow to fall into disrepair, and I did not wish to disperse them.

"I married in Australia, and brought up a family. One of my sons died a few years after his marriage, and his wife, who only survived him a year, left me guardian of their orphan daughter, then just seven years old.

"Mary was a happy little creature, a perfectly normal child (I mention this as necessary to remember in the face of what happened afterwards). . . . We became very fond of each other, so much so, that I decided to give her an English upbringing. There was the house at Bath ready to step into ; my affairs in Australia were so well ordered that our departure need not be delayed, my other children had made their own lives, and were not dependent on me. I had no ties.

"When Mary and I arrived at Bath, I found that my

instructions had been well carried out during these long years of absence, and the house and its contents were as well preserved as in my father's lifetime. Mary was too young to appreciate family portraits and period furniture, but she loved the old-fashioned garden, and as she wasn't lonely without playmates of her own age, I did not send her to school, but planned to educate her at home. For the moment it was one long holiday for us both.

"Autumn came, and when the days began to draw in Mary and I used to sit in the library, the child playing with her dolls, whilst I read. The library was a warm, comfortable room, and we spent many quiet hours there.

"One evening, just before 'lighting-up' time, Mary, who was nestling by my side before the fire, suddenly exclaimed :

" 'Look, Grandpapa, *whoever* is the old gentleman sitting in the big chair with "ears" ? He *does* look funny, he's dressed so oddly.' And she began to laugh.

" 'There's nobody there, you silly child,' I told her.

" 'Oh, but there *is*, Grandpapa,' she said. 'Why, he's just nodded his head. I *believe* he knows me. I didn't see him come into the room, did you ?'

" 'Run away, and see if there are any letters,' I said. I did not want to humour the child in strange fancies, so I lit the gas, and when she came back :

" 'Well, Mary, where is the funny old man ?' I asked.

"Mary looked round the room. 'Oh . . . he's gone—but he *was* here five minutes ago. Perhaps he'll come again. I *do* hope he will ; I *like* him, Grandpapa.'

"After this the visitor often returned, and Mary described his appearance and dress so minutely that I was convinced, against my will, that the appearance (unseen by me) was none other than my old father, wearing the clothes fashionable in the first years of the nineteenth century, which he had refused to discard for anything more up-to-date.

"It was useless to allow Mary to think that her friend was a ghost, so I let things take their course, hoping they would right themselves, although I could not imagine why my father had come back to haunt his former library, or why he wanted to get in touch with Mary.

"A few weeks elapsed, and, incredible though it may seem, Mary and her great-grandfather carried on long conversations, the substance of which she gave me verbatim, since, needless to say, I was never audibly, or visibly, aware of my father's presence.

"I have endeavoured to set down some of these conversations exactly as Mary repeated them to me, and when I told her to ask my father about certain family matters known only to himself and to me, the answers no longer allowed me to doubt the existence of a state of things beyond my comprehension. My last lingering doubts were eventually dispelled by the child herself.

"One day I said: 'Ask great-grandpapa what becomes of the little babies who die before they have time to open their eyes.'

"Mary looked at the invisible occupant of the chair with 'ears'; spoke to him, waited a few minutes, then: 'Great-grandpapa says that *still-born children* go on living in heaven,' whispered Mary; 'but what does *still-born* mean, Grandpapa?'

" 'It's another word for death,' I told her. After this I never doubted that these ghostly conversations were real, as the child had never heard the word '*still-born*' until my father used it. Proof conclusive, wasn't it?

"Winter passed and spring returned. Mary's first English spring, and one morning when the crocuses in the garden flamed in the sunlight, Mary said:

" 'Great-grandpapa told me yesterday that he isn't coming here any more, because he says I'm soon going to live with him. Where does great-grandpapa live? I hope it's not far away. Why *must* I go and live with him? I'm quite happy here—but'—brightening—'I expect I'll be able to come and see you every day.'

"My heart stood still. . . . I understood my father's meaning only too well, but I dared not tell the child that his 'house' was a grave in the churchyard of Bath Abbey, although the spirit which loved his little descendant was free of mortal environment. But Mary, all unknowingly, had received her summons to another world. Her great-grandfather never came again, and within a month she was dead.

"These, Dr. Edwards, are the outlines of the story—you will read the facts for yourself—but, after this, you will understand *why* I believe in ghosts."

"What became of the manuscript ?" I asked, hoping that I should be able to reproduce some of it.

"Unfortunately, when I left Camberwell House it was lost or mislaid," said Dr. Edwards ; "but beyond the outlines of what I have told you, it merely contained a mass of unimportant data which Mr. R. considered necessary to corroborate his statements. You've got the real gist of the story, but one curious thing, which I forgot to mention, is that Mary's great-grandfather told her he had visited Australia, and described her grandfather's and her father's houses in Adelaide. As he had never left England, this is rather extraordinary, but personally I have no doubt that everything happened exactly as Mr. R. told me."

. . . . .

I kept on thinking about this curious manifestation from another world; so much so, that I wrote to Dr. Edwards, asking his opinion why most of us apparently possess eyes which see not, and ears which hear not ? This is his reply :

"Cherchefelle,
"Reigate.
"4-4-'36.
"My dear Maude,
"There is no scientific proof of my suggestion that clairvoyance or clairaudience is due to a receptive faculty beyond that normally possessed, but it might well be so.
"The two senses, vision and hearing, receive their

external stimuli through vibrations, the former via the ether, the latter via the air. It is known that, in each case, perceptions of a certain intensity, or pitch, can alone be appreciated: with the light rays of the spectrum, for example, those on the two perspectives, infra-red and ultra-violet, are not so perceived. Should, however, some variation exist in certain individuals, they might see or hear that which is not for the common herd.

"The aura (*n.* ray) described so often by a medium is a simple example, and those more materialized forms (yclept ghosts) a more advanced one.

"So glad to have seen you yesterday.

"Yours, et cetera, et cetera,

"FRANCIS EDWARDS."

This pathetic tale of a strange friendship shows the fearlessness and friendliness of certain children towards visitants from another world, especially when these are in no way abnormal. Mary accepted her great-grandfather as someone who amused her, and talked to her so naturally that she was not at all worried when he told her she was coming to live with him. There is an old saying "For a little child, little mourning", and as "God is kind to children", Mary's grandfather has no doubt found her long ago in the starshine of the pleasant Playgrounds of Heaven.

THE LOVER AND THE BEAM

Contributed by Anne, Lady Selsdon.

IN a recent article written by Mr. Osbert Sitwell in *Nash's Magazine*, he says that "ghosts and spirit phenomena generally are very often the production of ennui. Imagination, generally of an elementary kind, asserts itself to relieve tedium : and then self-deception follows."

Whilst admitting that some ghost stories are fabricated to "relieve tedium", or to stimulate the imagination, I must beg to differ from Mr. Sitwell, as my own experiences of psychic phenomena were not connected in any way with ennui. They just *happened*, and (if one can apply the word normal to the supernatural) in a perfectly normal way.

A few years ago some friends of mine bought an old house in Buckinghamshire ; for various reasons I am unable to state its name, or the postal address—the county is correct.

The Hall is situated in one of the loveliest spots in the many still untrodden ways of Buckinghamshire. The house, originally late Carolean, and added to by some eighteenth century owner unconnected with this story, dominates the beech woods which surround it on either side until they gradually give place to undulating parkland. The grounds abound in imitation ruins, Greek temples, leaden and marble garden gods, and last, but not least, a lake of dreams, approached in springtime through groves of lilac, spilling fragrance and colour on your path. There is an old tradition that no ghosts will venture into a garden when lilac is in bloom, but tradition must be wrong. Any harmless "return" could not have a better *mise en scène* than a garden where lilac shows itself in clouds of rosy, pinkish mauve, gleaming like white coral in a sea

89

of emerald leaves, or flaunting the sullen, stormy reddish purples of the East.

The H.'s are immensely popular : the Hall wasn't difficult to locate, you received a welcome that gladdened your heart ; so no wonder most people often discovered some pretext or another to motor down from town.*

One particular month of May, when I was feeling more than usually fagged out, it suddenly struck me that a week-end with the H.'s would be the ideal rest cure. I rang up Dorothy, and proposed myself.

"I'm terribly sorry, Anne darling," she said ; "but we have a house full. Won't next Friday do as well ?"

I said how weary I was of the Town and all its works, adding : "I don't care if you put me up in one of the attics, I simply *must* come."

After this S O S I heard a hurried consultation, and Dorothy said if I didn't mind sleeping in the Long Room (as she called it) I should be as welcome as the flowers associated with the month !

I reached D. in time for tea and small talk, and the square open galleried hall from where one could look up to the top storey provided the setting for an effective conversation picture. The house party was in the best of spirits, preparing to enjoy every minute of the crowded hour, but to my surprise, Robert, usually one of the most charmingly selfish and self-centred of mortals, went out of his way to apologize for the impossibility of putting me anywhere except in the Long Room—to be more exact, he *fussed*.

"I never knew there was such a room, and I've stayed here many times," I said.

"We never use it," he replied. "You probably won't like it one little bit."

However, I liked the Long Room, which we reached after a stiff climb to the unconsidered regions at the top of the house, and, true to its name, the Long Room ran the entire length of the frontage. It was narrow, as well as long, and the square windows, like sleepless, lidless eyes,

---

* The Hall was eventually sold to a financier, who altered it beyond recognition and the Long Room exists no more.

looked down the beech-bordered avenue. Comfortably furnished, there was nothing unusual about the Long Room, except an immense beam which crossed the ceiling immediately over the bed.

"Are you *sure* you don't mind sleeping here ?" asked Robert.

"Mind—why should I mind ?" I retorted.

The evening passed in the pleasant intimacy inseparable from the H.'s week-end parties : we were not hurried off to dine and dance in some strange house, or driven forth into the wilderness to the nearest cinema ; we rested—talked— listened to good music—enjoyed the peace of the country-side, and realized the H.'s were past-masters of the art of entertaining.

Robert still persisted in his profuse apologies for the Long Room. I saw Dorothy look at him with an unspoken prayer for silence, but he paid no heed, and when good nights were being said, Robert almost insisted that he should once more show me the way to the Long Room.

The night was chilly ; a genial wood fire burned on the open hearth—the dancing flames showed up every corner, and I wondered for what reason Robert had "protested" so much.

The oak four-poster was evidently a survival of the Carolean era of the house: the crewel-work hangings were admirably preserved and the colours of the exotic flowers glowed as if they had been embroidered only yesterday. The remainder of the furniture was modern "period", and the only archaic note was struck by the absence of electric light—"too near the rafters, perhaps", I soliloquized when I saw the tall wax candles in the silver candelabra which had been placed in readiness to light me to bed.

Now let me assure Mr. Sitwell that, at this moment, there was no vestige of ennui about me. I was comfortably tired ; I had all kinds of pleasant memories of the good companions I had left downstairs. I got into bed, and drifted into the sea of dreams as soon as my head touched the pillow.

I do not know how long it was before I awoke with a sickening sense of terror, the like of which I had never experienced. It was as if existence had been suddenly destroyed and laid about me in ruins by a ruthless being who knew neither pity nor remorse. Added to this mental terror, I was physically afraid ; in dread, not only of my own life, but of that of someone inexpressibly dear to me.

I tried to control my nerves—when suddenly the bed-clothes were literally dragged off. I struggled to retrieve them; useless—somebody, unseen, was stronger than myself—so I lay in a huddled heap, my face buried in the pillows, whilst the heart-throbs of a hitherto unimagined passion vibrated around me, and formed dark unintelligible hints of some wild and despairing love.

At this moment I felt a cold rush of air from a hastily opened window, and in the expiring gleam of the fire I noticed something dark swaying to and fro from the great beam—something that twisted and struggled. *What was it?* —what re-enacted horror from Beyond was I witnessing ? Surely it was a man hanging from the beam! I was now too frightened to take refuge in the obvious and faint, but by some supreme effort of will-power I clutched the bedclothes, wrapped them around me like a cocoon, and waited, hardly daring to breathe, for what might come next. *Nothing happened.* I was left undisturbed, and at last I ventured to light the candles, which fortunately did not burn down to the sockets before the dawn.

The friendly daylight, and the song of the awakening birds, came as a benediction. I jumped out of bed, and as I did so I remembered the open window ! To my amaze-ment, the three windows looking over the drive were tightly closed! I knew I had not imagined the horror of the night. Where was the other window—what had become of it ? I carefully examined the wall, there was no trace of any window, past or present, not even a bulge or a seam in the wallpaper. I looked at the beam : solid, ancient, and uninteresting in the fast-growing light—the atmosphere of the room was as colourless as it had been vibrating, as dead as the cold ashes of the fire on the hearthstone. But nothing on earth would induce me to pass another night in the Long Room. I was now sure that I had been confronted with a sinister record of a drama affecting three people in some tragic triangle of the past.

At breakfast, Robert once again *fussed* in a way totally at variance with his character. "Had I slept well ?"

"Yes, admirably."

"Really ?"

I assured him that the simile of the "top" might well apply to my slumbers. He was doubtful, eyed me askance, asked Dorothy to second his inquiries, and was frankly dissatisfied when her queries brought forth no result.

During the morning I recalled myself to London— although I realized that no sensible person is ever recalled during a week-end visit. Dorothy, always the understanding friend, accepted my unconvincing explanation and did not mention the Long Room. Neither did I. Robert, like some stormy petrel, hovered in the wake of my departing car, registering a composite expression of mingled gloom, self-reproach, and acute curiosity.

A succession of unforeseen obstacles prevented me from week-ending at D. during the summer, as I went abroad and remained away many months. Curiously enough, when I came back to England, the first person I met was a mutual friend of myself and the H.'s, and one evening after dinner I heard the ghost story connected with the Long Room.

"I was sure you had gone through it, Lady Selsdon," said Colonel T., "when you left in such a hurry. Tell me, exactly how *much* DID you see ?"

I told him.

"Hm . . . yes, exactly so. . . . Well now, I'm quite justified in putting you wise."

He first explained something which I had always looked upon as a harmless "fad" of Dorothy's. "Have you noticed that Mrs. H. never lets her beloved bull-dogs 'sit up' until midnight, and always sends them off before eleven ?"

"Yes—of course, but what bearing can it possibly have on your story ?"

"Because she doesn't want anyone to see how terrified the dogs would become if they were to remain until midnight. I saw it once—couldn't do anything with them, the brutes were literally beside themselves with fear ; and *why ?* Because *they know* who comes back to the Long Room. There's no getting away from it."

I said, "Begin at the beginning."

"The beginning is the story of an old man's infatuation for a lovely girl of eighteen, somewhere about the late seventeenth century. At that time the Hall belonged to the last of the family, a detestable individual, whose sole idea in his old age was to amass more, and more, money, and beget an heir. The seventeenth-century Beauty, who loathed her Beast, and failed signally in her duty to carry on the direct line, was virtually kept a prisoner at D., and she was also ignorant that her aristocratic husband was a money-lender to young bloods with prospects, as well as gamblers and high livers at Whitehall, whose extravagant pasts made it necessary to face the present at an unholy rate of interest.

"Hence nobody suspected that Sir J. D. was the person known as Mr. Silas at his chambers in Lincoln's Inn Fields, and no one at D. was told whither he went on his frequent absences from home.

"I don't know how love eventually came into the girl's life. At first the lovers used to meet in the park, after-wards in the Long Room, as the Hall was run by an old housekeeper who was a martinet where her lady's out-of-doors liberty was concerned.

"One night Sir J. D. returned two days earlier than was expected. He entered the Hall by a side door of which he alone possessed the key.

"Having completely ruined a promising young peer, he had supped well, and, flushed with wine, and in fine fettle, he went into the great bedroom in a pleasant humour to awaken his wife. But the bed had not been slept in !

"Fuming at the whimsies of women, Sir J. hurried from bedchamber to bedchamber, only to discover no trace of his missing wife. He sat down to think things over, and, putting two and two together, he remembered that there was an upper room as yet unexplored. Wishing to leave nothing to chance, he first went into the library, where he unearthed a stout steel chain and a pair of handcuffs ; he then made his way silently to the Long Room.

"The lovers were asleep in each other's arms and at that moment the bad old man must have realized what he had missed in life. The knowledge made him see red. He slipped the handcuffs on the wrists of one of the unconscious sleepers and the wife awoke to see death staring at her out of her husband's eyes.

"To make a long story short, Sir J. dragged the unfortunate young man across the floor, and hanged him from the beam with the steel chain. You see, Lady Selsdon, the victim couldn't lift a hand to save himself, and Sir J.'s superhuman strength enabled him to truss him up, although one wonders how the dickens he managed it.

"The terrified girl covered her head with the bedclothes —and her husband left her undisturbed until his final preparations were complete. Then, when the something that had once been a *man* was throttling, and turning in agony, he tore the bedclothes away from his wife's face, and bade her look at her lover. . . . Every time she tried to hide her eyes she was forcibly "persuaded", until, in a fit of maddened desperation, she eluded her husband, and opening one of the windows, jumped out and was killed instantly when her body hit the stone steps below."

"So that explains the sudden inrush of air," I said. "But—there isn't any vestige of a window. . . ."

"It was bricked up from the outside in recent years. However," continued the Colonel, "the hauntings have always persisted in the Long Room, and that's the reason the H.'s keep it locked up."

I said most people would wonder why the H.'s continued to live there.

"Well," said the Colonel reflectively, "it's a lovely place ; the hauntings are only acute in one room, so—barring the little trouble with the bull-dogs—*why not* ? After all, if you hadn't slept in the Long Room, you would have known nothing about the lover and the beam. Leave it at that. . . ."

And I have done so, until I was asked to contribute a

true ghost story to this collection of psychic phenomena ; but as one story usually leads to another, I remembered a curious happening which befell me and my small son when I was staying with my "in-laws" at the Scottish castle they once rented for a term of years.

THE CASTLE WITH SEVEN STAIRCASES

Contributed by Anne, Lady Selsdon

I CANNOT give the name of this particular castle, which has existed for centuries. At one period it was one of the various residences of Cardinal Beaton, when his private life was somewhat akin to that of Henry VIII, and—like Henry—he inclined towards "variety". But, unlike Henry, when Cardinal Beaton tired of love he wasted no time in trials or investigations, and the lady, with or without encumbrance, was quietly removed.

The scene of these "removals" possesses no less than seven staircases, and the castle walls are so thick that, when alterations were taking place, we understood how simple it had been to brick up an unfortunate mother and her infant, whose skeletons were brought to light by the workmen.

One of the seven staircases was associated with a strange psychic phenomena. Whenever we came up or down this particular staircase, we always heard the sound of a child's toy-cart being slowly dragged across some unseen floor. Creak-creak went the wheels (how one longed to oil them!); but where was the cart, and what had become of the child who had played with it? Once again we owed the explanation to the workmen, as whilst repairing the wall under part of the staircase they discovered a cell-like, windowless room.

The floor was thick with dust, and a little wooden cart stood forlornly in the middle of the room—its child-owner represented by a pathetic heap of bones. "Starved to death," said someone. The cart is preserved today in the castle, the bones received Christian burial, and the ghostly creaking has ceased for all time!

I cannot say I encountered the castle's worst "return",

97

but my little son Patrick not only saw, but heard, things which to this day he has never forgotten.

As I mentioned before, Patrick and I first came to the castle on a visit to my husband's family, and my Victorian mother-in-law, who had arranged a nursery with a competent nurse for her grandson's especial benefit, was considerably displeased when I told her that as Patrick and I always shared the same room, we had no use for conventional nurseries or nurses.

Such a declaration, which swept away the tyranny of the Accepted Idea, and destroyed the law laid down in the detestable words, "It isn't *done*", caused endless discussion. But I was firm, and Patrick and I were installed in an ancient bedroom hung with tapestry, and a short, winding stairway in one corner of the room led to a door opening into a small ante-room on the next floor.

It was said that the conspirators who had pledged themselves to rid the earth of a bad man came up this staircase to reach their victim, but the dark deed of long ago didn't trouble me. Patrick knew nothing about it, so we slept peacefully until I was awakened by the child asking me in a whisper who were the men who had just gone up the staircase.

"You're dreaming . . . there aren't any men," I said.

"I *saw* them," he persisted; "the night-light showed them quite plainly. Listen—what's the noise over our heads ? Just as if people were fighting."

There was certainly a sound of some sort of a scuffle, which I dismissed as coming from rats, but when we were once more settling down to sleep, Patrick started up. "Look ! Look !" he cried. "What dreadful eyes they've got ! . . . *Do* make the men go away—don't you see them creeping down the stairs ? Oh, *that* one is the worst," and he clung to me in terror.

Although I did not intend to capitulate and accept the nursery, I could not possibly allow Patrick to be frightened out of his wits. I decided to give the room another try-out on the following night.

However, the same phenomena occurred, and the little

boy watched the murderers cautiously creeping up and down; he saw eyes filled with the lust of cruelty and revenge, and, as before, we listened to the scuffling overhead.

I was never certain whether my mother-in-law knew that she had put us in a haunted room—at any rate she made no sign when I asked for a change. "The tapestry is lovely, but *just* a little gloomy, don't you think?" I hazarded.

The majority of Scottish castles are associated with a long series of tragedies, many arising from feuds between the clans, or border warfare, and in Scotland haunted castles and hereditary apparitions linger more persistently, and have "longer leases of existence" than in the South.

Some bond of a bygone passion must certainly exist between *my* nameless castle and Claypotts Castle, near Dundee, which Cardinal Beaton built for Marion Ogilvy, daughter of the first Lord Airlie, after she became his mistress, in order that she could signal from one of the upper windows to her priest-lover, and advise him that she lived only for his return. On the anniversary of Cardinal Beaton's murder, the wraith of Marion Ogilvy appears at the "trysting" window, and calls in vain upon his name! But, whether the legend be true or false, I like it infinitely better than the stories of the Cardinal's light-o'-loves who "disappeared" in the Castle of the Seven Staircases when he tired of them.

TWO GHOSTS I HAVE SEEN

Contributed by Winifred Graham (Mrs. Theodore Cory)

AND

MRS. GRAHAM'S GHOST STORY

THE name of Winifred Graham needs no introduction to the reading public, which has always appreciated her striking novels, and I cannot do better than allow her to relate her experiences in her own words.

TWO GHOSTS I HAVE SEEN

I HAVE only definitely seen two ghosts in my life [writes Miss Graham] and in each case they chose an unromantic setting. No ancient baronial hall or romantic moonlight night in the still country for *these* apparitions. One of them appeared in the train; the other, many years ago, in an old-fashioned four-wheeler. So now for the occurrences: I will take the train first.

I was travelling from Hampton Court to Waterloo one morning, and was lucky enough to find an empty carriage at Hampton Court. At Thames Ditton, the next stop, quite an ordinary-looking man got into the carriage and sat down at the far end from me. We took no notice of each other, and in the usual course of events I should have continued reading my paper without giving him a thought. But I suddenly had a most dreadful feeling about him, in fact it was so strong that I could hardly support his presence, and something seemed to say : "Take in every detail of that man's appearance, because you will have to identify him again." Naturally, after receiving this psychic warning, I thought he might be going to attack me, and I decided I would get out at the next station (Surbiton), but in the meanwhile I obeyed the inward order. Without appearing to observe him, I registered in my mind his face and figure, the colour of his clothes, and especially a little pile of four books, fastened neatly together with straps.

So uncomfortable and nervous did I feel that I was ready to jump out of the train at the next station. But, rather to my amusement, before I had time to rise to my feet when the train drew in at Surbiton, my fellow traveller calmly took his books under his arm, stepped out and marched off. "So much for intuitions," thought I, and telling myself I was very silly, I dismissed the incident from my mind.

Surbiton is always a busy station in the morning, and a minute later some other people got into my empty carriage, and the train proceeded to Waterloo. I closed my eyes for a little, and opened them at Vauxhall to see which station we had arrived at, when to my unutterable horror, I saw the very same man seated in front of me. On his knee were the four books in the straps, and he sat very still, gazing quite calmly and normally at me.

At this time, being unacquainted with the psychology of ghosts, I was frozen with terror, as I knew he had left the carriage at Surbiton. I got out and ran the whole length of the train, desirous of nothing except to put distance between us. Then I jumped, panting, into a compartment, terrified lest I should meet him again at Waterloo.

Alas, this ghost story has no sequel, this experience was the beginning and the end of my phantom man, and I shall never be able to explain it to myself, or to cease regretting my folly in doing a bolt! Now that I am versed in psychic knowledge, and am deeply interested in the occult, if such a happening were to occur again, the last thing I should do would be to run away. How often I have longed to know what would have happened had I asked the "ghost" the time, or waited to see whether he would vanish when we reached our destination. Shall I ever see him again?—for I am convinced that he meant

ST. ALBANS, HAMPTON-ON-THAMES

THE HAUNTED MAGNOLIA TREE AT ST. ALBANS

Mrs. Graham's Ghost Story

BOSTON HOUSE, CHISWICK

The Ghost of Lady Boston at Chiswick and some other haunted houses

something in my life. Anyhow, this ends ghost number one.

. . . . .

The second occurrence took place in Norfolk Street, Strand, many years ago, when Mother and I, coming out of a business building one dark wet evening about six o'clock, had asked the hall porter to whistle for a four-wheeler. It was before taxis were to be seen regularly on the streets, and we stood in the porch of the building until the cab came up. Then I noticed the dark figure of a man, apparently wearing a loose black cape, who was leaning out of the window of the four-wheeler, gesticulating violently. I was certainly impressed by the strange blackness of his clothing, and it crossed my mind that he was either making signs to the driver to stop, or else wishing to indicate that he was going in the wrong direction—nothing uncanny entered my mind. Then, to my amazement, the cab drew up *empty*, and as the porter advanced to open the door, I said quickly to my mother :

"I saw the figure of a man in the cab, waving his arms. He must have been signalling to us not to get in. I'm sure if we do so, we shall probably be killed."

Again I had a surprise. My mother, who believes in ghosts, and is psychic, being the seventh child of a seventh child, entirely discarded my warning. She would not be advised, and she stepped into the cab. I had no choice but to follow, and we had not been two seconds in that four-wheeler before the horse bolted, swerved violently across the road, and came to a standstill on the pavement, landing the cab against the railings of the opposite building. Naturally we got out as quickly as possible, and I can only surmise that the man in the black cape deliberately frightened the horse and made it shy in order to clear us out. I cannot help believing if we had remained in the cab something very terrible would have happened and I should not be here today to tell the story !

. . . . .

Another ghost with whom I came in personal contact was, strangely enough, not seen by me, but by my great friend, the late Mrs. C. N. Williamson, the well-known authoress. This happened in the early days of motoring, when Mrs. Williamson and her husband had kindly invited me on a motor tour through England, and we were staying at an old-fashioned hotel in the country (I won't mention its name, as the proprietors might object). Once again the ghost appeared in the morning—it seems their favourite time so far as I am concerned—and just as Mrs. Williamson and I were walking down the winding staircase to the breakfast-room, she suddenly caught me violently by the elbow and pulled me on one side, saying in a very alarmed tone, "I saw a man rushing up the staircase, and I really thought he would knock you down, until he seemed to go right through you and vanished into that wall. He looked like a highwayman." I declared that I had seen nothing ; privately I thought she was a little bit imaginative, but we laughed and went on our way, without giving the matter another thought.

Some months later, we saw in a paper an account of a strange discovery in the same hotel. The premises were being enlarged, and when the wall on this very staircase was taken down it revealed the skeleton of a man, which the paper said was supposed to be that of a highwayman ! This was undoubtedly a very strange occurrence, and what Mrs. C. N. Williamson saw must have been the apparition of this unfortunate man. I wonder what tragic story was connected with the place ?

It often strikes me as strange that we should be so scared of spirit appearances, as according to hypnotists, and the testimony of psychical research, each of us has a ghost inside him, or her, and this kind of science insists that we are haunted by a Spiritual Presence of whose existence we are rarely, if ever, conscious. The theory is, that this spiritual presence is that of our Unconscious Personality, the nature of which, so far, has not been determined. We are now standing on the edge of a new world formerly unknown to us, and there are no papers so absorbing as those which deal with Psychical Research, and discuss the Personality of Man, "I—myself", "What am I ?", and "What is the Ego ?"

The spirit world is so closely connected with our own that we ought to be seeing "returns" all the time, and when once you begin to make inquiries among your friends, most of them have a true ghost story to tell you. As a fitting conclusion to my own experiences, I have asked my mother to relate her story of the ghost of the man who hanged himself on a magnolia tree in her riverside garden.

Mrs. Graham's Ghost Story

Many years ago my husband and I came to live at Hampton-on-Thames. We had the prettiest house imaginable, and one summer evening we were sitting in our punt, close to the edge of the lawn. The moonlight made everything as clear as day, and my husband suddenly exclaimed:

"Just look at the magnolia tree! Do you see anything on it ?"

"Why—of course," I replied. And I looked again. "Oh, dear !" I cried. "I believe a *man* is hanging there !"

We scrambled out of the punt and rushed to the tree, seeing the man all the time quite clearly. Then—he disappeared. Of course, we said to each other that we had *imagined* things, and put it down to the effect of moon magic.

The following week, when we went to a ball at Colonel Harfield's, my husband was introduced to a charming lady from Molesey, whom he presently asked to dance, and directly she heard his name she said, "Why, surely you must be the Mr. Graham who has just bought St. Albans, that lovely old house *where the man hanged himself on the magnolia tree.*"

My husband at first said nothing about what we had seen, but later in the evening he begged his partner to tell him the story. "I really don't know the details," she replied. "I believe it was a footman who got into some kind of trouble, either over money, or with one of the maids. It's quite ordinary, but people insist that his ghost haunts the garden." So it was *not* our imagination, and I don't mind acknowledging that I was glad not to renew the hanged man's acquaintance. We have never seen him since.

St. Albans was certainly an exciting house to live in. One day my maid rushed into my room to tell me that a new maid had seen a lady, wearing a low-necked dress, standing against the wall of her bedroom, surrounded by a bright light. Asked if she were frightened, she replied :

"Oh no—not a bit, she was so beautiful, that I was only sorry when she disappeared."

Hearing this, I thought at once of Nell Gwyn, who had lived at St. Albans (so named, I suppose, after her son the Duke of St. Albans), and I remembered that I had a photograph of her portrait in the Beauty Room at Hampton Court.

"Take this downstairs," I said to my maid, "lay it on the kitchen table, and see if Edith notices it."

The end of the story is curious. Directly Edith saw the photograph she said excitedly : "Why—this is my lovely lady, that's her exactly !" So I felt quite certain the vision beautiful was really that of Nell Gwyn, especially as the bedroom in question is in the oldest part of the house, and may well have been occupied by pretty, witty Nelly when she lived here.

Now for a very strange occurrence. Early one morning when I awoke I saw, to my surprise, three people standing outside my window, one of them was a woman in a dripping wet dress with her head hanging down, looking perfectly dreadful. She was supported by two men, and I had only time to call, "Whatever is the matter ?" before all three vanished.

I jumped out of bed and looked out—there wasn't a sign of a living soul, but when my maid brought my early tea, she said there had been a dreadful accident on the river, as a motor-car with three occupants had over-turned while being ferried across from the island close by.

Two men were alive, but it had been impossible to save a woman sitting in the car. Then I knew that what I had seen was in the nature of the supernatural, but, as it happened, I had specially noticed the face of one of the men.

A long while after, I read an account in a newspaper which said that Tommy Hann, a famous Brooklands motorist, had been found gassed, and it was believed he had lost his nerve, as a shock had caused him to give up his track career.

A motor-car, in which he was travelling with friends, had slipped into the Thames at the ferry at Tagg's Island. He was not driving, so he forced a door open, and remained in the car, under the water, trying to rescue his friend's wife. After he was dragged out, he insisted on diving repeatedly into the river, but it was too late, as the woman was already dead, so his efforts to rescue her were in vain. Above this account was printed a picture of the dead man, whom I instantly recognized as *the man I had seen holding up the woman on one side when the three persons appeared outside my window.* I kept the newspaper report and picture in my possession, both of which now "illustrate" my story. Here is the account of Tommy Hann's death.

THE ACE WHO LOST HIS NERVE

[*Daily Express* Special Representative.]

Widowed Lady Williams, in whose house Tommy Hann, famous Brooklands motorist, was found gassed, declared yesterday that he believed he had lost his nerve.

He had a top-room floor in Holland Park Avenue, Bayswater, W.

Lady Williams, whose husband was Sir William Willoughby Williams, told me :

"Tommy determined last year to make a come-back on the track at the age of forty-four. His heart and soul were in the game. He practically built the car himself.

"It was a failure. It was scratched by the authorities because it was not fast enough.

"Tommy never got over the disappointment. He said to me, 'I think my nerve has gone for racing.'

"The day before his death he discussed with me the report of a man who had committed suicide through financial trouble.

"I said it was a ridiculous thing to do. He smiled. But he never threatened to commit suicide himself.

"I saw him on Friday afternoon. Then I went out. When I returned I noticed that the bathroom door on the first floor was closed.

"I called a friend, and we broke a window in the door. A gas-ring in the room was on, and Tommy was lying dead on the floor."

Tommy's real name was Albert Percy Hann. In recent years he had been a consulting engineer.

But he could never forget the thrill and glamour of success on the track. In 1923 and 1924 he carried all before him at Brooklands.

Then came a shock which caused him to give up his track career.

The motor-car in which he was travelling home with four friends slipped into the Thames at the ferry at Tagg's Island.

Hann, who was not driving, forced a door open, but he remained in the car under the water trying to rescue his friend's wife. When they pulled him out he dived repeatedly into the river again.

But the woman had died from shock. His rescue efforts were in vain.

An inquest will be held on Tommy Hann today.

Two of the appearances were certainly ghosts of the living—the woman had already "passed"—and the only explanation seems to be that, the Thought Body is capable of transferring itself wherever it pleases. But after all, everything is possible when one happens to be (like myself) the seventh child of a seventh child, and for us the veil between the seen and the unseen is often very transparent. However, most human beings are either receptive, or insensible, to psychic phenomena—mediums, clairvoyants, and seers belong to the first named ; materially inclined, matter-of-fact people come under the latter category, although sometimes even matter-of-fact people have the supernatural forced upon them.

THE GHOST OF LADY BOSTON AT CHISWICK AND SOME OTHER HAUNTED HOUSES

By Maude M. C. ffoulkes

THE Thames at Chiswick is a very different proposition from the Thames at Hampton, but after I had read Mrs. Graham's ghost story I remembered an old house at Chiswick which in the days of my youth was a well-known finishing school.

Boston House is situated in Burlington Lane, Chiswick, and the dark passage which is a feature of my story, and runs underneath the lawn, is thought to lead to the river. The original house was probably some kind of a religious institution, and the numerous cell-like rooms which open out of the larger ones support the supposition. In the early and middle part of the nineteenth century Boston House became a finishing school, passing from one principal to another, until, during the late eighties and early nineties, it was run by Miss Wilson, who, later on, transferred the name, and the pupils, to the fashionable environment of Eastbourne.

It is a quaint place, standing well back from the road in a little square connected with the house, and the iron gates are those through which the immortal Becky Sharp hurled Johnson's Dictionary, when she left Miss Pinkerton's Academy, saying : 'Thank God I'm out of Chiswick."

It is a vexed question whether Boston House or Walpole House on Chiswick Mall represents Miss Pinkerton's Academy, but the former was a School for Young Ladies as far back as Becky's day; both houses, however, possess ghost stories. Walpole House is haunted by the phantom of the tragic old age of Barbara Cleveland, and Boston House by a lady who loved, not wisely, but too well.

When I wrote *My Own Past*, I mentioned the romance connected with Boston House, which for some reason was discredited by Lord Boston, who disapproved of my alluding to it, but as my claims to truthfulness were backed up by local tradition, and the testimonies of members of families who had lived in Chiswick for generations, Lord Boston did not dispute the question any further.

I came to Boston House as a schoolgirl of seventeen, incurably romantic, enthralled by the lure of Things Past, and especially intrigued with what I described to myself as *ghosts*. Once settled in my new surroundings, I found a ready-made ghost story waiting for me, and I was especially attracted by the large schoolroom, originally the ballroom, which had a beautiful marble bas-relief over the fireplace of Venus and Cupid, flanked on either side by medallions representing the Lord and Lady Boston of the old-time tragedy.

Lady Boston had soon fallen out of love with her husband and given her whole-time affection to General Lord Fairfax, who lived in a house bearing his name overlooking part of the gardens of Boston House. It was said that during Lord Boston's frequent absences the lovers met, unsuspected and undetected, until Lord Boston received a private warning of his wife's unfaithfulness, and one night when he returned unexpectedly to Chiswick he discovered Lady Boston in the act of writing a letter to Lord Fairfax, which left no doubt as to the nature of their relationship.

In those days aristocratic husbands were not the easy-going individuals of the present day, when the Divorce Court exists to help the non-suited. Seventeenth and eighteenth centuries aggrieved husbands either placed their wives out of reach of temptation, by transferring them to a Home from Home in the heart of the country, or else they promptly challenged the Home Wrecker to a duel. Occasionally some temperamental husband took the law into his own hands, and removed his wife, not to a country seat, but to another world.

This is what happened to Lady Boston. Her appeals for mercy fell on deaf ears, her cries for help were unheard.

But she fought desperately for her life, and the walls of the Print Room (so called from it being papered with curious engravings) were bespattered in places with her blood.

When Lord Boston realized that he had killed his wife, he was faced with the problem of how to dispose of her body, and, remembering the underground passage, he carried the corpse downstairs, forced open the entrance, and passing down the damp tunnel, he threw the dead body into the Thames. But Lord Boston had not reckoned with the unstable quality of any kind of water; the river rejected Lady Boston's body, which was washed up by the tide a few days later, and buried with great secrecy in a corner of the garden. How well I remember the ivy-covered mound, unmarked by any memorial, until years afterwards, when Boston House passed into Catholic hands, and the kind nuns placed a cross on the forgotten and nameless grave.

In my day it was considered a proof of great daring to slip out into the garden after dark and to pick an ivy-leaf from Lady Boston's grave, and I still have one of these badges of courage pressed between the leaves of the book in which I first told the story.

It was rumoured that Lady Boston "walked", but I never saw her, although sometimes there were strange noises at night which made us shiver and shake. After the tragedy Fairfax House remained uninhabited for years; it was definitely and badly haunted—in fact so badly, that some of the occurrences have been published in one of the monthly magazines dealing with psychic phenomena.

A few years ago Boston House came into the limelight when the *Sunday Express* published an interview with a Mr. Arthur Clayton, then living in the neighbourhood. Mr. Clayton told the *Sunday Express* representative that whilst cycling past the house on the previous evening he was startled by the sudden appearance of a woman in the road, wearing what he described as "fancy dress". The apparition, for it was certainly an apparition, stretched out her hands, her lips moved, and her face wore an expression of great terror. She then turned round, walked towards the house, and disappeared.

Miss Edith Rushwood also saw the ghost (undoubtedly that of Lady Boston), but this time she was not so kindly disposed towards the living. According to Miss Rushwood, the apparition raised her hand—in which was a tiny dagger —as if wishing to strike someone, and Miss Rushwood, too frightened to move, stared for some minutes at Lady Boston, who once again disappeared in the direction of her old home.

Boston House has been spared the fate of so many beautiful old houses through the public spirit shown by its present owners, Chiswick Products, Ltd., who have preserved it, not only as an interesting souvenir of Old Chiswick, but as an up-to-date club for their women and girl employees, without destroying, or disturbing, an inch of the original building.

The large annexe, which contains the restaurant and the theatre, is built out on one side of the garden, and it covers the actual site of Lady Boston's grave. This was not known at the time of the construction of the new buildings, as someone, ignorant of the tradition, had said that the artificial ivy-grown rocks at another spot marked Lady Boston's grave.

This was incorrect; the rockeries and grottoes only date from the nineties, when Roman Catholic nuns lived at Boston House, and these grottoes usually feature in most "religious" gardens.

The picturesque grounds with the ancient cedar, under whose dark shade successive generations of girls discussed what the future might have in store for them, are unchanged.

I cannot describe the Boston House of today as a club; in my opinion it is more of a school—essentially progressive —never "finishing". When I saw the extraordinary chances of self-development offered to these girl workers, and how no expense is spared by the directors of the company to teach, interest, and help those willing to help themselves, I could not help contrasting their advantages with those of the "young ladies" of my day.

A little less veneer, and some useful "Mansion Polish" training, might have made—who knows ?—all the difference in many of our lives—my own (once described by a candid critic as "good material spoilt in the making") included !

It would be ungracious to dismiss Chiswick without mentioning something more about Walpole House, where Barbara Cleveland passed part of her dishonoured old age, a creature hateful to herself and to others, who had removed to Chiswick after the nullity of her marriage to Beau Fielding had been pronounced, and lived in retirement with her daughter Barbara's illegitimate son by the Earl of Arran.

In July 1709, the Duchess developed symptoms of dropsy, which "swelled her gradually into a monstrous bulk", and terminated fatally on October 9. She was buried four days later. No monument marks her resting-place, and the vaults under Chiswick Church hold the remains of the worst, and fairest, of the mistresses of Charles II. Tradition has it that the ghost of the Duchess is occasionally to be seen at one of the windows of Walpole House, entreating someone unknown to "give me back my beauty".

It is curious that, as a child and a young girl, I came in contact with four haunted houses, three of them close to the Thames. I made the acquaintance of the first when, at the age of ten, I was sent to school at Hatton Hall, Wellingborough. Even at that time I was a dreamer of dreams, a strange little creature, buffeted hither and thither, apparently only useful in providing a family grievance, consequent on my mother's extraordinary methods of bringing up her only child.

At ten years old I understood the appeal of the beautiful, so I was able to appreciate the oak staircase at Hatton Hall, dominated by a marvellous stained-glass window, where, on sunny days, one could, figuratively, "bathe" one's feet in pools of living colour spilled on the stairs by downward reflections from the window, on which *Vive ut Vivas*, the motto of the Vivians, was repeated three or four times.

Even now Hatton Hall recurs to me as a very sinister

place. Some time in the eighteenth century, when the Hall was occupied by two brothers, the tragedy happened (like so many others, inspired through jealousy and greed), and the younger Vivian hated the elder so much that, on some flimsy excuse, he challenged him to a duel in one of the attics at the top of the house. Here they fought until the younger brother killed the luckless owner of the family possessions, and, terrified at the consequences of his deed, he hid the body in an oak chest and went abroad, where, so he gave out, his brother had preceded him.

Time passed, and Hatton Hall remained uninhabited, although I suppose it must have been maintained ready for the return of its owner, and there was no suspicion of foul play until the oak chest made its presence felt, and the decomposed body of the elder brother was found inside, with his broken rapier beside him. I do not know what became of the "moral" murderer, since a duel hardly comes under the heading of murder, but his earthbound spirit, and that of his equally earthbound brother's, were said to re-enact the duel at midnight in the old attic, and if you cared, and dared, to go to the foot of the staircase leading thither, you would certainly hear the clash of ghostly swords overhead.

Children are often super-sensitive to psychic things, and, looking back, I distinctly remember how peculiarly the environment of Hatton Hall affected me. There is no doubt that youth has a streak of cruelty in its composition, and the "big girls", as we called them, used to torture the nervous amongst the younger girls by shutting a selected victim in the haunted attic on half-holidays.

As often as not I was chosen for this frightfulness— and I see myself, a trembling child, sitting in the semi-darkness and dust of the attic, where successive generations of spiders had spun their silken ropes until they hung in festoons across the leaded windows. A quantity of old furniture which had been dumped in the attic took on grotesque shapes in the shadows, and I half expected to find some dreadful creature hiding behind it. But what I most dreaded was the possibility of seeing the wicked

Vivian wiping his bloodstained sword on his coat-tails, as we were told had been the case. When this ghostly ordeal was over, I fled into the garden which joined the parkland, and tried to forget the attic and its terrors . . . it wasn't possible, and I was thankful when my mother took me away and deposited me at Beaconsfield.

Before I went to Boston House, we lived at Petersham, and I was initiated in the foundations of music and education at Elm Lodge, Petersham, once the home of Charles Dickens, who wrote part of *Nicholas Nickleby* there.

Elm Lodge was essentially an Early Victorian house, with nothing ghostly about it, and the dear old Principal, the late Miss Frances Holland, who believed in ghosts, encouraged me, *sub rosa*, to believe in them.*

We were quite close to Ham House, lying dreaming in the meadows beside the Thames, and as no house in England possesses such wonderful scenic possibilities wherewith to stage a "return", Miss Holland never tired of telling me the story of the old Duchess of Lauderdale, who still revisits the scene of her worldly intrigues. Her boudoir remains exactly as it was in her lifetime, and the servants asserted that in the small hours they often heard her ebony walking-stick tap-tapping across the floor. Lady Lauderdale does not come back in the splendid arrogance of her beauty, but appears as an old woman, who once terrified the butler's little girl out of her wits, when she woke up and saw the Duchess scratching the wall near the fireplace with her yellow beringed fingers. Strange to say, when the wall was examined later, various important family documents were found hidden there in a secret recess.

Miss Holland and I used sometimes to wander down the long avenues leading to Ham House, when the rest of Petersham was asleep, hoping to meet Lady Lauderdale, who passed that way in the full of the moon. I shall never forget the thrilling joys of expectancy which these walks represented, especially as they were entirely unorthodox from

---

* In recent years, Mr. Jonathan Cape, the well-known publisher, lived at Elm Lodge, and Mr. Cape, who published my first novel, told me that he had always been interested in knowing that I was once at school there.—MAUDE FFOULKES.

an educational standpoint, and I had also stolen a march on my mother, who described the supernatural as "stuff and nonsense", often appealing to heaven to know the reason why she was afflicted with a "difficult" daughter. Miss Holland and I never encountered Lady Lauderdale, but we saw the old house transformed in the moonlight, when the statue of Father Thames seemed wrought in molten silver, and the busts of the Roman Emperors in their dark niches glowed in the cold fire of the moon.

At this time, Miss Cooper, a friend of my mother's, lived at the Old Palace on Richmond Green, where Queen Elizabeth died in the Gatehouse on the morning of March 24, 1603. Needless to say that the Old Palace was supposed to be haunted ; it was an amazing place, and I revelled in its memories and its "ghosts", especially as Miss Cooper told me, "almost in confidence", that she never willingly went into the Gatehouse after dark. . . . She also related a curious story about Elizabeth having been warned of her approaching death by the apparition of her "double", and whilst the Queen lay in a stupor on her heaped-up cushions this "double" was seen walking about the rooms and passages of the Old Palace. "Occupy your mind with something useful," said my mother, but I am glad I never followed the prosaic road approved of by her. I have always found my greatest happiness in things psychic. In these, the true believer is never disillusioned, and as the possibilities of the psychic world are unlimited, it never fails to "hold" those who adventure on its unknown "unpathed waters and undreamed shores".

THE GHOSTLY MONKS AT BILSINGTON PRIORY

Contributed by Mrs. Joseph Conrad and corroborated by
Mrs. Cherrie Macnamara

THIS true story, contributed by Mrs. Joseph Conrad, the widow of the famous author, happened in a part of Kent associated with many colourful stories of the past.

Canterbury and its traditions need no introduction or repetition, and within a thirty-mile radius the locality abounds in ghostly phenomena. At Ashford, there are hauntings in an old Manor House situated where the railway takes a dip as it skirts the garden wall, where the ghost of a murdered man willed that the woman he loved should discover his body, hidden in the vast space under the roof, and bring his murderer to justice.

It is believed that the ghosts of two brothers, both highwaymen, who lived in a cottage òff the main Ashford-Folkestone road, who were ultimately hanged at Tonbridge, haunt the locality where they left their horses during their last "hold up". The brothers were caught before they could return to the coppice, which, being secret and unfrequented, resulted in the poor beasts being gradually starved to death. Why the highwaymen never divulged the whereabouts of the horses remains a mystery, especially as Gentlemen of the Road were pro-verbially considerate of their mounts.

As you go down the hill road that passes Aldington Knoll—again a haunted spot—you find yourself on the lower road skirting Romney Marsh, the home of ghosts of smugglers and Preventive men, and, still keeping the lower road, you will reach Bilsington, the scene of Mrs. Joseph Conrad's ghostly experience a few years ago.

One late afternoon in early autumn, an especially lovely season in this wooded countryside, when Mr. and Mrs.

Conrad were driving in the neighbourhood, their pony cast a shoe, and Joseph Conrad looked round for some place where his wife could await his return with the pony from the village forge.

As luck would have it, the Conrads found themselves close to Bilsington Priory, part of which was then occupied by a farmer and his wife . . . the remainder, to all intents and purposes, was a ruin.

The farmer's wife, a hospitable soul, showed Mrs. Conrad into a lofty room heated by a large fire, and, whilst she went to fetch a lamp, Mrs. Conrad settled herself in an arm-chair and made friends with a companionable wire-haired terrier.

Although the Lady with the Lamp took an unaccountably long time to lighten the semi-darkness of the warm fire-lit room, Mrs. Conrad, glad to rest in such pleasant surroundings, did not notice her absence. Suddenly the dog beside her gave a low growl, graduating into a terrified whimper, then, to Mrs. Conrad's amazement, the opposite wall seemed to dissolve into nothingness, the clear firelight was obscured by a kind of dust haze, through which Mrs. Conrad gradually discerned the figures of a procession of monks.

The ghostly "returns" passed slowly towards a hidden staircase, and Mrs. Conrad could plainly hear their wooden pattens sounding in a kind of regular rhythm as they climbed upwards. When the last monk had disappeared, the haze lifted, the wall was once more visible, and the dog was no longer afraid.

Mrs. Conrad had not indulged in the merest suspicion of a doze, she was not thinking of monks, she knew nothing about the history of Bilsington Priory. So, wondering greatly, she waited for the farmer's wife to come back, determined to find out what monastic tradition of the past was associated with the vision in the firelight.

But the farmer's wife could not help, although she was able to corroborate Mrs. Conrad's story.

"Bless your heart, m'am, we don't take any notice of those monks. Why, they be so punctual that we tell the

THE OLD VICARAGE, GRANTCHESTER

THE EXTERIOR OF THE LATE RUPERT BROOKE'S SITTING-ROOM AT THE OLD VICARAGE

The Return of Rupert Brooke

BILSINGTON PRIORY

The ghostly monks at Bilsington Priory

time by their footsteps, and 'tis always six o'clock when they do go upstairs."

However, Mrs. Conrad's story has an interesting sequel.

Thirty years ago, Mrs. Cherrie Macnamara, as a small child, used to spend the summer holidays at Bilsington Priory with her brothers and sisters, when the Priory was rented by a farmer and his wife named Stonebridge. (I wonder whether, as old people, if they were still living there when Mrs. Conrad saw the ghosts?)

Mrs. Macnamara told Mrs. Conrad that one evening when they were exploring the ruins, and had reached the top of the ancient spiral staircase, with one accord they turned and fled, *because all of them had seen a bare foot in a sandal about to descend the steps.*

"It (the Priory) was a most attractive spot," writes Mrs. Macnamara, "to which I am always wanting to take my own family of five children, and I expect to be renewing the acquaintance of an artist, who used to come to the Priory with us for sketching expeditions, and when we acted a play in the banqueting hall he painted the scenery."

The other day I heard from a friend living at Ashford that within the last few years the Priory has been an hotel, and is now a private house. It is somewhat inaccessible, and picture postcards are difficult to obtain. The accompanying illustration, which shows the actual place where Mrs. Conrad saw the ghosts of the monks, is therefore especially interesting.

I should like to express my indebtedness to Mrs. Conrad, as not only did she send me particulars of her own and Mrs. Macnamara's experiences at Bilsington, but she put me in touch with Dr. Copeland of Theobald House, Rochester, whose ghostly adventure will appeal to those who admire the poems of Rupert Brooke.

THE RETURN OF RUPERT BROOKE

Contributed by Dr. A. I. Copeland, Theobald House, Rochester

DR. COPELAND'S acquaintance with the supernatural happened in January 1919, after he was demobilised, when he went back to Cambridge, and rented the rooms in the old Vicarage, Grantchester, formerly occupied by Rupert Brooke, which, by reason of his famous poem, is now familiar to all poetry lovers.

The sitting-room at the old Vicarage gave Dr. Copeland the impression of still being lived in; there was not the slightest feeling that the bright young life associated with the place had met with such sudden extinction. How well one knows the atmosphere of a man's room when he is the healthy out-of-doors type, and where the aftermath of good tobacco blends with the never-to-be-forgotten smell of leather-bound books, and you appreciate the "homeliness" of photographs, the favourite ash-trays, and the odds and ends so characteristic of the man.

Dr. Copeland was perfectly happy in the friendly, unchanged environment of Rupert Brooke's "den", which possessed one especially curious feature—a false bookcase which concealed a priest's hiding-place, probably dating from the Reformation.

One winter's evening, after Dr. Copeland had finished supper, he settled himself comfortably by the fire, reading and smoking in the soft lamplight, by which Rupert Brooke had also once smoked and read. Caesar, Dr. Copeland's bulldog, was snoring on the sofa. The stillness of a frost-bound night lay over everything, and a bright moon riding high in the serene heavens made objects in the Vicarage garden as clear as day.

Suddenly Caesar woke up, to the usual bulldog accompaniment of gurgles and snorts, and listened intently.

Dr. Copeland put down his book. . . . Slow, regular footsteps were coming round the house, making their way towards the french windows of the sitting-room.

The footsteps stopped—Caesar gave a non-committal growl, and Dr. Copeland jumped up and opened the windows, expecting to see his landlord, Mr. Neave, returning from a moonlight stroll.

No one was visible. The garden slept under a glitteriig sheet of frost ; there was no possibility of any person taking cover. Dr. Copeland and Caesar stood for a few moments on the path looking around them, and then went back to the warm lamplit room.

Presently, in answer to Dr. Copeland's ring, Mr. Neave appeared, and listened to the story of the weird footsteps.

"Can you explain it ?" asked Dr. Copeland.

Mr. Neave said : "We are used to these footsteps ; they've happened ever since Mr. Brooke was killed—they belong to his ghost, which up to now nobody has seen. The footsteps come close to the window, but there's ro one there. . . . I hope, sir, you've not been upset," concluded Mr. Neave, a little anxiously.

It is highly probable that Rupert Brooke returns to the place he loved and lived in before he looked at the bright face of danger, and took the great leap into the dark. How truly Rupert Brooke, and all those whose youth was given to England, can say : "I could not die by any nobler fate". And one recalls a verse in his poem on the old Vicarage, Grantchester, written in the same room where Dr. Copeland heard his footsteps seven years later, which perhaps explains something of the reason for his "return".

> For England's the one Land I know,
> Where Men with Splendid Hearts may go,
> And Cambridge-shire of all England,
> The shire for Men who Understand.

SOME TRUE ITALIAN GHOST STORIES

Of a Haunted Countryside

Contributed by Signor Arno Monducci

ITALIAN ghost stories are always interesting to lovers of the supernatural, and they are extremely difficult to get first hand, as the Roman Catholic Church sternly discountenances non-miraculous voices and apparitions. Hence few, if any, ghost stories are published in Italy, and the only possible way to collect psychic happenings is from people who have actually experienced them.

In 1932, when I was compelled to pass fifteen weary months in Bologna, I made the acquaintance of Signor Arno Monducci, who, like myself was devoted to psychical research, and I listened, entranced, to his stories of the haunted countryside on the borderland of Tuscany and Romagna.

"It is a lovely region," said Signor Monducci, "a paradise of vineyards and olive groves, with the Apennines for a background, from whence rivers and restless mountain streams flow into the valleys below.

"The peasants relate various legends of these haunted highways, but, as you want actual experiences, I will tell you about some that happened to my relations and friends, since, being a Romagnola, I have family interests in that part of the world.

"Let me first tell you about the earth-bound spirit of a priest, who lived and died in the Monte Fone district not so many years ago, whose hauntings are as persistent as they are *real*.

"One evening a girl friend of my sister's was passing the little cemetery, when she heard a voice saying an Ave Maria in tones of evident distress. There was nobody in sight, and as the cemetery, with its high walls and dark cypresses, must have looked ghostly in the gathering twilight, Guilia, who had every excuse to feel frightened, ran all the way home, always followed by the sound of the sad voice.

"Fortunately for her peace of mind she did not *see* the priest, who occasionally walks in the valley, reading his breviary ; and she was also spared from sharing the fate of one of my father's woodmen. This is what happened to him.

"After working late in the chestnut woods, Battista came back to his cottage shortly before dawn, and when he opened the door he saw the dead priest of Monte Fone sitting by the stove. Knowing the priest so well during his lifetime, he realized there could be no question of mistaken identity, so all that the poor man could find to say was :

" '*Are you not dead ?*'

"The priest looked at his former parishioner, who afterwards described the ghost's eyes as 'smouldering like red-hot charcoal'.

" 'My body is buried, Battista,' said the priest, 'but my spirit lives, condemned to expiate a mortal sin committed during my earthly life. This is my punishment. I must remain in this valley for a hundred years—finding no repose in the midday heat, or any shelter when the bleak winter winds sweep through the leafless woods. Know then, that Time and God will give judgment, and pray for me.'

"The figure disappeared, and the trembling peasant threw himself on his bed and tried to sleep, fearful every moment lest the dark form would return . . . and his superstitious terror augmented to such a degree, that an hour later he had a slight stroke which rendered him temporarily speechless. His condition was only discovered when some of the neighbours, wondering why Battista had not gone to work, found him lying in bed, vainly trying to make himself heard.

"Battista recovered sufficiently to tell my father what had happened, but the poor fellow developed jaundice, and died eighteen days later.

"The ghost of the priest has been seen by many reliable witnesses, and last year (1931), when military manoeuvres were taking place in our mountains, the priest appeared one night to a Bersaglieri who was passing the cemetery. . . . Wishing to ask for some spiritual guidance, the soldier waited for the priest at a little bridge higher up the road.

"On came the priest, but when he reached the bridge he vanished, and the Bersaglieri, who usually feared nothing and nobody, took to his heels and made for his quarters, where he related his strange experience and heard that the same thing had happened to several others of his company who had taken the cemetery road after nightfall.

"The restless presence of the priest has caused a great deal of uneasiness in the district—so much so, that the weight of excommunication was called in, as it was hoped by this means to make the priest change his locale. But excommunication availed nothing, and nothing will drive the ghost away until it has served its sentence of a hundred years ! One of its most unpleasant manifestations takes place in the forests, when peasants carrying loads of wood feel their burdens increased by the weight of an invisible man, who repeats the Ave Maria inseparable from the apparition.

"As you prefer up-to-date hauntings, I remember a certain wooden cross which stands close to an old bridge in the Toscana country, and marks the spot where, barely a dozen years ago, a traveller was killed when his horse, taking fright, jumped the low parapet and fell on the rocky bed of the river below.

"I was told that some of the peasants had often seen the ghosts of the horse and its rider, but I never imagined that I should come in contact with them and 'hear' them for myself. This happened one night when I was coming back from a local *festa* with four friends, none of us thinking about ghosts or hauntings ; as we approached the bridge we heard the sound of horses' hoofs, and saw in front of us a swift-moving ball of fire, which disappeared close to the wooden cross. At this moment a stifled cry of 'Help !' rose from the bed of the river. . . .

" 'It *must* be the ghost !' we exclaimed simultaneously, and I wasn't at all sorry when we had crossed the bridge and left the haunted road behind us. . . . But, tell me, Signora, are you interested in animal ghosts, because, if so, I can give you a good deal of information."

I said : "Any kind of 'returns' appeals to me."

"Well, phantom dogs, or the shadows of dogs, haunt the mountains ; these are quite harmless, and not half so terrifying as the spectral bloodhounds of Cannacio, which run in and out of the old *Castello* when the hunt is up before morning. It is well known that stables and cowsheds on lonely estates are haunted by spirits in one form or another, and a farmhouse on a property belonging to my uncle was haunted by the ghost of an industrious old servant, who used to cut up kindling wood in an outhouse, and afterwards came into the kitchen, where she threw the chairs about, something in the manner of a German poltergeist.

"A curious psychic occurrence at San Terno took place in the stables, when one usually quiet horse was often heard kicking and rearing in its stall, and my uncle at last made up his mind to investigate the cause. To his surprise he found the animal covered with foam, and its mane plaited in a grotesque way. On another occasion the shadow of a horse with a dog rider was plainly silhouetted against the white wall of the cortile, the shadow finally materializing *as* a horse, which galloped away in the darkness. I don't pretend to be able to offer any explanation of these things, but they are as true as the story of the tongues of fire once seen at a wedding *festa* near San Terno.

"The bridegroom-to-be was the only son of a prosperous agriculturist. He was already experienced in the ways of love, but in one instance he had carried his trifling too far, and the betrayed girl had taken what she considered to be the easiest way out. This tragic incident did not constitute any impediment to marriage with the daughter of a neighbouring farmer, and nothing unusual took place until the united families had assembled for the traditional Romagna wedding banquet and dance.

THE RUINED TOWER OF CANNACIO, SHOWING THE OPENING
THROUGH WHICH THE GHOSTLY HOUNDS COME AND GO

Some Italian ghost stories

THE HAUNTED COTTAGE

A haunted cottage in Mayfair

Suddenly terrible blows were heard overhead, and a late arrival, shaking with fear, rushed into the great kitchen, announcing : 'The house is surrounded by flames !'

"The guests crowded round the entrance, and sure enough the house was encircled by a ring of flickering tongues of fire, which disappeared in a single line in the direction of the river where the unfortunate girl had drowned herself. From that day all good luck left the farm, and the marriage represented the failure which it would probably have been in any case, even if the dead girl's 'fire' curse had not been laid upon it.

"Shadows of the past and shadows of another world are alike thrown on this beautiful blood-stained country, and although I know you prefer true ghost stories to ghostly legends, I feel I must tell you the story of the old bridge at Vatreno, now rebuilt as the only bridge in the world having a single arch span of 1100 feet.

"The old bridge was once the scene of constant fighting between representatives of the Tossignani and the Allidosi, two noble and strife-loving families, living on opposite sides of the border. Their quarrels and fights were accepted as a matter of course, until *real* trouble came when a brother of the reigning Allidosi fell in love with Laura di Tossignani, who refused to listen to his proposals, still less to see him. Becoming desperate, the young lord staged an abduction which would appeal to any modern scenario writer.

"One dark night a picked party of the Allidosi came over the border and camped out in the wooded country adjacent to the *Castello* of the Tossignani. Owing to a purposely false report that the *Castello* was undefended, the Allidosi forced an entrance, only to meet with such a determined resistance (accentuated by frantic ringing of the Castle alarm bell), that they fled in confusion, leaving two of their number behind them.

"Next morning the prisoners were brought before the overlord of the district, who interrogated them, at first to no purpose. Afterwards, when they knew that their continued silence would mean a very unpleasant death,

they confessed that the love-raid had originated solely with
the young lord of Allidosi.

"When this open confession became known over the
border, the haughty lover sent an envoy to demand the
instant return of the prisoners, saying that if this were
refused they would be taken by force !

"The Tossignani, enraged by this high-handed attitude,
sought assistance from their neighbours, and when the
Allidosi returned to the charge, headed by one of the family,
they were met at the river by the Tossignani and their
allies, and a desperate fight took place, a large number of
soldiers being drowned in the swift-flowing waters. The
young lord was saved, but after this wholesale drowning
the Allidosi decided to build a bridge, where, at least, they
could fight the Tossignani without getting wet !

"The old bridge, admirably planned, with a series of
rooms on either side for attack and defence, witnessed
many encounters, and the peasants declare that every year,
towards the middle of September, a long file of shadowy
men-at-arms, led by the young lord, may be seen crossing
the *new* bridge to renew the feud with their ghostly op-
ponents awaiting them on the other side of the water.

"A not unamusing supernatural experience recently
happened to an old man I knew well—a disagreeable
individual, the custodian of the Castle of the Cannacio,
who never allows the keys of the ancient Bell Tower to
leave his possession.*

"This cross-grained fellow lived in a corner of the
deserted *Castello*, and one night the peasants of the district
were awakened by the sound of the Great Bell of the
Cannacio, sending its brazen message of warning across the
countryside. Believing the custodian to have become suddenly insane, a number of villagers made their way to the
Castello, to the disturbing accompaniment of the alarm
bell, and when they arrived there, they met the custodian
literally foaming with rage, dancing about in front of the
tower, demanding the saints to tell him who had dared set
the bell in motion.

---

* The custodian of Cannacio died shortly afterwards.

"Next morning, the custodian, still beside himself, asked justice of the Mayor, explaining that as he invariably slept with the keys under his pillow, *someone* must have entered the tower surreptitiously, in order to annoy him.

" 'Wait and see if the disturbance happens again,' said the pacific Mayor. . . . And sure enough, three nights later, the Great Bell rang out at midnight! This was the last straw, and the custodian's wrath was only appeased by the wily suggestion of the parish priest, that the old Lords of Cannacio must be great admirers of Mussolini, and had caused the Castle Bell to be rung in order to summon the descendants of their vassals to place themselves, not under the jurisdiction of the Cannacio, but under that of the New Italy."

THE GHOST AT THE PALAZZO CAFFARELLI, NAPLES

(*Miss Mary Boyle's Experience*)

THIS occurrence happened some years ago, when Miss Mary Boyle was travelling in Italy with her mother and sister, but it may be taken as authentic, as Miss Boyle not only saw the ghost once, but many times.

The Boyles, who had wintered in Rome, went to Naples in the early spring, and it seems futile to enthuse about the Italian *primavera*—certainly not the English lass with the delicate air, who dances lightly over a carpet of bluebells, and leaves her gentle kisses on the trees and hedgerows, as *this* spring is a glowing passionate beauty, breathing a thousand heady perfumes, garlanded with many-hued flowers, embodying in herself the promise of the year's later luxuriant maturity. What sentimental memories cling round spring-time in Italy! I have only to close my eyes to see the Piazza di Spagna, a sea of colour and fragrance, and I possess an unforgettable memory of pinkish purple peach-blossom, set against the burning blue and gold of noonday in the Campagna.

A well-meaning friend had recommended the Santa Lucia Quartier at Naples as likely to suit the Boyles, but they found hotel life there impossible. Santa Lucia was neither harmonious nor healthy, being the principal resort of the fishermen, and not only their loud voices, but the continued presence of fish, made it difficult for the Boyles to appreciate the freshness of morning, or the sea breezes at night. This being so, they determined to take a flat, and were fortunate enough to find one on the lower floor of the Palazzo Caffarelli, at the corner of the Chiaja and the Piazza Caffarelli, close to the lovely gardens of the Villa Reale.

The rooms were spacious and lofty ; two of the bed-rooms had the disadvantage of being passage rooms, but Mary Boyle was too young to trouble over trifles ; she was delighted with her "dormitory" as she called it, which formed a corner, one window overlooking the Piazza, the other the Chiaja, and in after years she described how she used to watch the tideless sea, dazzling in the sunlight, silver and onyx in the moonlight. "It is never night at Naples", and Mary Boyle discovered this, when varying sounds, ranging from the rumbling of market carts to the twang of guitars, kept her awake. Unfortunately, the street noises were accentuated owing to the heat, which made it necessary to open the windows and allow plenty of fresh air to circulate through the flat.

There was a short space between Mrs. Boyle's bedroom door and that of Mary's sister, which were placed at right angles to each other in a corner of Mary's room, and every night for four months she saw the figure of a woman pass through these doors, which were always left open.

The young girl was not afraid when she first saw the form in the uncertain light. Its outlines and movements registered Youth, and, thinking it might be her sister, she called her, but, receiving no answer, she decided that she had not been heard. The figure came again. Mary paid little, if any, attention to its visits. There were four women beside herself in the flat—it might easily be one of them— but afterwards she gradually became attracted by the peculiar gliding movement of the unknown wanderer, whilst the fact that she never received any answer to the inevitable question "Who's there ?" considerably puzzled her.

One night when the figure made its usual appearance, Mary, taking her courage in both hands, jumped out of bed, and followed the figure as it went into her sister's room. It vanished on the threshold, and the mystery of its identity remained a mystery.

Again and again Mary followed the form, and at last she confided her adventure to her mother, hoping to find out whether Mrs. or Miss Boyle had also seen the "ghost". Her questioning was brushed aside.

"My dear Mary," said Mrs. Boyle, "you are talking nonsense ! How could anyone possibly come night after night into your sister's bedroom without her knowledge ? Your ghost is probably a reflection thrown by something outside. Don't let your mind dwell on such things."

Mary said : "I'm not frightened—only *curious*."

"This kind of curiosity is ill-advised," replied her mother—"and please remember not to breathe a word of this to anyone. Our Roman servants were fanciful enough in all conscience, but Neapolitans seem to be the last word in ignorant credulity."

A little offended and "snubbed" by Mrs. Boyle's want of sympathy, Mary did not allude again to the mysterious figure. As she said, she was not frightened, and she began to think the whole thing was a freak of imagination, until she heard the well-known rustle, and saw "Her" pass through the accustomed door.

As the summer, even for Naples, was exceptionally hot, Mrs. Boyle changed her bedroom for one with a cooler aspect, and Mary, who had moved into her mother's room, wondered if the figure would appear to her *there*. To quote her own words :

"Yes, every night : the hour varied, as was my time for going to bed, *but the visit was certain*."

One day when Mary was complaining of sleeplessness to Teresa, an elderly servant, who represented a kind of fixture in the Palazzo as *donna di faccenda* to one or another of the tenants, the problem of the figure's identity was partially solved.

"So, the Signorina can't sleep," said Teresa compassionately. "Well, I've often wondered how you manage to sleep at *all*—in this apartment."

"Why—for what reason ?" asked Mary. "It isn't always so hot, and I'm getting quite accustomed to the noises outside."

"Ah . . . the Signorina and her family have evidently never heard the sounds and screams which at times disturb the other inmates of the *palazzo*. Perhaps she has *seen* ?"

Intrigued by the possibility that Teresa knew something, and disregarding Mrs. Boyle's opinion of Neapolitan credulity, Mary burnt her boats, and told Teresa all about the figure.

Teresa listened attentively, crossed herself devoutly, implored the assistance of the Madonna, and whispered :

"The Signorina is the only person in the *Palazzo* who has actually seen the ghost. It is a sad story. In the very room occupied by the Signorina, a young English lady died broken-hearted for love of the (then) Prince of Capua."

More than this Teresa refused to disclose ; perhaps the love affair was taboo in the *palazzo*. And Mary Boyle, who could not speak Italian fluently, and had no Italian friends, was prevented from making investigations on her own account.

It was her first and last experience of the supernatural, but she never forgot the girl who died for love, and she always regretted that the true facts of the romance were lost to her.

A HAUNTED COTTAGE IN MAYFAIR

MY PERSONAL EXPERIENCES WHILST LIVING THERE

By Maude M. C. ffoulkes

SOME years ago (perhaps the happiest period of my life), I lived in a genuinely haunted cottage in Mayfair. The cottage was the queerest little swallow's nest, a survival of the period when that part of London was open country, and I believe it is marked on some of the earliest survey maps of the district.

Externally the cottage was uninteresting, and it gave no hint of hauntings or "returns" ; nevertheless it already possessed a "social" history of its own. In the early days of the nineteenth century it had served as the *pied-à-terre* of a notorious Regency rake, years afterwards the late Lord Rowton occasionally used it as a kind of sanctuary where he found solitude and rest, and I have also heard that Queen Mary, as Princess May of Teck, once stayed at the cottage for a night with her lady-in-waiting, when she went to a party given by some friends living close by. I cannot vouch for the truth of this—I merely repeat the tale as it was told to me. I suppose it must have been in Lord Rowton's time.

Madame Adelina Patti's niece, Guilia Strakosch, occupied the cottage before I took possession of it, and I remember how thrilled I was when I realized she had lived there, especially when I saw the imposing wardrobe cupboards on the top landing (designed for gowns *alone*) which, on opening the doors, breathed sighs of perfume which must have been especially created to express the wearer's personality.

As my new home was only represented by a number, my friend, Eveleigh Nash, gave it the name associated with it today.

The cottage was the quaintest place. The rooms had been originally divided, but at some time or other the partitions were removed in order to make one long narrow room on each floor. There was also a dark basement, which, in my unregenerate days, I never realized must have been horrible even for the most contented pre-war servants. The dining-room, with a wide window and a window-seat, was level with the street ; the drawing-room was on the first floor ; one bedroom was above it, and the top floor was arranged as a small bathroom and a maid's bedroom.

The stairs were almost as steep as a ship's ladder, and the doors slid on runners into the walls to save space. Altogether it was a most suitable home for anyone like myself, usually described as "so terribly peculiar, my dear".

I soon settled down, but gradually I became aware of an atmosphere of sadness in the house. This I dismissed as "fanciful", as surely no sadness existed where vivid and beautiful Guilia Strakosch had lived, but I was certainly a little puzzled by footsteps ascending and descending the stairs, either in the small hours or late at night. Occasionally I heard them in the afternoon.

Perhaps I should not have noticed anything unusual if I had not been deeply interested in Hauntings ever since I arrived at years of indiscretion, so I argued that the footsteps must belong to *someone*, and if I couldn't *see* the *someone*, it must be nothing more or less than a ghost.

I made inquiries. These elicited that there *was* a story about the cottage, but nobody seemed able to remember exactly *what* it was. Afterwards, I made friends with the pretty young wife of my landlord, who, more communicative than the rest of my little world, confided to me that at a certain time of the year it was impossible, owing to noises, and *"Things"*, for her children to sleep on the top floor of their house. As their house adjoined the cottage, I wondered whether the footsteps had any connection with the periodical disturbances next door.

I was very happy. Success after success came to me, and I like to remember the cavalcade of celebrities who visited the cottage during my tenancy. . . . Some of the names figure in European history, whilst there were others, the wonderful artists, authors, actors, dancers, and dreamers who alone make life colourful and worth while.

It was partly due to the suggestion of one of these "imaginative" friends, that I decided to hold a seance, with Vango as the medium, in order to find out the cause of the sadness which always persisted inside the cottage.

I have just heard that Mr. Vango is alive today and has written his reminiscences. He was one of the most genuine and interesting mediums I have ever met, and this particular seance was noteworthy, not only for the discovery that the cottage was haunted by the ghost of a girl who had committed suicide there (probably in the riotous days when George IV was Prince Regent), but also for the curiously intimate facts revealed to some of the "sitters".

The ghost, through Vango's control, said she resented anyone living in the cottage, and would continue to make her presence felt, hoping in this way to obtain undisputed possession of her old home with its bitter-sweet memories. This did not disturb me in the least ; at any rate I knew to whom the footsteps belonged. I was to see their owner later.

At this time I did most of my literary work in my bedroom, and when I sat at my bureau I faced the half-glass door that lightened the dark landing, and I was also able to see, and hear, anyone going up or down stairs.

One afternoon I heard footsteps on the floor below, and a few moments afterwards a woman went slowly up the last flight. Thinking this to be my maid, I called her, but receiving no reply, I went upstairs to her room. Nobody was there . . . and putting the figure down to a trick of the dim light, I went on with my work.

Three days passed before I saw the figure again ; this time there was no possibility of mistaking it, and its appearance was the forerunner of two very curious psychic happenings.

One Saturday evening, Mr. and Mrs. Frank Charley, who had previously dined with me, were sitting in the drawing-room recalling old times to such good purpose that we never noticed the lateness of the hour, and we were only brought back to earth by someone knocking at the front door . . . *hammering* is the word which best describes it, because my antique Medici knocker from a Florentine *palazzo* was only capable of producing such emphatic sounds.

My mother was then in very poor health, so I naturally supposed that someone from Kensington had brought bad news, and, as Frank Charley and I ran downstairs, the hammering became more and more intense. But when we opened the front door the little street was empty and as quiet as the grave. (And now I must digress for a moment in order to explain that on Saturday night our environment was usually deserted, as the business houses closed early, and few people passed through the passage-street.)

However, Frank Charley went one way, whilst I scouted in another direction, only to return to the cottage with the same information—no one was in sight.

This ghostly knocking was heard by three people, but, so far as I remember, it had no especial signification or premonition.

The next psychic occurrence took place when Dr. William Brown Thomson, then living in Brook Street, who often dropped in for a chat, to the accompaniment of a cigarette and a whisky-and-soda, was telephoned for one evening almost as soon as he had arrived. There was little chance of his return at a reasonable hour, so I said good night, and went back to the drawing-room to switch off the lights.

Directly I entered the room, I sensed the presence of something evil—something earth-bound, an invisible slave to formerly uncontrolled bodily appetites—and I received a distinct impression that this evil entity had once been a drunkard. It was summer ; both windows were wide open, and, impelled by I knew not what, I seized the untouched whisky-and-soda, and emptied it out on to the window-box. . . . The remaining spirit in the decanter found the same destination, and the pleasant flower-filled room became normal again.

Apart from this very unpleasant manifestation, I never came up against anything else of a similar nature. However, my maid, Kate Eden, was not so fortunate. Kate, who lived close by, was deputed during my summer holiday to go daily to the cottage and carry on as usual, and one afternoon when she was polishing the sides of the stairs, she heard a devilish laugh close beside her. She listened—a little frightened—but when the laugh was repeated, Kate bolted, and after this she brought her little daughter to bear her company.

Another psychic experience connected with the cottage concerns the famous historian, the late Major Martin Hume, who regarded the cottage with the same passion which inspired King David to covet Naboth's vineyard. The Major was always asking me to let him have the remainder of the lease, and the more I said No, the more persistent he became; in fact, it was customary with Major Hume to pass by my window once a week, on his way to the Devonshire Club, and gaze at the exterior of the cottage, which he hoped eventually to possess—after constant dropping had worn away the stone, represented by me and my tenancy.

I was sitting on the dining-room window-seat one Saturday afternoon, when I noticed Major Hume looking at the cottage in his usual possessive manner, and, as I wanted to speak to him about a book of Memoirs in which I was collaborating, I hurried to the front door, feeling sure he was still outside.

To my surprise there was no sign of Major Hume. It was impossible for him to disappear so suddenly, only a minute had elapsed since I left the dining-room, and, even if he had walked on, I should certainly have seen him before he reached the end of the little street.

A week later Eveleigh Nash told me that Major Hume had died on the very day, and I believe almost the same hour, when his "ghost" stood outside the cottage. He was taken ill on a week-end visit to one of his sisters. His friends had no knowledge of his whereabouts, so his death came as a shock to a great many people—myself included.

I lived at the cottage for six years—I have previously alluded to them as being the happiest period of my life— but as all things work together towards one end, Destiny decreed that I and the cottage should part company.

I have always regretted leaving it : the restless ghost did not affect me ; perhaps she was tolerant of me, for, like her, I was to know the heart's bitterness, and the dark waters which submerge the soul.

The subsequent "supernatural" history of the cottage is interesting, as it all goes to prove that it was definitely haunted.

I disposed of my lease to a well-known man, but for some reason he never lived in the cottage. Afterwards came a pretty, unhappily married woman, who died tragic- ally after a very short tenancy. She was followed by an American who admitted frankly that nothing on earth would induce her to remain a day longer than was abso- lutely necessary. "Much too disturbing" was *her* verdict.

The cottage was rarely occupied for any length of time ; at last it stood empty for months on end. I remember passing it on a bleak January afternoon, when all the world was covered with snow, and my pity went out towards the weather-splashed windows and the general unkempt appearance of what had once been so well tended.

The cottage was swept and garnished by another new owner, who, to do him justice, modernized it without destroying its delicate air of the past. But his wife refused to live there, so once more the little house was "up" for disposal at a rental of £250—ex taxes, and a premium of £1000. (I had paid £112 yearly, *including* taxes. Sir —— certainly wore *his* rue with a difference !)

Three years ago I looked over the cottage, then To Let, but alas ! not in hopes of living there. This time it was a pilgrimage of remembrance, and when memories which shall not be destroyed crowded on me, I distinctly heard the sound of familiar footsteps overhead.

Today the cottage is a shop, and the grey-haired aristo- cratic proprietress made me welcome, and forgave my non-business intrusion, when I went to see if my former home had been destroyed in the tempest of change which has swept over Mayfair. To my relief, the cottage was untouched! There was no shop window, everything was planned on gracious lines. . . . Modernity certainly existed, but it was not obtrusive, and the lovely display of femininities gained thereby.

I told the proprietress who I was, and, when we became better acquainted, she said that when she first came to the cottage she felt if anything inanimate possessed the power to *hate*, the place *hated* her. "But," she smiled, "I love it, so perhaps I shall be 'allowed to stay'."

This story begins with a psychic mystery; it shall end with a material one.

"It's curious you should have called today," said my charming acquaintance. "Only last week, such a nice man asked if he might sit in the 'shop' for half an hour. 'I spent some of the happiest times of my life in this cottage, when Maude ffoulkes lived here,' he told me."

I wonder which of my sentimental pasts he represents?

THE CAPTAIN'S RETURN

A True Ghost Story of the Island of Inishinny

Told to the Rev. *Archdeacon St. John Seymour, B.D., Litt.D.,*
by Mr. T. Macfadden

THE REV. ARCHDEACON ST. JOHN SEYMOUR, well known as
a writer on the supernatural, has been kind enough to allow
me to use the material contained in a letter sent him from
Mr. T. Macfadden, in which the writer gives details of a
true ghost story, the incidents being vouched for by Mr.
Macfadden's father, one of those who witnessed the
Captain's "return".

The little Island of Inishinny is one of the most picturesque places on the Donegal coast, and, with its sister
islands, Gola and Inismaan, it provides a natural harbour
and a safe anchorage for storm-tossed vessels.

A few years ago, about a fortnight before Christmas, a
small sailing ship put into the Gola Roads in the height of a
prolonged storm, and, as the supply of provisions was
almost exhausted, the Captain and two sailors came off in
one of the ship's boats to "fill up" at Bunbeg. They were
quite at home on the island, and the people from the main-
land, resident at Inishinny, knew them well.

The old harbour bar, never very safe even at the best of
times, was a seething cauldron of foam on the evening of
the Captain's arrival. However, the small boat managed to
get inside the bar, and the Captain and his men were
warmly welcomed by the islanders. But the oldest inhabitant, whose knowledge of weather lore excelled the wisdom
of King Solomon, prophesied some dreadful calamity
should the Captain venture to return to his ship that night.

Captains are always courageous, and sometimes fool-
hardy . . . this Captain was both. He had already lost time

141

through the storm, he couldn't afford to wait any longer. Once amply provisioned, all would be well, and he'd soon call back at Inishinny to tell his friends what a lot of silly old women they had been.

The oldest inhabitant shook his head, and a chorus of entreaties to stay arose on every side. The Captain, bent on his own destruction, refused to listen, although the storm was increasing and the wild white horses of the sea tossed their manes as they dashed furiously towards the land. The winds roared encouragement, the stars went out, and darkness, deep and impenetrable, fell on Inishinny.

The Captain's scanty knowledge of the difficulties of the channel, doubly increased by the force of the tempest, brought about the final catastrophe.

The morning after the storm was comparatively serene. Skies, shading from a sullen leaden colour to faintest pearl grey, flecked with occasional bars of primrose, showed the whereabouts of the imprisoned sun ; the wild white horses were stalled deep in the ocean, and the sea, encumbered with a load of wreckage, was casting it ashore with the incoming tide.

One of the islanders, early astir, was busy gathering in the harvest of the sea, when, as he waded out to pick up a piece of wet driftwood, he saw, lying in a shroud of glistening brown seaweed, the body of the Captain who only a few hours previously had laughed at the possibility of danger. Lower down, lay a battered boat rejected by the sea, but no trace existed of the sailors who had accompanied their Captain on the face of the waters.

There was keening and mourning at Inishinny throughout the dreary winter's day. Word was sent to the Captain's wife in Derry, and kindly women arranged the corpse, and left it temporarily "chested" in the little church.

A few days later the widow arrived at Inishinny, and took away her husband's body, to bury it with those of his own people, seafaring folk like himself who had also gone down to the sea in ships.

Gloom still hung over Inishinny, and sorrow showed her tear-drenched face at the blessed Festival of Christmas.

But this condition was not entirely due to the recent tragedy—the islanders were too much accustomed to death to fear it ; what now obsessed them was a subconscious dread of the *Unknown*.

Mr. Macfadden's father happened to be at Inishinny at the psychological moment when the islanders, afraid of solitude and darkness, usually spent their evenings together in one house.

On the evening of the Captain's "return", they were seated round the peat fire, chatting, and enjoying a "dhrop of the crathur", when they heard the sound of approaching footsteps. This caused the more imaginative to glance at each other apprehensively. The house was literally built on sand, which hitherto had deadened any description of footsteps. *These* rang as clear as if coming over hard and frosty ground.

No strangers were staying on the island. Who, then, could it be ?—and Mr. Macfadden and the others sitting by the red fire faced the door expectantly

On came the footsteps. The watchers, whose expressions now showed various kinds of emotion, waited for further developments, and at last the door opened. The cold north wind lifted pieces of peat ash, scattering them like grey snowflakes, and a tall stalwart form filled the doorway—that of the Captain who had been buried in the graveyard at Derry several days previously !

The apparition wore the same kind of clothes which the Captain always wore on board ship, even down to the cheese-cutter cap. There he stood—looking at his terrified friends, until a woman, sitting in a corner opposite the door, broke the icy silence, by saying in a low voice to Mr. Macfadden :

"Oh God !—Patrick, shure there's the Captain !" These everyday words helped Mr. Macfadden to regain his courage and in a spirit of recklessness he addressed the dead in Irish.

"Come in," said he.

No sooner did Mr. Macfadden give the invitation than the figure moved backwards and disappeared. No retreating footsteps were heard ; the wind continued its fantastic progress through the living-room, and, the nerve tension becoming unbearable, one of the men seized a lighted storm-lantern set against the wall, and ordered those present to follow him into the night.

The search continued well into the small hours, during which time no stranger was discovered within the confines of Inishinny.

This is a true account of the Captain's "return", when he appeared to Mr. Macfadden and other reliable witnesses present on that wild December night at the house on the sand. For what purpose did the spirit of the drowned man appear ? Perhaps he desired the prayers of the living, or he may have been grateful for the care shown to his earthly body. It is entirely a matter for conjecture. The ways of "returns" constitute a law unto themselves, and only those who have devoted, and are still devoting, a life's work to Psychical Research can answer these conjectures, which possess the advantage of stimulating independent thought by suggesting various sidelines of strange inquiry. To quote the words of Archdeacon St. John Seymour :

What limits God in His Providence has seen fit to put upon us we cannot tell, for every moment the horizon is receding, and our outlook becoming larger, though some still find it difficult to bring their eyesight to the focus consequently required. The Marvellous of Today is the Commonplace of Tomorrow.

SOME GHOST STORIES FROM INDIA

"You don't believe in ghosts, Lord Beningfield ?"
"No one who has lived in Egypt or India disbelieves in 'em altogether, let me tell you. After all, what is a ghost ? Not a turnip and a sheet. Some houses are full of 'em, though you can't swear to a shadow that the sun and moon won't account for. There are creaks on the stair behind you—voices that whisper over your shoulder."—*Regency*, D. L. MURRAY.

THE mention of India opens up an unknown world of immense and unplumbed psychic possibilities, to say nothing of more ordinary ghostly "returns", of which the name must be legion. First-hand ghost stories, however, are difficult to obtain, perhaps owing to the fact that the majority of Anglo-Indians are extremely insular, and consider it their duty as Britishers not to encourage what they term "superstition".

Hence, authentic ghost stories are few and far between. Those well-known novelists, the late Mrs. B. M. Croker, Mrs. Alice Perrin, and Mrs. Penny, who have made military and civilian life in India romantic for those "at home", occasionally touch on the supernatural, whilst Flora Annie Steele, who knew English and native India like a book, could have told a thousand and one tales of haunted cantonments, and strange occurrences at rest-houses. But one must be grateful for small mercies, and, in connection with haunted bungalows, Mr. Douglas Hume, late Commissioner for a district in Abyssinia, contributes this story of an inexplicable and habitual occurrence at an old Government rest-house at Nanigundi, in Kadesh, Bombay Presidency.

Mr. Hume writes :

The house consists of four rooms in a row, with wide verandas all round the building, which is raised about two feet above the ground on a solid plinth made of old masonry.

The floor is of hard beaten earth. There are no windows, as the doors also serve for these, and are composed of teak about two inches thick. There is a teak ceiling just under the tiles, which are mostly old ones made locally.

The doors of the end room on the right in approaching the bungalow can never be kept shut at night. This room has six doors ; four being outer ones, one leading to the bathroom, and one leading to the next room, and they are the usual Indian type of double door opening in the centre. These doors are fastened by a bolt running into two staples, and on nearly every door there are several other hasps and staples, put on by various visitors. Most of these hasps and staples are screwed in with one-and-a-half-inch screws which are not visible from the other side of the door.

A man I knew once took his own hasps and staples, and screwed them in with strong screws, and before getting into bed he put on two $1\frac{1}{2}$-inch Chubb padlocks. Five minutes after he had extinguished the light he suddenly felt a breeze, but when he lit the lamp, he found all the doors wide open—not a sound was heard, and the locks were still locked on the staple. In the ordinary way it would be impossible to open the hasp without undoing the lock, even if the screws were unscrewed.

My friend felt nothing unusual, except that the first gust of breeze was very cold—there is always the same sensation of cold in psychic phenomena—but that may be put down to his imagination. However, the Indians will not go near the house at night, and no dog will enter the room—they even dislike going anywhere near the bungalow.

THE LATE MAHARANI OF COOCH BEHAR'S EXPERIENCE NEAR CAWNPORE

THE late Maharani of Cooch Behar had a strange experience when, as a child, she was travelling by road with her parents across country, as her father, whose name is known throughout India as a great reformer who aimed at abolishing child marriages and the tyranny of caste, often made long journeys with his family in order to give public lectures and addresses in out-of-the-way places.

One evening the party arrived so late at a small town not far from Cawnpore, that it was decided to pass the night in a disused Government building, placed at their disposal by the authorities. Mr. Sen was not only a reformer, but also a philosopher, accustomed to make the best of things, so the coolies proceeded forthwith to unload the baggage and prepare for the night.

When the future Maharani—then little Sunity Sen—began to look round the large, dimly lighted building, she noticed that the walls about ten inches upwards from the floor were covered with brown stains, as well as being scratched and cut about. However, this conveyed nothing to her; I suppose she only thought their quarters were rather dirty, and then forgot all about it. After the tired travellers had enjoyed some badly needed food, they made themselves comfortable in their improvised beds (probably hammocks), and settled themselves to sleep.

The Maharani told me, although it was the hot season, the hall was uncomfortably cold, and she could not close her eyes. . . . She felt frightened, but she could not have explained *why*, especially as she was not alone. Her uneasiness persisted. She heard a door being cautiously opened . . . and she understood that there were quite a number of people in the hall. It was now dark ; burning any kind of lights during the night had been prohibited, so she could see *nothing*, although she was well aware of stealthy movements which seemed to come from every corner of the building.

Her father and mother were fast asleep, and little Sunity did not like to disturb them—even when there came noises of scufflings, and stifled cries—whisperings—thuds—an occasional groan, and a choking prayer for mercy.

Afterwards all was quiet, and the child, too terrified to stir, and not daring to close her eyes, waited for the coming of dawn, when once again she saw the stained and scratched walls, but nothing, or nobody else, was visible.

Later, she told her parents, who made inquiries, which
disclosed what had happened in the building during the
Mutiny of '57, when a number of English ladies had
sought shelter there (the building had no connection
with the House of the Ladies at Cawnpore), and were murdered almost as soon as they had found "sanctuary". The
stains and scratches spoke for themselves, and it was well
known that the place witnessed periodical repetitions of the
horrors which had occurred there. It was with feelings of
relief that the travellers went on their way, but the late
Maharani always insisted on the truth of her story, especia-
ally as she said she could never forget what the sounds in the
darkness must have represented.

THE MAN IN THE TURBAN

A HAUNTED BUNGALOW IN CEYLON

(By courtesy of Miss Estelle Stead)

MR. WILLIAM PATTERSON HENRY is responsible for an
authentic Indian ghost story, this time from Ceylon, when
he and his family were living at a bungalow on a large tea
and coffee plantation of some hundreds of acres.

The Henrys found existence in Ceylon, with its fragrant
winds and delightful climate, ideal. The charming
bungalow, situated on a hill overlooking a valley, formed
three sides of a square with a wing at each end, a veranda
ran the entire length of the house, and continued round the
north, or nursery, end. Mr. and Mrs. Henry slept in the
middle of the building, and it was customary with them to
go to the nursery wing every night before going to bed, to
see that everything was well with their two children.

One night Mr. Henry awoke with the feeling that
someone was in the room. . . . He switched on the light,
but, except for himself, the bedroom was empty, and he was
just dropping off to sleep, when he heard the sound of

knocking, proceeding from the door of the children's room. At this moment Mrs. Henry came in.

"Whatever is the matter?" said she. "Whoever can be knocking at this time of night? Do go and find out."

Whereupon her husband, hastily putting on a pair of slippers, went outside to discover the cause of this deliberate knocking of six distinct knocks, one after the other.

Nothing was visible! . . . and the puzzled Mr. Henry was just about to go back to bed, when he caught sight of someone crouching under a large shrub, who, on being discovered, stood upright, bolted along the path, with Mr. Henry in close pursuit, until the retreating figure put on such speed that he was obliged to give up the chase. Shouting lurid threats of shooting, arrest, and imprisonment, Mr. Henry returned empty-handed to the bungalow.

He described what he had seen to his wife. "It was certainly a native," said he, "and a native well over the average height. He wore an enormous turban, and, as far as I could make out, a robe of Madras muslin——" But he stopped short, remembering something more than curious about the flying figure.

"What's the matter?" asked Mrs. Henry, alarmed at her husband's expression. "Are you ill?"

Mr. Henry said: "My dear, it has struck me that *I could see no lower limbs*, and I never heard the suspicion of a sound of footsteps, as I watched *it* speeding down the road."

After this the Henrys very wisely said no more—and so (again) to bed.

Next day when Mr. Henry came back after a tour of inspection round the plantation, he found that his wife had been employing part of the morning in trying to find out who the midnight visitor might have been. To her surprise, her inquiries were taken entirely as a matter of course.

"Why," chorused the household, *"that's only the ghost"*— apparently taking it for granted that the ghost "went" with the bungalow as a supernatural fixture.

The tea-planter was nothing if not thorough. He summoned the newly engaged servants, mostly Tamils and Cingalese, to his office, and subjected them to a gruelling cross-examination.   But one and all agreed in a startling manner to the presence of the ghost in their midst.

The gardener, the first witness for the "ghostly" defence, asserted that one morning when he came to work in the cool hours of dawn, he had seen a figure creeping round outside the nursery door, but, thinking it was some stray coollie, he took no notice, until the following morning, when he saw it again and hailed it, to receive no reply. On the third morning, thinking that the mysterious person was up to no good, he tried to seize hold of it, but his hand grasped the air, and he hurried to the kitchen in a state of mingled panic and excitement.

"There's nothing whatever to be frightened of," said the Cingalese natives of the country. "You've only met the ghost !"

"*What* ghost ?" asked the Tamil gardener.

"Why—the bungalow ghost—everybody sees it."

The evidence of the keeper of the cattle, and Mr. Henry's groom, went to show that the figure occasionally haunted the road leading to the cattle shed, and the groom had seen it standing at the stable door. The butler, the cook, the kitchen man, and the "boy" gave similar evidence, and one and all described the ghost as that of a tall man dressed in white, the exaggerated size of whose turban would make him noticeable anywhere.

More than ever mystified, the Henrys decided to question the children's ayah privately on her return (she had been away at her village for a few days) and prevent any collusion with the other ghost seers ; but when the secret inquiry took place the ayah told her employers quite unconcernedly that she was often awakened by knocking on the nursery door.

"Sometimes," said she, "there is nothing—sometimes I see a tall man in white robes, who walks away when I open the door. But," she continued, "the knocking is always strange. Just *six distinct knocks*."

"Always the same number ?" asked Mr. Henry.

"Always six knocks," replied the ayah.

"And when did you last hear it ?"

"It happens so often, that I never take any notice of it," said the ayah.

All subsequent inquiries proved useless. The ghost presented an unsolvable mystery, and the "legless" man, dressed in Madras muslin, continued to make periodical visits to the bungalow. For months Mr. Henry vainly tried by every means in his power to throw some light on this recurrent phenomena, but as it was impossible for him to give up his position on the estate, and as the children were spared meeting the ghost, the Henrys decided to see things through. However, it was not conducive to a steady "nerve" condition—to fall asleep, knowing that they might be awakened at any moment by the six knocks, and also, that somewhere in the tropical darkness an uneasy "return" from another world wandered, seeking rest, and finding none.

THE DEAD RIDER ON THE "GHOST" PONY

AN EXPERIENCE IN THE "HILLS"

(From records in the possession of the Society for Psychical Research, and by courtesy of Miss Estelle Stead)

WHEN General C. Barter, C.B., was living in the Indian hill country, he met with a supernatural experience, when not only did he see the ghost of a former acquaintance, but also that of the pony which he used to ride during his lifetime.

One evening when the General was returning from a day's shooting, he noticed a man on horseback, accompanied by several servants, coming slowly down a bridle-path, which sloped gradually to join the wider way on which the General was riding. It was bright moonlight, and the first warning of the unusual was given by the dogs, who ran to their master and crouched by his side, apparently frightened of the people on the bridle-path above.

On they came, and General Barter had a good view of them. The man on horseback, who was wearing dinner

dress, sat his powerful hill pony as if he were listless and
weary past endurance; the reins hung loosely from his
hands, and whilst a syce led the pony on either side, a third
servant supported the rider, to steady him in his seat.

What most concerned General Barter was the fact that
this particular road only led near his own house, and, not
expecting any visitors, he hailed the little group and asked
them what they wanted, and what they were doing hereabouts.

As he spoke, the rider stopped, and, gathering up the
fallen reins, looked General Barter full in the face, and
the latter, not knowing what ôn earth to make of the stillness and strangeness of the travellers, recognized, to his
surprise, a Lieutenant whom he had known some years
previously, and afterwards lost sight of.

General Barter remembered his former acquaintance as
a clean-shaven normal young man—this was a dead face,
its ghastly pallor and its encircling dark fringe of hair
accentuated by the tropical moonlight, which made the night
as bright as noonday; the body was more or less bloated.
And the General, startled, but not scared, rushed up the
steep bank to investigate for himself.

Unfortunately, more haste and less speed resulted in
General Barter falling forward in the loose earth, but
he eventually stood near the place where he had first seen
the waiting group—there was now not a trace of anybody.
As the direct road stopped at a precipice twenty yards
further on, the General, retracing his steps, ran down the
road to warn the little party, only to find no one in
sight.

Puzzled and annoyed by an occurrence for which he
could give no explanation, and finding it impossible to get
the "face" out of his mind, General Barter sought out a
friend of the Lieutenant, and gradually brought the conversation round to his name.

Said he : "How stout B. has become lately, and whatever possesses him to wear a beard in the ugly 'fringe'
fashion ?"

His friend stared at him.

"*How stout B. has become lately, and why does he sport such an ugly beard?* My dear fellow . . . don't you know that B. belongs definitely to the *Past*, and hasn't any Present, so far as we, and himself, are concerned ?"

"At any rate," replied the General, "I saw him last night, riding a dark brown stocky pony, with a hogged mane and tail."

"*Impossible*, or, if it be true, you've seen *two* ghosts !" exclaimed his genuinely surprised brother officer. "Why, B. has been dead a couple of years, and you certainly never set eyes on the pony during its lifetime. Perhaps I'd better explain. You know, as well as I do, that B. exceeded any kind of speed limit moral or otherwise, so what with drink and the seven devils which possessed him, he gradually became as swollen as a drowned dog. When he was on the sick list, he allowed his beard to grow as a hideous face fringe, in spite of anything we could say, and he took the fringe with him to the grave.

"As for the pony, which you never saw, *as a pony*, B. bought him in Peshawar, and it killed him one day when he was riding ultra-recklessly down the Trete Hill. And now, for the Lord's sake, tell me *your* story."

The General related all that had happened on the previous evening, and the two officers were at a loss to account for the phenomena, especially as they had never been really intimate with the dead man.

Once again truth is stranger than fiction, as well as proving the insistence of the supernatural in ordinary life, although the reason for such a manifestation occurring to someone who was not interested in the one who had "passed on" is incomprehensible. But as there still remains so much to make clear in the whys and wherefores of psychic phenomena, we must leave it at that, knowing that in the life after death, those who live on this side of the grave retain their identity in the other world, and "there is nothing hidden which shall not be revealed".

The late Mr. W. T. Stead (surely one of the wisest and most broadminded of men in his outlook on the supernatural ?) has said :

Whatever drawbacks there may be to the theory of the future life, there is at least one enormous compensating advantage in knowing that the accounts between Man and his Maker are not finally closed when he ceases to breathe on earth, and that the Almighty has still the infinite expanse of Eternity in which to vindicate the justice of His dealings with every human soul.

TWO IRISH GHOST STORIES

The Story of Wilful Warrender, the "White Lady" of Charles Fort, Kinsale.

(By the courtesy of the Rev. Archdeacon St. John D. Seymour, B.D., Litt.D.)

The military station of Charles Fort, near Kinsale, erected in 1667 by the Duke of Ormonde, is unquestionably haunted, and from time to time authentic accounts of the hauntings have been published.

The tragedy which accounts for the continuous psychic manifestations at Charles Fort, happened shortly after its construction, when Colonel Warrender was appointed Governor. The Colonel was a severe disciplinarian, and his daughter, anticipating the glamorous publicity of a name, was called "Wilful" . . . but, remembering her father's reputation, it is more than likely that "Wilful" was "a name and nothing more".

The beautiful girl was betrothed to Sir Trevor Ashurst, and their marriage was celebrated at Charles Fort with a great display of military pomp and circumstance. On the evening of the wedding day, after the last of the guests had departed, and Charles Fort had resumed its habitual orderliness, the bride and her husband were walking alone on the battlements, when suddenly Wilful's attention was attracted by some wild flowers growing between the clefts of the rocks on which the Fort is built.

"I have never seen anything so lovely," she said. "I wonder what kind of flowers they are ? I must certainly possess a bouquet. Won't you climb down and pick them for me ?"

This kind of climb down did not particularly appeal to the bridegroom, still wearing his wedding finery of velvet and brocade, but a sentry posted close by, who

155

had heard Wilful's words, and who, like the rest of the garrison, was one of her willing slaves, at once offered to get the flowers.

"But . . . what about your duty ?" said Wilful. "And what about my father ?—he'd set you against the wall, with a firing squad, for less than this."

"If his lordship will take my place whilst I gather the flowers, shure there won't be any throuble at all, at all," replied the cheerful Irishman. "And the General, God bless him, won't come this way for a long time."

The idea of this exchange of identities appealed to the high-spirited girl. "Bravely spoken !" cried she. "Trevor, I insist. . . ." And as no husband of a day could refuse his wife's first request, unconventional though it might seem, Trevor Ashurst put on the sentry's military coat, and shouldered his musket, whilst the soldier hurried off to find a rope. Having done so, he began the descent, and was soon lost to sight.

The search for the flowers was longer than Sir Trevor anticipated. Wilful, tired of waiting, had gone indoors. The evening air was strong . . . the wine which he had drunk was equally strong. It had been an arduous day—and because of these things, the bridegroom fell fast asleep in the sentry-box.

Another half-hour passed, and Sir Trevor still slept, unconscious of the approaching footsteps of Doom, represented by General Warrender, and ignorant that the wedding day, so happily begun, was destined to end in the night of tragedy.

Striding along the battlements came General Warrender, tall, distinguished, and overbearing—the typical seventeenth-century officer, who believed that severity and brutality were the only ways in which to train a soldier. His fury when he challenged the sentry and received no reply may well be imagined.

Once again came the curt challenge. Once again there was no answer ; and when the angry General had charged like a bull of Bashan into the sentry-box, he discovered that the offender was *asleep* !

It was impossible, owing to the semi-darkness, for General Warrender to see that the sleeper was his son-in-law—and I doubt whether his rage would have allowed him to grasp anything but the disgraceful fact that the sentry on duty was asleep.

Desperate diseases demand desperate remedies. General Warrender drew his pistol and shot the supposed sentry through the heart.

The sound of the shot echoed and re-echoed all over the fort, and a soldier at that moment clambering over the battlements with a bunch of wild flowers cried out wildly : "For the love of God, sir, what have ye done ?—ye have surely shot your son-in-law !"

The horrified General called for help. Lights flashed. Soldiers ran hither and thither ; and the fort surgeon, who, having dined and wined to perfection, was dozing in his own quarters, hurried to the scene of the tragedy.

When the surgeon unbuttoned the heavy overcoat, he realized that the cambric shirt with its Mechlin lace ruffles did not belong to any sentry, but had formed part of the wedding garments of Sir Trevor Ashurst, whose features were plainly recognizable in the fitful gleams of the lanterns

The unspoken question on the lips of the spectators— "Who would tell the bride ?"—was speedily answered. Scream after scream pierced the darkness like a succession of sword-thrusts, and Wilful—who, as soon as she knew something had happened, had rightly guessed the worst— threw herself on the body of her husband.

"He's dead !" she sobbed. Then, looking at her father : "*You* killed him! You killed him!" And rising to her feet— a tragic figure in her white satin wedding-gown, now stained with her husband's blood—she took a step forward, and, before anyone could prevent her, Wilful Ashurst flung herself over the battlements, and the rocks and the flowers received her in their embrace.

Confusion ran riot ; but later, the corpse of Trevor Ashurst and the broken body of his young wife were decently composed, and placed side by side on the canopied bed in which they had thought to pass their wedding night. . . . Then silence fell, and discipline reasserted itself. But in the small hours, General Warrender, after taking leave of his beloved Wilful, went into his study and shot himself.

He was found next morning by his orderly, a forlorn, huddled-up heap, lying prone on the floor, with his pride departed, and his dreams of preferment at an end—just an ordinary man, who hadn't the courage to face life and what it signified.

So much for the triple tragedy, of which Wilful represents the only "return"; but it is well known that, after her passing, reports were current at Charles Fort that her ghost haunted the house and battlements, and we owe the first authentic account of her appearance to Fort-Major Black, who served in the Peninsular War, and related his personal experience to a Dr. Craig.

Major Black told the doctor that one summer evening he saw a lady (who at first he thought to be the wife of one of the officers) going upstairs, and, as he glanced at her, he noticed she was wearing a gown made in the fashion of the previous century. Curious to know who was masquerading in fancy dress, he followed her into one of the rooms, only to lose sight of her!

On another occasion, when two sergeants were packing some stores, the little daughter of one of them called out: "Who is the lady looking at us over the balusters?"

The child's father glanced upwards. There was no one on the stairs.

"You silly little girl," said he, "you're dreaming . . . I can't see any lady."

The child persisted. "Oh, but there is. She's all in white, and she's smiling. I'm sure she thinks *you* are silly, not to be able to see her, just like I can." The next moment the child said the lady had "gone away".

Another true story connected with the return of Wilful Ashurst concerns a Staff officer—a married man, living in what is known at Charles Fort as the Governor's House. His children and their nurse slept in a bedroom near his own, and one night as the nurse lay awake she was surprised to see a lady in white standing by the youngest child's cot. After a little while the lady placed her hand on the child's wrist, and the little sleeper awoke, as frightened as it was cross.

"Take your nasty cold hand off my wrist," it sobbed.

Fifty-six years ago, when Captain Marvell Hull and Lieutenant Hartland were stationed at Charles Fort, the two officers were going to Captain Marvell's rooms when, as they reached a small landing, they noticed somebody in a white dress standing there.

Remembering the stories connected with the fort, the officers did not know whether to pass the ghost or to beat a retreat. Then Wilful turned and looked towards them, and they saw a lovely girl, with an ashen white face, and eyes like deep wells of sorrow, *who passed through a locked door*, leaving them with such badly shaken nerves that it required a stiff peg to restore their usual equilibrium.

Other psychic disturbances took place at Charles Fort which cannot be attributed to the agency of the White Lady, disturbances somewhat in the nature of a poltergeist mani-festation, when the spirit responsible for them always remains unseen, but I cannot put forward any reason to connect these with Wilful Ashurst, unless something malignant associated itself with the usual ghostly phenomena.

A few years ago, when an army surgeon was quartered at the fort, he met with an unpleasant experience after a belated return from snipe-shooting. As he did not appear at mess, an officer went in search of him, and found the medico lying on the ground in a dead faint. According to him, he had stooped down to get the key of his door, which he had placed under the mat, when he was dragged across the passage and thrown down the flight of steps.

A certain Captain Jarvis met with a similar experience. Hearing an odd noise in his bedroom, and finding the door locked, he suspected he had been selected by some practical joker as the object lesson of a hoax, and shouting a command to stop what he called "fooling", he felt a cold wind pass him, and, like the surgeon, he was thrown down the stairs and left senseless !

If one were able to choose the nature of the hauntings at Charles Fort, I am sure the majority of us would vote for the White Lady, who, Wilful by name, and wilful by nature, sold her earthly happiness, and her rest beyond the grave, for a handful of flowers, which, like the bodies of the long-buried loves, returned long, long ago to the earth from which they sprung.

THE HAUNTINGS AT LOFTUS HALL

ANOTHER well-authenticated Irish ghost story (and their name is legion) is given on the unimpeachable authority of a Rural Dean in the Established Church of Ireland. It possesses additional interest because, being *true*, it was related to Queen Victoria by the late Marchioness of Ely, and the old Queen always believed that the hauntings had actually happened.

The scene of the story is Loftus Hall, Co. Wexford, which came into the possession of the Loftuses somewhere about 1641 ; in the middle of the eighteenth century the owner of the Hall was Charles Tottenham, a member of the Irish Parliament, who once rode to Dublin in hot haste in order to give the casting vote which saved £280,000 to the Irish Treasury.

By his first marriage Charles Tottenham had two daughters, Elizabeth and Anne. Elizabeth married shortly before her father took up his residence at Loftus Hall, so the family only consisted of Charles Tottenham, his second wife, and his daughter Anne. Anne's father was austere, and her stepmother disagreeable, so existence was not happy or "artistic", as Loftus Hall was a house with no architectural pretensions ; there were "miles" of passages, unwanted nooks and corners, much heavy panelling, and a Tapestry Room—the only beautiful feature of the place. The county gentry were few and far between, travelling was difficult, and Anne Tottenham's life was almost as cloistered as that of any nun professed.

One wind-swept night, when the Tottenhams were sitting in the huge draughty drawing-room, they heard a loud knocking (a most unusual occurrence at that hour), and the butler announced that a gentleman on horseback who had travelled far, and lost his bearings, begged for a shelter from the storm raging outside.

Charles Tottenham, if austere, at any rate was hospitable. He made the stranger welcome, and as he proved himself not only a gentleman, but also a congenial companion, his stay was prolonged. It goes without saying that he and Anne fell in love, but Charles Tottenham absolutely refused to give his consent to their marriage, and as Mrs. Tottenham acted up to the best traditions of the cruel stepmother, the rejected and offended suitor left Loftus Hall and nothing more was heard of him, or from him. As the result, Anne Tottenham's reason gave way. She became hopelessly insane, and she was confined in the Tapestry Room for the rest of her life.

A ridiculous story was afterwards spread about the countryside, probably by the Tottenhams, in order to give some plausible account for Anne's dementia. In the eighteenth century brain troubles were not understood, or properly "treated", and it was considered rather disgraceful to admit madness in any conventional family. It was hinted, therefore, that the stranger guest was none other than Satan himself, and the shock of discovering that, in common with most men, he possessed a cloven foot, accounted for Anne's sudden illness.

Perhaps the Spirit of Evil resented being blamed unjustly for poor Anne's insanity, and retorted in true-to-type manner. Be that as it may, Loftus Hall became the scene of such alarming psychic disturbances that the Tottenhams called in Father Broders, the parish priest, who, armed with the might of the Church, most considerately confined the activities of the Powers of Darkness to . . . the Tapestry Room.

All further reference to Anne was avoided, and eventually the hard father, the unkind stepmother, and the mad
girl, went the way of all flesh, and years afterwards the
father of the Rural Dean who is the authority for this true
ghost story was invited by the then Mrs. Tottenham to
stay at the Hall. On arriving he found a "House Full", and
his hostess, with many apologies, told him that she had been
obliged to give him the Tapestry Room.

"But why apologize, dear lady?" said the puzzled visitor,
who did not know anything about the room or its history.

However he found out that all the apologies in the world
would be insufficient to compensate for the ghostly discom-
fort of the Tapestry Room. Hardly had he fallen asleep,
when something heavy jumped, growling, on the bed—the
curtains were torn apart, and sheets, blankets, and coverlets
lay in a heap on the ground. . . . When the exasperated
sleeper awakened, struck a light, there was no sign of
anyone, or anything, and his temper having in no wise
cooled down by breakfast time, he excused himself from
passing another night in such an unrestful place. . . .

Once again the fingers of Time turned over the pages
of the Book of Years, and the Marquis of Ely of that period
came to the Hall. For some reason his valet was allotted
the Tapestry Room, but in the middle of the night the poor
man's cries of terror awakened the household.

"I had been in bed for about half an hour," he said, on
being questioned by the irate Marquis as to the reason for
his panic, "when the rings on the bed-curtains rattled—the
curtains were pulled aside, and I saw a tall lady dressed in
brocaded silk. . . . Her expression was so dreadful that I
dared not stay a minute longer, and not a mint of money
would tempt me to go inside the room again."

Shortly afterwards the Rural Dean (then a youth) and his
father, a great friend of the family, visited Loftus Hall to
enjoy the excellent sea-bathing in the vicinity, and the
Rural-Dean-to-be chose the Tapestry Room as his bedroom.
For a time nothing happened, but one night he saw the door
open noiselessly, and the tall figure of a woman passed
through the room, apparently on her way to a powdering

closet at the opposite corner. In the words of his own story—for he placed on record everything which happened— "I rubbed my eyes. Every possible explanation but the true one occurred to my mind, for the idea of a ghost did not enter my head. I quickly reasoned myself into a sound sleep, and forgot the matter.

"The next night I sat up late in my bedroom, preparing a gun and ammunition to shoot sea-birds early next morning, when the door opened and shut in the same noiseless manner, and the tall lady proceeded to cross the room as quietly and deliberately as before. I instantly rushed at her, and threw my right arm around her, exclaiming, '*I have you now !*'

"To my utter astonishment, my arm passed right through her, and came with a thud against the bed-post, at which spot she then was. The figure quickened its pace ; as it passed me the skirt of its dress lapped against the curtain, and I marked distinctly the make and pattern of the gown—a stiff brocaded silk !

"The ghostly solution of the problem did not yet enter my mind. However, I told the story at breakfast the next morning, but my father, who had suffered from the lady's visit long beforehand, said never a word, and it passed off as some folly of mine. So slight was the impression it made on me at the time, that though I slept many a night in that room I never thought of watching or looking out for anything."

This record, set down in an entirely impartial manner, goes on to say that some years later the narrator was once more a guest at the Hall.

"The Marquis of Ely and his family, with a large number of servants, filled the house to overflowing, and one day, as I passed the housekeeper's room, I heard the valet say: 'What—sleep in the Tapestry Room ? *Never !* I will leave his lordship's service before I do.' At once my former experience flashed across my mind ; I had never thought of it during the interval, and I was still quite ignorant of the story of Anne Tottenham.

"When the housekeeper had gone, I spoke to the valet

'Tell me,' I said, 'why you will not sleep in the Tapestry Room; I have a particular reason for asking.'

" 'Why, sir,' he answered, 'is it possible that you do not know that Miss Tottenham passes through that room every night dressed in a stiff flowered-silk dress, and enters the powdering closet in the corner ?'

"I told him that I had never heard a word of her till now, but a few years before I had seen a figure exactly like what he described, and passed my arm through her body.

" 'Yes,' said the man, 'that was certainly Miss Tottenham ; she was shut up in that room ; she died there, raving mad, and people say she was buried in the powdering closet.' "

Once again the pages in the Book of Years increased in number, and another Marquis of Ely owned Loftus Hall, this time a grandson of the Marquis who had known the Dean and his father.

At that time the new Marquis was quite a child, and he came to stay at the Hall with his mother and his tutor (the Rev. Charles Dale) for the bathing season. Mr. Dale appears to have been a solid, steady, highly educated English clergyman, entirely devoid of imagination, who had never heard the name of Anne Tottenham ; on his arrival at Loftus Hall he was given the Tapestry Room.

"One day in the late autumn of that year," continues the Dean, "I received a letter from the Marquis' uncle saying :

"Do tell me what it was you saw long ago in the Tapestry Room, for something strange must have happened to the Rev. Charles Dale, as he came to breakfast quite mystified ; he will tell us nothing, and, in short, he is determined to give up his tutorship and return to England. Every year something mysterious has happened to persons who occupied that room, but they have always kept it a secret. Mr. D., a Wexford gentleman, who slept there a short while ago, had a wonderful dressing-case fitted with gold and silver articles, which he left carefully locked at night, and in the morning he found the whole of its contents scattered about the room.' "

Upon hearing this, the Dean made up his mind to write to the Rev. Charles Dale, then the newly appointed Vicar of a country parish near Dover, relating what had happened to him in the Tapestry Room, and saying, that as the evidences of supernatural appearances were so strong, and had continued for several generations, he wanted to piece them together. He would therefore consider it a personal favour if the Vicar would tell him exactly what had been his experiences in the room.

The Rev. Charles Dale's reply is included in the Dean's own story.

"For three weeks," he wrote, "I experienced no inconvenience from the lady, but one night, just before we were about to leave, I had sat up very late. It was just before one o'clock when I retired to my bedroom. I locked my door, and saw that the shutters were properly fastened, as I did every night. But I had not lain myself down more than five minutes, when something jumped on the bed, *making a growling noise*, and the bedclothes were pulled off, although I strongly resisted the pull. I immediately jumped out of bed, lighted my candle, looked into the powdering closet, and under the bed—but saw nothing."

Mr. Dale went on to say that he endeavoured to account for this in some sensible way, just as the Dean's father before him had tried to do—but, like him, he had failed! There *was* no explanation.

Here is the testimony of an unemotional English Vicar, repeating in 1867 almost the same words used by the Dean's father in 1790. Moreover, the Vicar had never heard of Miss Tottenham's doings eighty years previously.

The Dean goes on to say :

"In the autumn of 1868, as I was at Dunmore, on the opposite side of the Waterford estuary, I went across to the Hall to see what alterations Miss Tottenham had forced the present owners to make in the Tapestry Room. I found that the powdering closet into which poor Anne had always vanished had been taken away, the room had been enlarged, the tapestry removed, and a billiard table occupied the site of Anne's bed. I took the old housekeeper aside, and asked

her to tell me how Miss Tottenham liked the changes
in her bedroom. She looked quite frightened, and was
most anxious to avoid answering the question, but at last
she hurriedly whispered :
    " 'Oh, Master George—don't *talk* about her—why,
last night she made a horrid noise knocking the billiard balls
about ! "
    Knocking billiard balls about seems rather *infra dig.* on
the part of a ghost with such a romantic past, who was far
more dignified as a tragic "return" in a flowered silk gown
than as a billiard player.
    I will conclude the story in the Dean's own words.
    "I have traced," he says, "with strict accuracy, this most
real and true tale, from the days of 'Tottenham and his
Boots' down to those of his great-great-grandson. Loftus
Hall has now been wholly rebuilt, but I have not heard
whether Anne Tottenham has condescended to visit it, or
is wholly banished at last."
    This ghost story is one of the best authenticated that we
possess, and, like the hauntings at Fort Charles, two
distinct phenomena occurred—*the Seen,* and *the Unseen.*
In both cases the ghost appeared in the likeness of their
one-time physical bodies, and were quite harmless. On the
other hand, the *disturbances* were *felt,* and the noises were so
definite that it was possible to describe them as *growls* and
knockings—and the apparitions of Wilful Ashurst and Anne
Tottenham had no connection with them.
    Such is the true ghost story that the Marchioness of Ely
told the late Queen Victoria, and which greatly interested
Her Majesty, as few royal residences, with the exception of
the Tower of London, Kensington Palace, and Hampton
Court, are haunted, although Hampton Court certainly
makes up for what Buckingham Palace and Windsor
Castle lack. In connection with the latter, one of the com-
pilers of this volume wrote to His Majesty, asking his permission to get in touch with the Librarian at Windsor
Castle, in order to ascertain if any ghost stories beyond that
of Herne the Hunter were associated with the Castle.
    His Majesty graciously gave the required permission,

but, alas for "ghostly" hopes : the Librarian replied that, to the best of his knowledge there are no ghosts at Windsor.

Balmoral, so essentially Victorian, must be singularly free from hauntings, and the ghost story about St. James's Palace has been told so often, that it needs no repetition. I believe Marlborough House is "supposed" to possess two ghosts, but it was a great disappointment when Windsor Castle drew a blank . . . especially when one remembers its crowded past, and the dramatic scenes it has witnessed in the ever-changing pageant of the centuries.

TWO GHOST STORIES FROM AMERICA

THE ROCKING-CHAIR

Told to Maude ffoulkes by Mr. Edward Stewart of New York

THIS American ghost story was told me in Paris some years ago by Mr. Edward Stewart of New York, who stated positively that the facts were absolutely true, as he had had it first hand from the man who witnessed the "return" of a murderer.

"Ned" Stewart's friend formed one of a syndicate who rented a shoot in Louisiana, and as the rice swamps harbour quantities of snipe, they had every prospect of a worth-while "bag". Unfortunately, one day the shooters missed their direction and wandered for hours hither and thither, wondering where on earth they were ; and, to make matters worse, twilight fell whilst they were still without any prospect of getting a night's shelter.

At last they found themselves at the end of what had once been an avenue leading to a house ; many of the trees had been cut, or had fallen down, and a rush of crowding evergreens filled in the gaps. Progress was difficult, as in parts the avenue was choked with loops and tangles of wild grape-vine and grasses. But the shooters pushed on, and presently they saw a long, low, Colonial house, set high in a series of terraces and deserted lawns.

Realizing that they were in luck's way, the shooters cheerfully followed a flagged path leading to the house, and stood outside the columned portico. There was no sign of life, the rows of shuttered windows were like eyes of the dead, and the worn-out men hammered and hammered unavailingly. Nobody came. At last, they made their way round to the back of the house. Here everything was apparently derelict, until Ned Stewart's friend saw a tiny star twinkling somewhere in the outbuildings—and, following the star, they discovered it to be a lamp in a dilapidated cabin, from which an old negro emerged, and asked them, for the land's sake, what they were doing hereabouts.

On being told that they were lost, and wanted a night's lodging, the ancient at first flatly refused to discuss the matter.

"There's no one in dat dere house, sah ; no one hab lived there since old Massa's time. No good to sleep there neither."

Money, and its powers of persuasion, are keys which open every door. The negro, Jake by name, hesitated, and was lost. Finally, he agreed to make a fire in the hall of the house, where the shooters could sleep until morning.

"Specs I can contribe some hot coffee, and produce some sweet potatoes and waffles from somewheres," remarked Jake, as he led the way back to the entrance. And, after he had unlocked the massive and sadly stained mahogany doors, the little party followed him inside.

At this moment a curious thing happened : the two setters, who until now had behaved according to the best sporting traditions, ran a yard ahead, stiffened, growled, and darted first to the right and then to the left, circling uneasily and shivering violently.

"Merciful powers, what's de matter with them darned dogs ?" muttered Jake . . . Then, as if remembering something he shook his head ominously.

Ned Stewart's usually unimaginative friend told him that directly he crossed the threshold of the mysterious house he felt uncomfortable . . . wished he was outside, couldn't explain *what* he meant—but *there it was*, etc., etc. He was able to see by the light of Jake's lantern that the hall was large and panelled, with a wide main staircase leading to the upper floor, and the bedchambers opened on to a circular gallery, from where you could look down into the hall. The oak floor was thick with dust, decay was everywhere, parts of the panelling were full of dry rot. It was a melancholy place, this once fine southern mansion, which in the past had witnessed the lavish hospitality and movement that made life colourful and gay.

Presently there was the delicious smell of woodsmoke, and after the cold chimney had "warmed", the logs caught ; waves of golden flame roared upwards, and tongues of fire sent ruddy reflections to and fro.

Luckily there were some dilapidated arm-chairs and a settee in the hall, so the tired-out men sat down and waited impatiently for Jake's reappearance with their scratch supper.

Not so Ned Stewart's friend, who, possessed with some spirit of unrest (he said afterwards that the house gave him the impression as if it had been asleep, and had just opened its eyes), went upstairs to reconnoitre.

All the bedchambers, except one, were empty of furniture, and, to his surprise, this particular room was almost fully furnished. Tattered chintz hangings still hung on the great four-poster ; a rocking-chair, upholstered in what had once been velvet, was close to the fire-place ; a dressing-table and a tarnished mirror stood in one corner. And when the young man threw back the shutters, and looked out over the pale lawns, with masses of yew and box etched sharply in ink black silhouettes against the moonlight, he decided that this would suit him better than any communal shakedown. . . .

Afterwards, he descended, to find the others enjoying steaming hot coffee, laced with cognac, whilst the ancient hovered around with offers of rum, waiting first on one, then on another, tears glistening in his old eyes, which he hurriedly explained away.

"Specs Ise thinkin' of poor old Massa, and de doings here, before things went wrong," he quavered.

"Well—*I'm* going to sleep upstairs," said W. (for so I shall call him). "Here you, Jake, look slippy, and light a fire in the room with the four-poster."

"Oh, sah, don't say you'm going away from dese obber gentlemen ?"

"Why ever not ?"

"*Cos not*," answered Jake. "Do you believe in 'hants', sah . . . ?"

"I certainly don't. What 'hants' the four-poster ?"

Jake wagged his woolly pate. "Waal, if you see anything that frights you, don't be a-blamin' *me*."

The rest of the party were highly amused. "Pity we can't get the Plaza Hotel down here—too superior to share our humble dug-out, are you ? Which of us will Your Majesty graciously permit to light him to bed ?"

But as W. adhered to his resolve to sleep elsewhere, his friends left him alone, and, wrapping themselves up in the horse blankets which Jake had provided, they soon made themselves as comfortable as possible.

Preceded by Jake, W. followed him to the chintz bedchamber, where a fire was quickly ablaze, and, after the old man had closed the door behind him, W. threw himself on the bed, made a pillow of his coat, rolled himself in a couple of blankets, and lay awake, watching the pine cones and hickory logs glowing on the open hearth.

He was just dozing off, blessing the foresight which had provided him with a bed instead of a shakedown, when *something happened* that recalled him to wakefulness. The rocking-chair beside the fire suddenly jerked backwards, as if someone had just sat down, and it began to rock slowly to and fro.

W. stared. The chair continued to rock! It must be some trick of the firelight. He got up and proceeded to investigate, but when he did so there was no sign of any movement—of *course* it was the firelight—and, cursing himself for a silly fool, W. went back to bed.

No sooner had he done so, than the rocking recommenced. But after a few minutes the chair jerked backwards in the way peculiar to rocking-chairs, and W. heard soft padding footsteps going across the room towards the window. . . . Now, thoroughly wakeful, and, to say the least of it, a little troubled, W. asked himself uneasily what was going to happen next.

The unseen presence was evidently standing by the window. W. could hear the restless tapping of fingers against the panes, someone was getting impatient. For what purpose was "it" waiting ? But W., who, to do him

justice was no coward, was totally unprepared for the
horror which materialized. The tapping ceased, and was
succeeded by the unmistakable sound of a knife being
slowly sharpened. . . . (W. said afterwards that all the hatred
in the world was concentrated in this slow deliberate
sharpening.)

All at once W. was aware that a gigantic negro was
standing in the shadows of the window.

So lifelike and so menacing was the negro, that at first
W. thought he, and his friends, had dropped on a nest of
criminals hiding from justice in the fastnesses of the
rice swamps, and in all probability others were staging a
hold-up in the hall. He listened ; everything was silent,
but when he forced himself to meet the eyes of the figure,
he understood he did not enter into the picture of the Past,
and that he was about to witness a psychic tragedy once
connected with this room.

The negro took a step forward—stopped, as if listening
for some movement from the occupant of the bed—then,
satisfied that his victim was asleep, he advanced with a
terrible relentlessness of purpose, the long blade of the
knife plainly discernible in the dying firelight.

W. watched him, much in the stupefied frozen way of a
rabbit when it meets a snake. Then, regaining his self-
control, he sprang out of bed, calling loudly for help. (It
would never do to acknowledge that he had been scared
stiff by a ghost.) Hearing his voice uplifted in this unexpected manner, his friends unrolled themselves from their
blankets, and raced upstairs, followed by the temperamental
setters.

W. hastily explained that a negro had come into his
room. "About as bad as they make 'em," he said. "I'm
sure he was up to no good—sorry I yelled, but the feller
startled me some." And whilst he lied man-like to shield
himself, the two setters once more showed signs of unmistakable terror, and bolted out of the gallery down the
stairs.

The "syndicate" hunted through the empty rooms ;
they explored echoing passages, they threw open windows,

and looked out—but nothing was to be seen. The neglected gardens slept in the moonlight, the trees by the lake, seen through a light ground mist, seemed hung with pearls, the whole landscape was the embodiment of peace.

"I guess I wouldn't live in this old place as a gift," said one of the men. "There's something wrong here. Let's make up the fire, and yarn until it's time for a dip in the pool before breakfast." Thereupon they went back to the warm hall, and, between dozing and talking, the hours passed, until Jake, and a small piccaninny, introduced as "my grandson, sah", bearing trays loaded with fried ham and eggs and piping hot coffee, brought the fine air of morning into the house.

"Say, Jake," remarked W., "who's your darky friend who came into my room last night and did a bit of knife sharpening on the q.t. ?"

The ancient let the cup he was holding fall with a crash, and, staring at W. as if he could not believe his ears, he exclaimed :

"*Did he come?* Oh, sah, for de dear Lord's sake, don't say this thing."

"Did he *not* come ?—why, certainly he came—the wor looking cuss I've ever seen. Thank goodness that kind never leave 'the chair' vacant for long. What particular brand of wickedness does he fall for ?"

"Him not live nigger," wailed Jake, "him dead and drowned in the swamp more then seventy years. Him dead sure-ly—but Pete can't stay quiet noways ; ˡ.e murdered ole Massa, cut his throat when he was asleep—poor ole Massa, the last owner of dis house and plantation."

"What's the trouble ?" said the others. W. told them, and Jake went on to say that Pete, who had acted as "ole Massa's" valet, tired of waiting for dead men's shoes, had made up his mind to step into their living owner's as soon as possible. "Ole Massa", in direct contrast to his forebears, who had made their hour as crowded as possible, was a miser, and a disagreeable tyrannical miser at that. So one night Pete cut "ole Massa's" throat, when he was doubtless dreaming of gold, and still more gold, and, taking all the money and valuables he could lay his hands on, the murderer made his way up-country.

The murder and Pete's flight were discovered next morning.

"There were a fine commotion," continued Jake, "and then someone loosed ole Massa's bloodhounds. . . . I was younger than dis piccaninny, but I proper recollects it all. Waal, sah, dey dogs picked up Pete's scent, and tracked him to de swamp, and sakes, it were tarrible to hear that darky screaming and cursing as he ran. But suddenly he let fly a worse screech, and said that ole Massa were running alongside of him. . . . 'Twarn't ole Massa noways, but one of dem dogs. Howsomever, Pete ran for dear life—and nebber noticed he was in the swamp till he sank deep in the water, screaming out that ole Massa was pulling him sure down to hell.

"But de debbil don't want Pete fixed up with him, so he sends him back to hant dis house—a nasty trick, sah, cos nobody can live here 'cept Pete—and he must get weary of creepin' around ole Massa's bedroom.

"He don't show in the marning, so there's nothing to scare you—and thank you all kindly for them greenbacks—reckon I'll set up swell."

A little later, the syndicate, accompanied by a guide who knew every inch of this particular lay of the land, set out in search of sport ; and W. told Ned Stewart that, when he glanced back at the old house, he was sure he saw a wicked black face looking out of "ole Massa's" bedroom window.

A HAUNTED FARM-HOUSE

(By the courtesy of Miss Estelle Stead)

THIS is the account of a haunted farm-house at Oakville, a small town on the Savannah river, and, like *The Rocking-Chair*, the story hails from the south, where environment seems favourable for psychic manifestations. As a matter-of-fact, until now, American ghost stories are not plentiful, but there must be an unexploited mine of wealth for an enterprising and painstaking psychic prospector, especially since dangerous living, and swift dying, have become every-day occurrences in the U.S.A.

Some years ago, Mr. Walsingham, a gentleman farmer, bought a farm which, on the surface, appeared to be a very good investment, and for a few months after the Wal-singhams moved in they were not troubled by any kind of disturbances. Then, unaccountable noises made sleep impossible, furniture was overturned, and the door-bell pealed loudly and incessantly. The Walsinghams, being practical people, looked for a practical reason for these troubles, which they decided arose through mischievous neighbours, but this sensible solution soon had to be definitely abandoned.

One particular inmate of the farm who resented these nightly upheavals more than anyone else was a huge mastiff, Don Caesar by name, whose life was made un-bearable by perpetual wakefulness, and at last his temper began to show signs of wear and tear. No doubt he argued that although the duty of a house dog was to protect the life and property of his owners, he could not be expected to cope with invisible intruders. Don Caesar's fate was tragic. One morning he was found in the hall, barking loudly, bristling with rage, his eyes fixed on somebody facing him. At last he leaped forward—only to fall back, throttled and flung down by a powerful hand. His neck was broken.

The sinister Presence was on the best of terms with the house cat, and whilst dogs either show the extremes of rage, or fear, when they come up against the supernatural, cats, on the contrary, positively enjoy psychic phenomena, and I have often seen a cat intent on watching something unseen by others, its eyes following the some-thing's every movement. Thus the Walsinghams' cat would stand near one of the doors as if showing some visitor in, and it occasionally climbed into a vacant chair, purring and rubbing itself against the invisible occupant. But the cat's strange behaviour was infinitely preferable to what happened afterwards.

One night when Amelia Walsingham was brushing her hair, and creaming her face before going to bed, she felt a hand laid softly on her shoulder, and, thinking it to be that of her mother, or sister, she glanced in the mirror—at first to see no reflection but her own! She looked again—a man's hand was lying on her arm, a hideous hand, covered on the back with a growth of coarse black hair.

The terrified girl's continuous screaming brought her family upstairs, but when they arrived there was no sign of the hand, and Amelia, told by everyone that she must have "dreamt it", began to think she had dropped off to sleep, and that the hand had only been part of a nightmare.

Mr. Walsingham, however, was no dreamer of dreams, and one morning, after a light shower, when he was walking in the pleasant garden which sloped down to the river's edge, he noticed footsteps forming beside his own, which showed up plainly in the light soil. The footsteps were those of a man's naked feet!

The same evening, another incident occurred when some friends were having supper with the Walsinghams, and a loud groan proceeded from the room overhead. Everyone looked at his or her neighbour, but although the groan was not repeated, Mrs. Walsingham noticed a mark of something moist and red staining the white tablecloth. Where did it come from? She looked upwards, and saw a liquid slowly dripping on the table from the ceiling.

Everyone stopped eating to watch the slow descent of the red drops, and then Mr. Walsingham and his guests ran upstairs to the room directly over the dining-room to discover the source of this horrible dripping.

The floor of the room was completely covered, but, wishing to satisfy himself thoroughly, Mr. Walsingham ripped up the carpet, only to find the boards perfectly dry, and covered with a thin top layer of dust. There was no trace of any blood. Whilst the floor was being examined, those below still saw the continuous drip, drip, and a stain the size of a large plate formed before it ceased. (The stain was examined next day under the microscope, and pronounced to be *human blood*.)

The Walsinghams left the farm as soon as possible, and the premises were given over to the Unseen. All kinds of stories were now current, and Horace Gunn, one of the Bright Young People of Oakville, accepted a wager that he would not pass twenty-four hours alone in the haunted house. He eventually did so, but he said afterwards that not all the money in the U.S.A. would tempt him to pass another night there.

This is what happened.

Horace Gunn arrived at the farm shortly after twilight, and set to work to kindle a fire in one of the rooms. He had provided himself with a lamp, but when he tried to light it, an icy breath from someone standing by his side extinguished each match as soon as he struck it. The same thing happened with the fire. This unexpected commence-ment would have provided a good excuse for him to forfeit the wager and make tracks for Oakville, but the wager was considerable, and although Horace Gunn was afraid of ridicule, he was sufficiently courageous to make up his mind to sit it out.

For some time all was quiet—when suddenly a yell of pain came from the cellars under the house. This was the signal for a general pandemonium. Running feet passed up and down the stairs, as if some person were fleeing in fear of their life from the pursuit of a second. This frenzied chase lasted well over an hour. Then it ceased, and Horace, alone in the darkness, devoutly hoped that the manifestations were over.

All at once his attention was held by a luminous white spot which gradually materialized on the opposite wall, and continued to lighten, until it shone at last as a disc of white fire, and the terrified watcher saw that the light encircled a human head, which, without any body or means of support, was moving slowly along the wall about the height of a man from the floor.

This dreadful head was covered with long grey hair,

matted together over one temple with clots of blood from a jagged wound. . . . The expression of the face was one of incalculable suffering and misery, and the wide-open eyes, glowing with unearthly fire, were fixed on Horace Gunn, until the head finally disappeared, and the room was once more in darkness.

It was impossible to remain in the place any longer, and Horace Gunn pulled himself sufficiently together to try and make his way out. It is easy to imagine his apprehension as he groped his way, inch by inch, along the wall, wondering what horror his outstretched hand might encounter, dreading to see *what* he believed filled the room. . . . And he had nearly reached the door, when he was seized by the ankle, and thrown violently to the ground ; clammy hands felt for his throat, and notwithstanding his struggles he was choked into insensibility. . . .

When morning rode high in a cloudless heaven, some of Horace Gunn's light-hearted friends drove out from Oakville to see what had happened to the ghost seer. As they approached the farm, they were surprised not to be met by Horace with a demand for spot cash payment of the wager ; nobody was visible, and when their knocking remained unanswered, the cynical amongst the party decided that, after all, Horace, unable to see things through, had vamoosed !

However, the spirit of fair play insisted it would be only sporting to force an entrance. This was done, and the young men hurried into the dining-room, where they discovered Horace (who for a few moments they imagined to be dead) lying on the floor, and, bending over him, they noticed that his black and swollen throat was covered with the marks of long thin fingers terminated by hooked nails.

Horace Gunn was brought round with some difficulty, but he never recovered from the shock of his dearly bought experience as a psychic investigator, and the farm was abandoned to the evil entities who possessed it.

All kinds of reasons have been put forward to account for these hideous manifestations, especially as—to the best of everyone's knowledge—the farm's past for the last seventy years was beyond suspicion. Previous to that period something dreadful may have occurred, that constitutes one of the many unrevealed tragedies which have no known history.

One fact might have some bearing on the strange manifestations. Three months after Mr. Walsingham purchased the farm, a quantity of bones were unearthed in a corner of a small plantation. These bones were declared to be those of a human being, but Mr. Walsingham thought otherwise, and the bones were thrown into an adjacent limekiln, and quickly consumed.

The hauntings did not begin until *after* the discovery and disposal of the bones, so perhaps the outraged spirit of the person to whom they belonged in life may have resented such summary treatment, and punished the Walsinghams in this manner.

This strange story is well authenticated, and long accounts appeared in the Press when the hauntings became generally known, especially as Mr. Gunn's account of the wager, and its result, provided South Georgia with plenty of food for thought and conversation. I have included it in this collection of ghost stories, as it presents many similarities between psychic disturbances as we know them in the Mother Country. The ways of cats and dogs are alike all the world over, the noises are also familiar, and the sensation of cold is never dissociated from certain manifestations. The horrors are perhaps a little on the "American" side, but on the other hand, many haunted houses in England excel the Grand Guignol in gruesome happenings. Be that as it may, the psychic history of the Oakville farm-house is undoubtedly well worth recording.

SOME CLERICAL GHOST STORIES

(*By the courtesy of Miss Estelle Stead*)

THE PURSUER

The Rev. H. Elwyn Thomas' Experience

SOME years ago the Rev. H. Elwyn Thomas was acting as second minister on a Wesleyan circuit in the South Wales district. The circuit consisted of eight churches, and Mr. Thomas had to preach in each of them once a month, beginning his ministrations at Llanelly ; from there he went to Crickhowell, arriving at Llangynidr about six in the evening. A good "hiker", Mr. Thomas usually did the distance between these places on foot.

One fine Sunday evening in June Mr. Thomas told the friend with whom he usually stayed at Llangynidr that he would not be back at his house until nine o'clock, as he intended walking part of the way home with some other acquaintances.

At twenty minutes to nine Mr. Thomas said good night to his friends, and was making his way back to Llangynidr when he saw what he thought to be a beggar, standing on the banks of the canal which runs parallel for six miles with that particular road.

The canal and the road were lonely ; the nearest house was a quarter of a mile away. The intense stillness of a summer night brooded over everything, and Mr. Thomas, wondering what had brought anyone to this spot at such an hour, stopped to have a good look. No sooner had he done so, than he wished himself a thousand miles away. Within half a yard of him, he saw a startling and dreadful sight, that of an old man over whose face the leaden-coloured skin was tightly stretched : the lips were thin and bloodless, and the half-open mouth toothless. Two piercing and semi-luminous eyes, set far back, stared at Mr. Thomas, who could not avoid noticing that the "beggar" was dressed in a very peculiar way—perhaps the word "wrapped", not "dressed", better describes two bands of stained calico, one of which passed under the old man's chin, and was tied at the top of the head; the other was drawn round the forehead and fastened behind.

So horrible was this extraordinary object, that Mr. Thomas actually ran away from it. He was an absolute disbeliever in ghosts, and as he had no patience with any kind of superstition, it never occurred to him that the beggar was not of this world, and he only realized this when after, as he thought, outdistancing the figure, he turned round, to find it close behind him.

Mr. Thomas looked up and down the road, and the deserted canal banks. Not a soul was in sight; the night seemed only to hold him and his pursuer. By this time the wrappings had merged into a column of intense blackness, and there was nothing visible between the face and the ground. Raising his umbrella, in the unreasoning panic which seizes even the bravest, the minister hit out blindly, only to encounter air, through which his umbrella easily passed.

Thoroughly frightened, Mr. Thomas once again took to his heels, and ran as quickly as possible down a road which branches off the main road, going directly through the centre of the village of Llangynidr. And feeling that he had arrived at a spiritual crisis in his life, Mr. Thomas conquered his fear and confusion, and spoke to the pursuer, whose footsteps made no sound on the silent highway.

The "Thing" had stopped in the centre of the main road, and when, secure in his newly found moral strength, the minister walked towards it, he saw it moving swiftly until it reached the lower end of the road which runs parallel with the boundary wall of the churchyard. It then appeared to float over the wall, and vanished in the dense foliage of an ancient yew tree near the lych-gate. After this, Mr. Thomas fainted.

He came to himself two hours later, lying in the same place where he had fallen ; he was very cold, and he felt bodily ill. Fortunately, motor traffic on Sunday night was practically non-existent, otherwise he might easily have been run over by a passing vehicle. Picking himself out of the dust, Mr. Thomas took the road which led to the sanity and safety of human companionship.

The reaction from this mental ordeal proved too much for the minister ; it was over an hour before he reached his friend's home, barely a quarter of a mile away. When he did, his changed appearance alarmed his host and his daughter so much that the young girl screamed when she saw him, especially as Mr. Thomas was incapable of saying a word of explanation of his condition.

He tried to speak, but his words ran into each other and formed an unintelligible babel of sound, and it was not before five in the morning that some kind of speech returned to the stricken minister, and then, only in broken and meaningless sentences. After this Mr. Thomas spent the whole of the following week in bed, laid up with a bad attack of nervous prostration.

The strangest part of this strange story remains to be told. When Mr. Thomas was himself again, his host questioned him closely about the events of that unforgettable Sunday.

"Did you notice anything particular about the place where you first saw the figure ?" asked Mr. P.

Mr. Thomas thought—and thought again. "Well," said he, "I seem to recollect a ruined cottage a little lower down."

"Hm . . . someone answering the description of your pursuer once lived there. He was by way of being a recluse, lost to all sense of personal respect and decency. His garments were a collection of odd lengths of indescribably filthy calico and I believe he was buried in them, as, owing to his reputation as a 'wizard', nobody would go near him during his last illness. He was buried in the exact spot in the churchyard where you saw the figure disappear, and the cottage, already ruinous, became more and more so, until the greater part fell to the ground. It has never been re-built."

During the time Mr. Thomas remained on the circuit he never saw his pursuer again. . . . Perhaps the spirit was made manifest to rebuke his obstinate disbelief in "returns", and from that time the minister never discountenanced the reality of dwellers in the Unseen World.

.   .   .   .   .

It seems strange why ministers of any denomination should not believe in ghosts. There are endless stories of haunted vicarages, that of Epworth representing an "epic", and the phenomena which I am going to describe, which takes place at a vicarage near Cashel, have been experienced by the Vicar himself.

Twenty years ago, soon after the Vicar's arrival at D., his servants complained of odd noises in the top storey of the house, and his wife had to change servants so often that at last the Vicar spoke to the friendly parish priest, "as," so he writes, "I suspected that the idea of ghosts might have been suggested to the maids by neighbours who had some interest in getting rid of them.

"After a while," continues the Vicar, "my wife and I began to hear a noise, which, while in no sense alarming, has proved to be both remarkable and inexplicable.

"This noise sounds like a heavy coach rumbling up to the hall door; sometimes we hear it several times in the same night, and then perhaps we won't hear it again for months. We hear it best on calm nights, and, as we are nearly a quarter of a mile from the high road, it makes it difficult to account for."

The Vicar and his wife gradually became used to the "phantom coach", but one hot July day, between twelve and one, the Vicar was cutting hay in a small field near the tennis-court, which looked down the avenue for about four hundred yards.

Making any kind of hay while a scorching sun is shining must be tiring work, and the Vicar, pausing in his occupation, saw what appeared to be a high dog-cart, in which were two people, turning in at the avenue gate. As he had discarded both his coat and waistcoat, he took cover behind a newly made haycock, and watched the approach of the dog-cart until a clump of trees and a turn in the drive hid it momentarily from view. It did not reappear, so, hastily putting on his coat, the Vicar went as far as the bend in the avenue to investigate. Nothing was to be seen.

Returning to the Vicarage, the Vicar told his housekeeper (an old servant of many years' standing) what had occurred, and heard from her that she had seen the very same dog-cart, but did not like to tell her master as he "would have laughed at her".

All this happened in the summer, but when the winter of 1912 came the Vicar had another uncanny experience one dark evening, when he was working at the engine of his car. The chauffeur-gardener had gone down to the village with a message ten minutes previously, so, when the Vicar heard heavy footsteps in the yard, coming over to the motor-house, thinking them to be those of the man who had perhaps come back for something he had forgotten, he called out, "Hallo—what's brought you back so soon?"

There was no reply. Snatching up his electric lamp, the Vicar made a thorough search of the motor-house and the yard, but he could discover no one. A week later he heard the footsteps again, and renewed his search, with no better results.

According to the Vicar, a number of people have heard the coach, and some have "felt" it pass them—but there is no explanation, and the manifestations still continue.

．　　　．　　　．　　　．　　　．

In 1908, the Vicarage of East Rudham, a small unattractive village near Fakenham, witnessed a supernatural occurrence when the ghost of the living Vicar appeared to three people—the Vicar in charge, the Vicarage housekeeper, and a maidservant.

The Rev. Dr. Astley, who had left East Rudham to take the chaplaincy of Biskra for the winter months, was unfortunately detained in hospital at Algiers on his way to his new duties, as the result of injuries received in a railway accident.

The accident happened on December 10, and the same afternoon Mrs. Hartley, the housekeeper at the Vicarage, was about to close the shutters in the Vicar's study when she saw Dr. Astley coming across the lawn towards the window. The Vicar was hatless, seemingly in the best of tempers, as he smiled at Mrs. Hartley, and beckoned to her with the piece of paper he was holding.

When a country vicar, supposedly comfortably settled abroad, returns home without any kind of warning, the mind leaps to the unusual, and Mrs. Hartley, to say the least of it, was flustered.

However, when she opened the front windows, Dr. Astley made no attempt to come beyond a little recess— and, thinking this rather strange, Mrs. Hartley called one of the maids.

"Do you see anyone outside ?" she asked, in what she hoped represented merely a casual inquiry.

"Of course I do," said the girl. "Why, it's the Reverend arrived sudden like . . . but why ever don't he come inside ?"

Mrs. Hartley, with admirable presence of mind, stopped any further surmises, and told her surbordinate to fetch Mr. Brock, who was deputizing for Dr. Astley at East Rudham.

Partly enlightened by Mrs. Hartley's messenger as to the reason why he was wanted, Mr. Brock came to the study, and Mrs. Hartley's pointing finger indicated the figure in the recess.

Mr. Brock had only met Dr. Astley once, but he possessed a flair for details, and in a letter published in *The Times* of December 28, 1908, he described this extraordinary phantasm of the living.

When I was called into the study [he wrote] I clearly saw the figure outside, which I recognized as that of Dr. Astley, who seemed

to be sitting in a chair with some books before him. I noticed his
Cuddesdon collar, and his way of wearing his watch-chain straight
across his waistcoat, high up. The figure had the appearance of a reflection in a mirror. The time was about 4.40 p.m., with no light in
the room. I could see the figure quite clearly. It gradually vanished.

One of the curious facts connected with this return is
that if the Vicar had *really* been seated in his study with a
light in the room, his reflection would have been seen in the
window exactly as Mr. Brock described it.

In order to make this living ghost story convincing,
Dr. Astley ought to have "passed" at the time when he
appeared on the Vicarage lawn, but fortunately for his
wife and his parishioners he recovered from his severe
bruises, and returned to East Rudham, as a substance, and
not as a shadow.

The publication of Mr. Brock's letter aroused widespread interest, being corroborated by three independent
witnesses ; but there are quite recent instances of this kind
of psychic phenomena, and the late Mr. W. T. Stead, in
taking what he described as his "Census of Hallucinations",
obtained some curious stories of ghosts of the living, two
of them from clerical sources, the first given him by his old
schoolfellow, the Reverend Mr. Talbot, whose mother
possessed the faculty of seeing forms invisible to others.
On this occasion she saw a friend of hers coming up
the garden path, but, when she went to welcome her,
Mrs. Lister (for this was her friend's name) had disappeared.

Feeling certain that something had happened, Mr. and
Mrs. Talbot hurried off to the Listers' house, where they
found the unfortunate woman had been nearly killed by
her husband in a sudden fit of insanity.* No doubt, in her
terror and extremity, Mrs. Lister had thought of her friend,
and, in some way or another, her visual phantasm had
appeared in the Talbots' garden.

.   .   .   .   .

---

* This is true.

The Reverend Father Fleming told Mr. Stead how two figures from Woolwich (the scene of his labours) appeared to him when he was staying in Dublin, saying that they had died on certain dates, and begging him most earnestly to give them spiritual comfort.

As the "death dates" had not yet come round, Father Fleming asked the figures what this meant. He was informed that it had been done to "fix" his attention, and the priest was so troubled that he asked his hostess to allow him to cut short his visit, as he felt obliged to return to Woolwich.

On his arrival, he was immediately sent for by *one* of the "ghosts", a stranger to him, who was dangerously ill, and who died on the exact date mentioned at Dublin. The second summons came a few days later, and death ensued on the date predicted. The two men did not know each other, but, curiously enough, in both cases there was a great wrong to be undone, and both individuals had set their hearts on confiding the trouble to Father Fleming, who told Mr. Stead he regarded this experience in the light of a solemn warning, as their Spiritual Adviser, on no account to neglect the opportunity of saving two unhappy erring souls.

. . . . .

Fifty years ago, another Norfolk clergyman, the Reverend Dr. Jessop, met with a supernatural experience at Mannington Hall, when he was on a visit to Lord Orford, in order to consult some works of reference only to be found in the Mannington Hall Library.

Dr. Jessop, and a party of four, dined with Lord Orford, and at eleven o'clock Dr. Jessop shut himself in the library and began work in earnest, comfortably seated at a table near the fire, poring over an ever-increasing pile of books by the light of four candles in tall silver candlesticks.

At one o'clock Dr. Jessop rested awhile, opened the last volumes and commenced his concluding notes. After this I will let his own testimony, published in the pages of *The Athenaeum*, speak for itself.

I had been engaged upon it about half an hour [says he] and I was just beginning to think that my work was drawing to a close, when, as I was actually writing, I saw a large white hand within a foot of my elbow. Turning my head, there sat the figure of a somewhat large man, bending slightly over the table, and apparently examining the pile of books that I had been at work upon. The man's face was turned away from me, but I saw his closely cut reddish brown hair, his ear and shaved cheek, the eyebrow, the corner of the right eye, the side of the forehead and the large high cheekbone. He was dressed in what I can only describe as a kind of ecclesiastical habit of thick corded silk, or some such material, close up to the throat, with a narrow rim or edging of satin or velvet, about an inch broad, serving as a stand-up collar, and fitting close to the chin. The right hand, which had first attracted my attention, was clasping, without any great pressure, the left hand ; both hands were in perfect repose, and the large blue veins of the left hand were conspicuous. I remember thinking that the hand was like the hand of Velasquez' magnificent "Dead Knight" in the National Gallery. I looked at my visitor for some seconds, and was perfectly sure he was not a reality. A thousand thoughts came crowding upon me, but not the least feeling of alarm, or even uneasiness : curiosity, and a strong interest, were uppermost. For an instant I felt eager to make a sketch of my friend, and I looked at a tray on my right for a pencil : then I thought : "Upstairs I have a sketch-book ; shall I fetch it ?" There he sat, and I was fascinated, afraid, not of his staying, but lest he should go."

Stopped in my writing, I lifted my left hand from the paper, stretched it out to the pile of books, and moved the top one. I cannot explain why I did this—my arm passed in front of the figure, and it vanished ! I was simply disappointed, and nothing more. I went on with my writing as if nothing had happened, perhaps for another five minutes, and had actually got to the last few words of what I had determined to extract, when the figure appeared again, exactly in the same place and attitude as before. I saw the hands close to my own ; I turned my head again to examine him more closely, and I was framing a sentence to address him, when I discovered I did not dare to speak ! There he sat, and there sat I. I turned my head again to my work, and finished writing the two or three words I had to write. The paper, and my notes, are at this moment before me, and exhibit not the slightest tremor or nervousness. I could point out the words I was writing when the phantom came, and when he disappeared. Having finished my task, I shut the book and threw it on the table. It made a slight noise as it fell—the figure vanished. . . .

Throwing myself back in my chair, I sat for some seconds looking at the fire with a curious mixture of feelings, and I remember wondering whether my friend would come again, and, if he did, whether he would hide the fire from me ? Then first there stole upon me a dread and suspicion that I was beginning to lose my nerve. I remember yawning; then I rose, lit my bedroom candle, took my books into the inner library, mounted the chair as before, and replaced five of the volumes; the sixth I brought back, and laid upon the table where I had been writing when the phantom did me the honour to appear to me. By this time I had lost all sense of uneasiness. I blew out the four candles and marched off to bed, where I slept the sleep of the just, or he guilty—I know not which—but I slept very soundly.

So ended Dr. Jessop's experience. I do not know whether Lord Orford gave him any explanation of the library "ghost", but it says a good deal for Dr. Jessop's nerves that he was able to face this spiritual encounter calmly, and to remember every detail connected with it; but he always insisted that during the whole of dinner no reference was made to occult subjects.

JASMIN

(The facts are contributed by Mr. Aslett Baldwin, F.R.C.S., and the story narrated by Gwladys Townshend of Raynham)

ALL stories connected with ghosts of children make an especial appeal to the heart. They are rarely unhappy, these sweet "returns", who occasionally escape from the nurseries of heaven to revisit places associated with their brief sojourn on earth. For what reason do they come back ? I have heard of one ghost-child, who, during the night, tidied a room and arranged the flowers as she used to do. Another small child, rescued from drowning, only to die an hour later, haunts the house where it died, and the patter of its tiny feet is constantly heard in the tiled hall.

At one time Beaminster School was haunted by the apparition of John Daniel, a schoolboy who appeared to five of the pupils, one of whom had not even seen him when alive, and who proved his identity by a wonderful piece of circumstantial evidence. It is pathetic to think of the murdered lad reappearing in a place where he used to play with boys who now only knew him as a shadow !

Certain rooms in Trinity College, Cambridge, are haunted by a child who wanders about moaning, with the palms of its hands turned outwards. And in a house in Yorkshire, many visitors have seen the figure of a little dark-haired girl, always wearing her night-dress, who seems to be in great trouble, and who never comes twice into the same room.

A boy and a white rabbit, only seen by children living in the house, haunted an old manor in Somerset. And who does not appreciate the poignancy of the story of the ghost of a newly buried child who "returned" to entreat its broken-hearted mother not to weep so much.

"Your tears have made my shroud so wet, I cannot

sleep," it complained, exactly in the same way that a living child would become peevish if its night's rest were made uncomfortable. It is a homely little ghost story—pointing a moral, not to grieve overmuch, especially for the joyous band of children who will never know the sufferings entailed by sin, or, happiest thought of all, will never meet the worst of enemies, in their own sins armed against them.

I do not know whether Mr. Aslett Baldwin believes in ghosts, but he has contributed these startling psychic experiences, told him by someone who stayed in the house with the haunted garden, and vouches for the truth of everything set down in the story of Jasmin—a little flower gathered by the Master many years ago.

The house associated with the hauntings had been bought quite recently by Mr. S., a friend of the man—let us call him "C."—who knows Mr. Aslett Baldwin.

The delightful old Hall was an ideal retreat for a bachelor with bookish tastes, and C. congratulated his friend on his "find". After dinner they strolled about the admirably kept grounds merging imperceptibly into pine woods, at this hour dark caves of mystery, which partly surrounded the house.

All at once C. noticed a long winding path, so neglected as to be almost overgrown. Yew hedges bordered it, and climbing roses, on the other side, had pushed their way through the hedges, and waved imploring arms, weighted with scented loveliness, to attract the attention of those who walked in the garden. This blatant disorder in the midst of the studied order of the other part of the grounds puzzled C. His host saw the silent note of interrogation registered in his face.

"H'm—looking at that path, are you? Well . . . you couldn't miss it. However, I've a fancy to let it run wild. In another year nobody will be able to walk down it. . . ." He paused significantly. "I have good reasons for razing it level with the ground, but somehow I can't bring myself to do it. However—I always give it a wide berth. *It's haunted*, and I'll tell you what happens there, if you have patience to listen, without thinking I'm heading for the road where madness lies."

They were now standing some distance away on the soft velvet of the lawn facing the path. The evening sky was jade green, the trees etched sharply against it ; bats circled in the soft air ; the sickle of the crescent moon would presently reap the harvest of the stars.

Suddenly a child's laugh, piercingly sweet and clear as a blackbird's note, came from the direction of the path. "You heard that ?" said S. "Let's go indoors."

It seemed to C. as if part of the house were asleep—but he felt life still went on behind the dark observant windows.

"That wing looks uninhabited," he said.

"*It certainly is,*" replied S.

They closed the ancient entrance door, and shut out the perfume of the flower incense rising from the pale tobacco flowers, the passionate fragrance of the magnolia, the cloying sweetness of syringa, and the clean scent of many roses. The library, where the friends sat and smoked, was comfortably remote. No sounds penetrated its cloistered calm, and the old books looked like watchful rows of brown-gowned Franciscans.

"I believe this place is making me fanciful," said C. . . . "Or else it's waiting for your story."

"Well, you shall have it. I bought this property a year ago. . . . nothing odd about it, except that for years it hadn't been let or sold, and it was in very bad repair. I got it for a song. . . . I wanted to make it beautiful and dignified again—some old houses can stand their faces being lifted. . . . I made a thorough survey.

"The wing you saw had evidently been given over to generations of children . . . all sorts of reminders of them remained : pencilled marks and dates of their heights, initials cut in the panelling ; and we found a derelict eighteenth century doll in a walled-up cupboard. I am sure that little boys had knelt on the wide window-seats and flattened their noses against the panes on wet days, counting the raindrops chasing one another down the glass, and

little girls had sat in front of the wide fire-place (I suppose
it once had one of those high brass fenders), and played
hide-and-seek in the long passage which connects this wing
with *our* part of the house. But directly I set foot there, I
felt that there was something impossible to grapple with
. . . something that drove me away—didn't want me. So
I had the place made sound, and left it at that . . . I'm quite
all right on this side of the house."

C. said, "What a waste of space."

"Possibly, but, strange to say, nobody hereabouts was
surprised. However, things began to happen when I took
the garden in hand. At first I used to motor down from
Town, and spend a few hours with the builder, and a
gardener who understood gardens. One afternoon last
spring I thought I'd like to be alone. It was a heavenly day,
a jolly little wind investigating every corner, clouds
chasing each other across the sky—everything waking up,
even the dignified yew had put forth tiny green shoots.

"It was then I heard a rustle behind the hedge, as if
children were in hiding ; I say children, because the 'rustle'
was quite low down—I was being 'stalked', watched,
hidden from. . . . *And I had been told there wasn't a cottage,
or a child, within a mile radius.* Afterwards came a confusion of
voices, falling over one another in rippling cascades of
laughter—shrill sweet laughter—you heard some of it an
hour ago. I went back to the house—spoke to the old
caretaker.

" 'Look here,' I said, 'I won't have strange children
running about the grounds.'

"The cross-grained ancient stared. 'God love 'ee, sir,
did 'ee say *children*? I tell 'ee there beant none of them
audacious little varmints—none of 'em would show their
faces here—scared stiff they be of them others—and a good
thing as summat can scare 'em.'

" 'But I heard children talking and playing.'

"He laughed—a rusty, creaking chuckle. . . . 'Take no
notice,' he said . . . and he refused to be drawn. 'I'm a-
telling 'ee to take no notice,' he repeated.

"The first day I came to live here, I went to the path.

This time the footsteps and the voices were insistent, and words—afterwards sentences—detached themselves from the confusion of little tongues. Somebody said : 'We want to hear about your sister.'

"I took no notice.

" 'Yes,' chorused the voices, 'do tell us where she is ; we would like her to come and play with us.'

"I said sharply (conscious that I was making a perfect fool of myself), 'I *haven't* a sister.'

"The path echoed with derisive laughter. 'Of course you have—you *know* you have. You mustn't tell lies . . . it's *wicked.* Liars go to hell.'

" 'You know more than I do,' I retorted. "If I had a sister, tell me her name.'

"And—all the unseen children shouted : 'It's *Jasmin,* we'll spell it for you—J A S M I N.'

" ' Jasmine, without the E,' said a voice—' such a pretty flower—it smells so sweet.'

" I didn't want to hear any more—I wasn't frightened, but I was more or less annoyed and puzzled. Evidently that particular path belonged to the ghosts of the children who had died here in childhood . . . and I remembered having noticed many wall tablets in the old church com-memorating the names of those who 'died in their infancy '. The former owners of the Hall had been prolific parents, but the majority of their large families did not reach maturity—an old decadent stock, so I was informed, which finally flickered out more than fifty years ago.

" Still, I couldn't forget the name—Jasmin. I had supposed myself to be an only son, born at a period of her life when my mother had never expected to bear a child. I had not heard of the existence of any other. My mother is now a very old lady, living with her memories. Hitherto I had never ruffled the serene surface of her thoughts. Now I decided to do so.

"I went to see her. There's a nurse always in attendance, but Mother's not senile, only remote and self-absorbed. Outwardly, her life is bounded by the Bible (parts of which she knows by heart) and the satisfaction of seeing a few selected friends. She thinks 'back' a great deal when she lies awake at night, and gets frightened by age and death. She doesn't want to die when it's dark. Nurse declares she won't.

"'I'm pleased to see you,' she said ; 'and how is your house progressing ? It is a pity I am not able to help you in your arrangements—at my age the journey would kill me.'

"I drew a bow at a venture. 'If I only *had* a sister, how *useful* she would be.'

"'A *sister*—did you say a *sister* ? . . . Let me think. . . .' Submerged memories were evidently rising from the sea of the past. . . . 'But, John, you *had* a baby sister. I never talk about her . . . I never have . . . it was a great sorrow. . . .' Two difficult tears trailed their slow course through the furrows of old age. . . . 'Yes—a pretty little thing . . . hair like spun silk . . . I called her Jasmin—after the jasmine growing round our bedroom window . . . but I spelt her name differently. She did not live . . . it's many years ago. . . .'

"There's not much more to tell, but that little is curious. A week later, when I was sitting outside in the twilight, a child's hand crept slowly into mine—a little hand, with the helpless clinging fingers which appeal so much to women, and a sweet far-off voice said, 'I am Jasmin. You must not let the children trouble you. The next time they ask about me, please say, *I have nothing for you*, and then they will go away.' Afterwards—the little hand was quietly withdrawn.

"I could not wait . . . I went to the path. No sooner had I done so, than I was surrounded by the unseen children . . . pressing hard on one another's heels.

"'Now you *know* that you had a sister, but why does she not come here ?' said the leader.

"I answered : 'You were quite right. I *had* a sister : her name *was* Jasmin. I've been talking to her—she has sent you a message.'

"'What is it ?' clamoured a score of voices.

"'Just this—*I have nothing for you.*'

"The effect was electrical. A long tense silence. Afterwards a general stampede. Children taking cover, scampering away in all directions like frightened rabbits. The yew walk was deserted."

"As Jasmin had promised, they never came back, at any rate when I was anywhere near. I've thought it over, time after time, and it always becomes more and more fantastic. Although everything is true. You can't get away from the name, and the fact that I had a sister called Jasmin.

"I don't expect you to believe such an impossible story," said S., apologetically, "but"—evidently trying to excuse himself for having unburdened his mind—"hang it all, old fellow, *you* heard a child laugh, didn't you ?"

THREE GHOST STORIES

Contributed by H.H. Princess Marina Chavchavadze

THE HAUNTED HOUSE ON THE VASSILEVSKY ISLAND

IN Russia, ghosts and ghost stories are not the traditions of centuries, as is the case in Western Europe. With us, the belief in the supernatural is usually based on natural phenomena and the emotions which they inspire, and this condition, besides representing a survival of paganism, creates friendly and inimical beings who take part in the daily life of the Russian peasant.

Any close communion with Nature is bound to result in a belief, which necessitates giving a supernatural explanation of those forces which especially stimulate the imagination, in fact all over the world the worship of Nature Spirits persists in one form or another.

The best known Russian Nature Spirit, associated solely with woods and forests, is known as the Lieschy, whose whole-time occupation is either to make travellers lose their way, or else to frighten them out of their wits. In this aspect he somewhat resembles the Fata Morgana of Italy, the Feu Follet of France, the Erl King of Germany, and the English Will o' the Wisp and Jack o' Lantern. Another spirit, the Domovoy, who frequents all inhabited places, is more or less the companion of the Russian peasant. The Domovoy is a frivolous, irresponsible creature, who indulges in all kinds of practical jokes in the farms and cottages, but, unlike the Pixies, the Brownies, and the Irish Leprechaun, the Domovoy does not believe in work, so he never helps, but only hinders. He specializes in hiding things when they are most needed, he loves to bang doors, and startle harmless old people dozing by the fireside, although, to do him credit, he thoroughly succeeds in putting fear into the hearts of incorrigibly naughty children !

The Domovoy touches the heights of his semi-malicious activities when he appears in the kitchen and meddles with the cooking, spoiling the cakes and bread by making the "batch" as flat as the proverbial pancake or else as heavy as lead.

All domestic worries, great and small, are put down to the Domovoy, but as this joyous scapegoat possesses a back sufficiently broad to bear the multitudinous charges laid to his door, he continues, even in modern Russia, to pursue the uneven tenor of his way.

The reason for the dearth of ghosts in Russia may be due to the changeable conditions of life throughout her history, and, more prosaic still, to the comparatively recent use of stone in building, which not only has prevented the creation of ancient houses and castles, but has deprived new ones of the traditions inseparable from antiquity. But wherever the boundaries of Russia touch on the older civilizations of the Caucasus, or Baltic Provinces, ghosts and ghost stories immediately enter into local legends.

I do not wish to give the impression that ghosts do not walk in Russia. In most important houses dating from the seventeenth and eighteenth centuries you find the usual family ghosts, omens and warnings, and some of our well-known authors—Gogol in particular—have made ample use of the supernatural element in their midst.

No doubt the atrocities and poignant dramas of the revolution accounts for many present-day "returns", some of which haunt the scenes of their violent exits from life. Hauntings in the prisons are a foregone conclusion, and the wraiths of the murdered Imperial Family must be inseparable from Ekaterinburg. Even in 1924 the place was enveloped in an aura of tragedy, and when Isadora Duncan visited it she described it as a living nightmare. "You have no idea what a living nightmare is, until you see this town," she wrote. "Perhaps the killing of a certain family has cast a sort of Edgar Allan Poe gloom over it. The melancholy church bells ring every hour, fearful to hear. . . . We saw the house and the cellar where they shot a certain family. *Its psychosis seems to pervade the atmosphere. You can't imagine anything more fearful.*"

And there are many other tragedies of those days which have left their imperishable record on souls, and on environment.

My first ghost story, which provided one of the greatest sensations of pre-war Petersburg, concerns a haunted house situated on the Vassilevsky Island opposite the Nicolaevsky Bridge.

The house had been unoccupied for many years, and externally it lived up to its sinister reputation as "a house under some prodigious ban of excommunication". However, two students, who disbelieved in any kind of superstition, and scoffed at supernatural manifestations, planned to destroy the legend, by passing the night there, holding themselves in readiness to tackle any ghost bold enough to appear.

The owner of the property, anxious to reinstate the house as a selling or letting proposition, gladly gave permission to the ghost seers to stay as long as they liked, and he made arrangements to have a good fire lighted in what was known as the "haunted" room, besides supplying two chairs and a table, as the friends proposed having supper before commencing to "watch out". Everything was soon in readiness. Provisions and wine were sent in, and a goodly supply of candles to lighten the darkness, completed the equipment for the night.

C. (for it is better to describe him as an initial) arrived punctually at the time fixed for the meeting. Apart from his mulish obstinacy where the supernatural was concerned, he was a nice young fellow, who entered into the spirit of the adventure on this cold rainy autumn evening, and, as he liked his "comforts", he was cheered by the thought that the vigil would not take place in a fireless room. He therefore unlocked the front door with pleasurable anticipations, not only of being "thrilled", but also of being warmed

The hall was in darkness, and when C.'s electric torch flashed here and there, he understood how different "empty" houses *feel* at night. During the day they are just *empty* : at night they become alive, and belong to the unseen —or to the shadows of those who have lived and died within their walls. At night, the complainings of any old house are *pathetic*, especially when its creaking old bones resent the burden of the years and the dry rot which gradually eats into its heart. To suffer like this a house *must* be old, and few modern buildings possess the capacity either for suffering or for endurance.

Upstairs, someone was singing, and C. recognized his friend's voice in company with a curiously distorted echo.

"Keeping up his spirits," said C. to himself; but suddenly the Echo set in movement something definitely malignant ; the house became a receptacle for an immense resistless power, and C. sensed an imperishable record of Incarnate Evil.

Reproaching himself for possessing imagination, C. went upstairs, and opened the door of the room from whence the voice, and the echo, proceeded.

A fire of ships' timber blazed on the open hearth, and flames of red, blue, green, and faint lilac danced and pursued each other upwards in a carnivalesque riot of colour. The table was set for supper, and lighted candles in heavy candlesticks stood on a marble side buffet—a relic of the house's former State. In this aspect, the room had nothing approaching the supernatural about it.

Taking off his heavy overcoat, C. greeted P., and asked him how long he had been waiting.

"I didn't know you meant to steal a march on me," he said.

"Merely my fancy," answered P. "I wanted to get in touch with the Unseen."

"And—did you ?"

"Yes—and no." And he began to sing in a voice lacking all youth and clearness, the sound cleaving the warm wood-scented air like a meteor. C., hitherto only accustomed to hearing P. sing students' songs, with an occasional excerpt from musical comedy, was, by turns, attracted and repelled; he even experienced a vague feeling of panic; for a moment it seemed as if a devil were making music. With something of an effort he said:

"Well, let's have supper. By the way, in what language were you singing? I couldn't understand a word of it."

"Naturally *not*," and P. smiled at him across the table, a wicked, cynical smile, which perplexed the already perplexed C. This might be P. who sang and smiled, but it certainly was *not* the familiar light-hearted P. of the daily round. He said nothing, and tried to think, and act, normally, but from time to time he looked at his friend, who was enjoying his supper with a healthy appetite, whilst C. ate sparingly, and only drank a couple of glasses of wine.

At last P. began to talk about the house. "I wonder what we shall see," he said. "Don't you think it is a little presumptuous to disturb well-buried evil by reason of senseless curiosity? Perhaps this house belongs to one who is adored through fear, whose strength lies in destruction, and who might *resent* our intrusion."

"But you were the first to propose to investigate the hauntings," said C. "Have *you* by any chance become a convert to the religion whose god is adored through fear?"

P. threw him a dark look. "We won't discuss religion. Better by far to toast midnight in a libation to Evil." He tossed off the contents of his glass, refilled it, and flung the red wine on to the merry flames. "A Libation to Evil!" he cried. Suddenly his whole personality changed, and with a snarl he turned to C. "You poor fool," he cried, "to attempt to measure your strength against those whose strength is invincible. You thought to destroy the indestructible, to uproot, as easily as weeds, forces whose roots are older than Time. Do you not think that you deserve punishment?" As he spoke, P. rose from his chair, still smiling his cruel, mocking smile, and C. stared at him, incapable of thought or movement, conscious only that he was a helpless prisoner of the Powers of Darkness.

The last thing C. remembered was P.'s tiger-like spring. His throat was seized by fingers which burnt like acid into his flesh, then darkness fell.

.   .   .   .   .

Next morning C. and P. were absent from the University, and, as they had missed a special noonday lecture important for both, some fellow-students, who knew about the experiment at the haunted house, decided to go and see what had become of the ghost hunters.

To their disappointment, there was nothing "frightening" about the place—the silken curtains spun by successive generations of spiders waved across the windows, and when the door opened to admit the autumn air, an inquisitive ray of watery sunlight darted across the floor and up the broad staircase, followed by the little group.

When they went into the room on the first floor, cold grey ash and burnt-out candles met their eyes; afterwards they noticed an overturned table, and broken plates, and pieces of food strewed the floor, where the spilt wine looked like a stream of congealed blood.

Something lay under the debris. This was C.—evidently in a dead faint—or worse. There was no sign of P., so whilst two of the young men busied themselves in bringing C. round, the others hurried upstairs to see if P. was anywhere in hiding.

The rooms were empty, save for gigantic bloated spiders scuttling away in the gloom. The dust of years rose like musty incense from cracks in the boards as the searchers hurried over them, and, in the garrets, battalions of bats clung to the worm-eaten beams.

The students concluded that P. had gone suddenly mad and attacked C. in a moment of frenzy. There was nothing else to do but to take C. back to his home (he was now somewhat restored, but incapable of giving them any information), make inquiries at P.'s lodgings, and, if necessary, report the affair to the police.

A closed carriage was fetched, and C., looking as if

he had passed the night in Hell, and not in an empty house, was restored to his family, who, although alarmed at his condition, could not resist the chance it gave them to repeat the familiar formula, "I told you so", on every possible occasion.

The next halt was at P.'s lodgings a few streets away. The inquiry as to whether he was at home instantly produced a running commentary from the landlady. "*Was* he at home? Yes, he *was*, and, judging from his appearance, likely to remain at home for the next few days." She didn't know whether too much learning, or too much seeing life, made anyone sleep like the dead. "He came in at two o'clock yesterday afternoon, went straight to bed, and has not got up since. Sleeping all the time." It would be a good thing to rouse him—so far she hadn't been able to do anything with him.

More than ever amazed, the young men went to P.'s room. Sure enough, there he was, sleeping, and snoring heavily.

"And yet she says he went to bed at *two o'clock* yesterday afternoon," said the leader, and, with another willing helper, he shook the sleeper as one shakes an apple on the topmost bough; P. reluctantly opened his eyes.

"What on earth are you fellows doing in my room?" he grumbled.

They explained the reason, and, awakened to some purpose, P. sat up, and stared at them uncomprehendingly; at last the gravity of their story gradually dawned on him. "Then it *was* yesterday that we planned to go to the house on the island?" He was assured that it was so. "And you come and tell me some cock-and-bull story about finding C. half murdered, and that there were evidences of two people having eaten together . . . Are we all mad? *I've never stirred out of this place*—my landlady can prove it. I forgot the appointment, but I remember I felt curiously tired, and had a sort of drugged sensation, when I came back to lunch; in fact I became so drowsy that I went to bed. I never gave a thought to C., or to any haunted house, so if there *were* two people at supper *the second one wasn't me.*"

There for the moment the matter ended. P.'s twenty-eight hour alibi was provided by his landlady and her servant, as well as by a friend who had called later in the evening.

On the other hand, C.'s incredible story was confirmed by the condition of the room, his own pitiable state, and the statements of eye-witnesses; but, strangest of all, the imprints on his throat could never have been made by the spatulated fingers on P.'s rather pudgy little hand.

The mystery of this authentic story of the supernatural has remained unsolved. It created an immense amount of talk and speculation in Petersburg, but no clue was ever found as to the identity of C.'s supper companion. It was a clear case of like and unlike, with something deeper still, something that made even unimaginative people *afraid*, and when shortly afterwards the owner of the house on the island decided to pull it down, not one stone was left upon another of the ill-omened place with its evil entities and unsolved mysteries.

THE STAIRLESS TOWER

"THE Stairless Tower" is *not* a ghost story, being only associated with death warnings peculiar to certain families in one form or another, and this particular warning concerns friends of mine, Baron and Baroness R., who owned a beautiful estate in the country, where the ruins of an ancient tower stood in the gardens surrounding the house. The tower had only one window, and, as the stairs had long since been destroyed, it was merely a picturesque inaccessible "shell", covered with ivy, and a few wind-sown wild flowers.

According to tradition, whenever a member of the R. family died a light gleamed through the tower window, although nobody could give a practical reason to account for it.

One summer evening, Baron R.'s two daughters and a friend went for an after-dinner stroll, and, not noticing how far they had walked, found themselves to all intents and purposes lost in the soft darkness of a moonless night. Fortunately, the woodland paths on their father's estate were well kept and clearly defined, so it was not difficult to "feel" their way back to the gardens, and as they walked up the avenue dominated by the Stairless Tower, the girls stopped, and a little shiver passed from one to the other. They had both seen *a light shining in the Tower window*, with a curious searchlight effect, partly phosphorescent, and partly flame, which streamed like a white ribbon on the night. The sisters looked at each other. . . .

"Do you see anything?" whispered the elder girl.

"Yes," faltered her sister, "there's a light in the Tower."

To their friend, who did not know the story of the Death Warning, she said, trying to speak naturally, "surely there's a light somewhere?"

"Of course there is," he laughed; "why, it's in the Tower—however has anyone managed to get up there? Perhaps they've flown in," he added.

The light was still shining in the barred window when they returned to the house, and it continued to shine until an hour later, when a telephone call came through, informing the Baron of the sudden death of his eldest son.

Afterwards the Stairless Tower became part of the darkness.

The Warning Given to a Member of My Family of the Impending Assassination of the Emperor Alexander II

On Saturday, February 28, 1881, another and more ghostly kind of warning occurred in our family, the recipient being the young Countess S., and it is necessary, in the cause of truth, to say that on this particular evening no discussion of any kind had taken place about ghosts or psychic phenomena, and the Countess had gone to bed in a perfectly normal frame of mind.

The first hour or so she slept soundly, then she awoke with a start, to see by the dim light of the vielleuse someone leaning over the low bed-rail.

The figure was that of a pale-faced old man with a long white beard, wearing some kind of a flowing dark robe. His expression was gentle, mingled with a sense of tragedy, and the Countess heard him say, very solemnly :

"Tomorrow, at noon, the Emperor Alexander II will be assassinated."

He then disappeared, and the terrified Countess awakened her husband, and told him of her vision and the old man's ominous words.

The ordinary type of husbands have no use for the supernatural, and they do not show much sympathy when it becomes a question of dreaming dreams or seeing visions. Count S. listened patiently to the story of the old man's warning, laughed a little, comforted his wife, and told her to go to sleep.

The young wife was *not* imaginative, she *wanted* to go to sleep, but the old man appeared twice more during that nerve-shattering night, and each time he reiterated his statement of the approaching assassination of the Emperor. After the third visitation, she lay weeping silently, with frayed-out nerves, by this time absolutely convinced that it was the Emperor's last day on earth.

That morning Count S. was on duty with his regiment for the trooping of the colours at the Mikhailovski Manege. This ceremony was to take place in the presence of the Emperor, and, knowing the time when it would be over, the Countess hurried along the Embankment to meet her husband as he came back. She was more than ever impressed with the drama of the night, and she felt the only way to combat her fears was to face matters, and not to wait for someone to tell her the best, or the worst.

Directly she saw her husband riding towards her she knew from his expression that the old man of her vision had spoken the truth, and although Count S. was a soldier, with a soldier's self-control, a little of his composure failed him when he saw his wife's pale face, and read the unspoken question in her frightened eyes. So he said, very quietly :

"You were right. The Emperor has been murdered."

I wish I could finish this true family record with some more interesting details, but none are available. It is a fact that Countess S. saw the apparition three times consecutively, and her husband always corroborated her statement. In any case, the Count could not have prevented the assassination of the Emperor, and it is doubtful whether anyone in his entourage would have listened or paid any attention to the story of a waking dream. But those who query the importance of the supernatural in daily life may justifiably argue that the ghostly warning ought to have been given direct to the Emperor, or to one of the officials responsible for the arrangements on that fatal morning.

However, in many cases of supernatural manifestations the real reason often remains unexplained.

THE GHOST AT HUNSTANTON HALL
AND THE HAUNTINGS OF
DAME ARMINE LE STRANGE

(The facts contributed by Bernard le Strange, Esq., the present owner of Hunstanton Hall, to Gwladys Townshend of Raynham)

THE Norman Manor House which originally stood on the present site of Hunstanton Hall belonged during the reign of Henry I to Ralph de Hunstanton, mentioned in the Doomsday Book as holding certain lands in Norfolk, and when, about the same time, Roland le Strange, a Frenchman from Anjou, settled near by in 1110, it is not surprising that in due course he married Matilda le Brun, heiress of Hunstanton. Their descendants have lived in Hunstanton down to the present time (1936)—over eight hundred years.

In 1853 a great fire destroyed the Elizabethan wing of the building formerly joined on to the Plantagenet block, and it is grievous for those who love the traditions of the past to think of the old furniture, the family pictures and the stained glass, which perished in the fierce blaze which consumed the ancient stairway, each step a solid block of oak.

The Grand Staircase and the Great Drawing-Room still exist as "features" of the Jacobean portion of Hunstanton Hall, and the drawing-room is a long panelled room with stone mullioned windows, looking over the Green Court, and the Inigo Jones Gateway. The decorations above the fireplace were carved by Grinling Gibbons, whose genius made dead wood live, and round the cornice, small shields bear the arms of the owners of Hunstanton Hall since Roland le Strange's day.

Everybody who comes into the Great Drawing-Room stops before the portrait of Dame Armine le Strange. They can't explain *why*—it just happens. I have even heard super-sensitive people say that it needed all their will power to confront it, as this long dead woman seems tremendously alive, and perhaps she possesses a quiet sense of amusement in her power over others.

When Dame Armine le Strange sat to Heins for her portrait, she was no longer in her first youth, and the artist's conception of her reveals character and great strength of will.

Armine le Strange married Henry Styleman, and lived quietly with him at Snettisham Old Hall until her husband, devoted to his home and estates, died broken-hearted, after the sea, which knows no respect for kings or landowners, broke through one of his marshes at Snettisham and did irreparable damage.

His widow then took up her residence at Hunstanton Hall, which she had inherited through the death of her brother. But the home of successive generations of her family was destined to witness the tragic sacrifices demanded from her by her eldest son, Nicholas ; sacrifices so appalling that it is difficult to understand how she faced them, even with the help of the strong personality that still makes itself felt in the place where she lived out her life—the victim of the wilful, pleasure-loving individual known throughout Norfolk as "The Jolly Gentleman".

Nicholas Styleman—otherwise "The Jolly Gentleman", born in 1722, was educated at Trinity College, Cambridge, and became a B.A. In 1743 he married the daughter of Henry Hoste Henley, of Leigh, Somerset, he was appointed D.L. in 1759, and in 1776 he served as High Sheriff of Norfolk. He was a man of many parts, who took his fill of life, and kept open house at Hunstanton. There is a suggestion of kindness, good temper, comradeship, and light-heartedness in the name by which he came to be known. "The Jolly Gentleman" makes one think of a delightful fellow, with lovable failings, who hardly ever troubled to excuse his conduct. In his day people did not stop to reason about the pros and cons of their daily actions, and the great livers were rarely troubled either by conscience or by criticism.

However, the case for the defence of "The Jolly Gentleman" must be that he began life in a difficult period, when the excesses of the Restoration had given place to a full-blooded, non-squeamish trend of existence, especially in the country; moreover, "The Jolly Gentleman" was also a gambler born; one of those who, "lest he should lose, does not stop losing".

The fear of "losing" made "The Jolly Gentleman" sell everything of value he could lay his hands on, and Hunstanton Hall, at this time, represented an Open Sesame of precious possessions easily convertible into cash. His mother, alternatively raging, sorrowing, and benumbed, saw the gradual dispersion of the wonderful library, the horrible "gaps" in the plate-room, and—crowning enormity to a woman with a background of traditions—the sale of the historic jewels worn successively for centuries by the ladies le Strange.

One of Dame Armine's cherished possessions was a large antique carpet, a poem, woven in a riot of colour and design, said to have been given her by a Shah of Persia. It is a little difficult to understand why her affections were set on a carpet—certainly not a magic one. It may have been that it was unique in Norfolk, but the carpet became so great an obsession that, when she lay dying in her despoiled home, her thoughts continually reverted carpetwards. "The Jolly Gentleman" knew its value; would he—horrible thought—sell it, after his mother, taking her last rest in the Church of Saint Mary the Virgin, could no longer gainsay him?

Dame Armine sent for "The Jolly Gentleman", who came into the sick-room, after a day's hunting, bringing with him the tang of the sea and the earth scents of the country. He was a little curious as to the reason for this unexpected summons, and as he perhaps cared for his mother in his casual, selfish manner, he must have been genuinely grieved to know that she was dying.

"I wish to speak to you, Nicholas," said Dame Armine, "because my time is short, and my heart is full of foreboding."

Her son looked at his mother, said never a word, and tapped the floor uneasily with his hunting-crop.

"I do not wish to reproach you," continued the dying woman; "there is so little left with which to reproach you, that it would be idle to do so. You have sold nearly everything, and I am told that if I were able to look out of the windows of my bedchamber I should miss the deer in the Park."

"It's true," said "The Jolly Gentleman" cheerfully. "I lost 'em at play last week."

His mother disregarded this candid confession.

"There is something—as yet unsold. *My carpet*. And because of my carpet I have sent for you. It possesses a saleable value. You will dispose of it after my death."

"Stap me, Madam," exclaimed the slightly scandalized "Jolly Gentleman", " 'fore heaven, I have never given it a thought."

His mother smiled acidly. "The deer in the Park were at one time unthought of as being worth staking. However, I have been powerless to stop anything you have chosen to do. But, as your mother, I am empowered to ask you to give me your solemn promise never to sell *the* carpet."

The "Jolly Gentleman", relieved at the simple conclusion of what he must have mentally described as "much ado about nothing", readily gave the required promise.

"Here's my hand on it," he said.

Dame Armine held her son's powerful hand in her own. "Remember, Nicholas—if you break your promise, and if you or anyone else commit the enormity of selling the carpet, or letting it go out of the Hall, *I shall return and haunt this house*. I swear it, and I know I shall be permitted to do so."

Later, as the "Jolly Gentleman" went through the great drawing-room, he stared at the Shah's carpet, and wondered greatly at the incomprehensible vagaries of women.

Dame Armine died, and her son, inspired by a belated remorse, and not feeling too sure of his "moral" strength, decided not to be led into temptation, where the carpet was concerned. He gave orders for its removal from the drawing-room, and caused it to be nailed up in a wooden box, and placed somewhere out of sight, acting on the precept that what the eye does not see, the heart does not grieve for.

Faithful to his spoken word, the carpet remained unsold during the lifetime of the "Jolly Gentleman", who, dying in 1788, was buried at Snettisham, and its existence was forgotten by those who came after him until eighty years later, when Mr. le Strange's grandfather, Hamon le Strange, owned Hunstanton Hall.

Mr. le Strange's grandfather, who rebuilt the Elizabethan portion, married Emmeline Austin, of Boston (Mass.), a lovely girl, known as the American Beauty, whose portrait by Watts hangs, with that of her husband, in the great drawing-room. Mrs. le Strange evidently possessed the pioneer spirit, as well as the natural desire to explore her new home, and as ancient houses often represent unexpected "finds" in pictures or furniture, she was thrilled when she discovered the dust-covered box containing the forgotten carpet.

I am afraid she was a little disappointed when she saw it, and, as she had never heard the story, she merely looked on the carpet as a harbourage for moths. This being so, she decided to cut it up into hearthrugs, and distribute it among the cottagers, and one day, laden with a largish bale of hearthrugs, Mrs. le Strange drove out to present them to deserving homes.

It was getting late when she returned with the consciousness of having been lavishly generous, where hearthrugs were concerned, and as the carriage approached the Gate House Mrs. le Strange saw a woman glaring at her from one of the windows whose expression was so forbidding that the bride was positively frightened, more especially as the face seemed somehow familiar. Who could it be? Then, with sudden recollection, she knew that the face at the window was that of Dame Armine le Strange. Whatever had brought her spirit thither?

Mrs. le Strange ran indoors to consult her husband, who suddenly remembered the "Jolly Gentleman's" promise, and related the story to his pretty wife. "It's evident Dame Armine has been as good as her word," he said. "I'm afraid we shall have to replace the carpet in its box, and leave it undisturbed."

Mrs. le Strange's New England common sense, no doubt, led her to say something about "silly" superstitions, and at first she refused to contemplate the carpet's return. She spoke too soon. That night, and for several nights, the ghost of Dame Armine wandered about the Hall like a restless fury, striking terror into the hearts of those unlucky enough to encounter her, and at last Mrs. le Strange, yielding to general pressure, exchanged the scattered pieces of the Shah's carpet for a corresponding number of good Axminster rugs.

Delays are dangerous, and whether Mrs. le Strange delayed unduly, or whether Dame Armine resented the American invasion, her ghost still walks at Hunstanton. Mrs. le Strange never cared to discuss the incident, and neither Mr. le Strange, nor his uncle or great-uncle, can remember what the carpet looked like. In Mr. le Strange's recollection, two of the housekeepers have actually seen Dame Armine; on one occasion he can fix the date as November 25, 1910—his grandfather's birthday.

This curious instance of a whole-time obsession for an inanimate object can claim to be an authentic ghost story, although entirely dissociated with any kind of bad luck following the removal of the carpet. The present-day hauntings seem consequent as the result of the American Beauty's ignorance of the "Jolly Gentleman's" death-bed promise to Dame Armine le Strange. Rather a poor revenge; but, after all, few women possess the saving grace of sweet reasonableness, and, in this case, certainly not a ghost!

WHERE DID SHE COME FROM?

Contributed by Sir Ernest Bennett, M.P.

THIRTY-FIVE years ago, when Sir Ernest Bennett was an Oxford Don, he accepted an invitation to spend Christmas with some friends—the fortunate possessors of a beautiful country house in Gloucestershire. There were also the inducements of a County Ball, a sympathetic house-party, and his hostess' three charming daughters. Sir Ernest had every prospect of thoroughly enjoying his visit.

At this time Sir Ernest was, as he now is, a member of the Psychical Research Society, and when, on the evening after his arrival, the conversation turned on spiritualism, his hostess, Mrs. B. H., asked him if it would be possible to get a medium down from town and hold an informal seance, Sir Ernest was not keen on the idea. In his opinion paid mediums were usually fraudulent; but not wishing to appear ungracious, he told Mrs. B. H. that he knew of one genuine medium, a Mrs. Corner, *née* Florence Cook, who had often sat for Sir William Crookes and obtained wonderful results.

"If we can get Mrs. Corner," he said, "we shall be sure of our spiritualistic ground; but, should she come, I must make two stipulations—one is that, beyond her expenses, she receives no money, and the second, that she is invited as a guest, and not as a medium."

Two days later Mrs. Corner and her daughter, a pretty girl of sixteen, arrived, and it was arranged that she should give an after-dinner seance the following evening, notwithstanding the fact that the majority of the guests were quite ignorant of spiritualism, and one of them, a sceptical young doctor, frankly denounced it as "rot". A room on the ground floor was arranged for the seance, part of it being curtained off to form a cabinet, whilst the sitters formed a semi-circle facing the curtains. The remainder of the furniture consisted of a few chairs and a piano. A window looked out on to the gardens, which were just below the level of the room, and this window was sealed and fastened in such a way as to render it impossible to open it from the outside or inside. It was also agreed that, during the seance, the door of the room would be locked, Sir Ernest holding the key, whilst the presence of an unemotional footman posted on guard in the hall would ensure fair play.

Mrs. Corner had no idea of the geography of the large rambling house, and, by way of proving her genuine disinterestedness, she insisted on being searched by some of the ladies present before entering the cabinet. This was well and thoroughly done, and afterwards Mrs. Corner put on her pretty semi-evening gown, and sat down in the chair facing the drawn curtains.

Sir Ernest Bennett had taken the most elaborate precautions to prevent the slightest possibility of fraud. Mrs. Corner was enclosed in a perfect network of strands of filoselle silk, her ankles and wrists were fastened to the chair, a steel chain, padlocked to the chair, encircled her waist—the key being retained by Sir Ernest Bennett, who explained to the sitters that the reason for using filoselle silk was on account of the difficulty of unfastening knots made in it.

Everything was in readiness : the sitters took their places, Sir Ernest on the right, the disbelieving medico next but one to him, and Miss Corner sat in the middle of the semi-circle.

The medium soon went into trance ; her head drooped ; presently she seemed absolutely unconscious and, during this time, the door and window fastenings were finally tested. The cabinet was in darkness except for a red lamp, which lit up the faces of the sitters, and marked the time by Sir Ernest's watch. As nobody except himself had ever assisted at a seance, people talked quite normally during the ten minutes which ensued before anything "happened", and it must be noted that, before entering the cabinet,

Mrs. Corner had made everyone promise not to *touch* any figure, should one "materialize".

In due time the curtains parted, and a curious vision wearing a turban, a tunic, and white trousers tied below the knee, appeared before the opening. Her legs and arms were bare, and at first "she" (for it was certainly a woman) kept on darting in and out between the curtains, until, gradually gaining courage, she emerged into the space in front of the cabinet, and closed the curtains behind her.

The amazed sitters had hardly recovered from the surprise caused by the appearance of this curious individual, when the stranger began to speak in French, and informed them her name was Marie, and that she was an Algerian dancer!

Marie was not a serious-minded materialization; she carried on a desultory conversation in "slangy" French, she thrilled the sitters by executing a few daring dance steps peculiar to Algiers, then, becoming suddenly shy, she darted behind the curtains, and remained hidden for a few moments.

The effect produced by Marie was devastating, especially as she did not resemble in the very least the accepted idea of a return from the Spirit World. She was good-looking in a coarse way, and the most charitable person could not describe her as "appealing". Marie was also about as disagreeable and peevish as it is possible to imagine, but when she became better acquainted with the sitters, she went up to one of them and offered to shake hands. Too nervous to refuse, he accepted Marie's hand-shake. . . . "Her hand was absolutely flesh and blood," he said afterwards.

Sir Ernest, like everyone else, found it exceedingly difficult to "place" Marie, and when he asked her to show him her feet, this somewhat unusual request angered the dancer, who bounced forward and placed one foot on a small stool, glaring at Sir Ernest, and telling him in fluent "argot" her unvarnished opinion of him. However, undeterred by this "directness", Sir Ernest carefully examined Marie's foot, which, if not resembling that of Trilby, at any rate was small and nicely formed. The inspection was punctuated by jerky talk from Marie, who finally announced her intention of seeking "cover", as she was "fed up" with life and people in general, *"Je suis fatiguée à mourir de ces mornes vrais types Anglais."*

"The very next time you go behind those curtains, I'm coming *too*," said Sir Ernest.

This decision brought forth a volume of mixed Algerian and Montmartre abuse, and a frightened expostulation from his hostess, reminding Sir Ernest that he had promised Mrs. Corner not to touch what Mrs. B. H. described as "the exhibit".

"I certainly promised not to *touch*, but I never promised not to follow," said Sir Ernest, but whilst arguing as to what a promise actually signified, the golden opportunity passed. Marie went "behind", and when Sir Ernest, delivered from the weight of a vow, rushed in pursuit, all he saw was Mrs. Corner enclosed in her network of filoselle in a deep trance condition, with padlock and knots intact.

Marie had vanished as completely as if the earth had swallowed her up. The footman had remained continuously in the hall during the seance ; nobody had passed him, the door was still locked, the seals on the window were un-broken—*where was Marie ?* This was the burning question which agitated every mind with a single thought, and everyone asked :

Who was she ?

Emerging from her trance, Mrs. Corner could give no information, as she remembered nothing that had trans-pired . . . thus Marie became a subject for endless con-jecture, and she was responsible for a certain amount of nervousness, as vanishing ladies are not usually invited to conventional English homes, especially when they are associated with the spirit of the dance as featured in Algiers.

The first impulse of the sitters was to suspect Mrs. Corner, either of dressing up as Marie, or of collusion with an outsider. The first doubt was quickly ruled out, as after the thoroughness of the Search Committee it would have been impossible for the medium to have concealed even a quarter of a yard of muslin undetected. Marie and Mrs. Corner were also of different build, and there was not the faintest resemblance between them. It was suggested that Marie might have been a huge doll, worked in some incomprehensible way by wire-pulling and ventriloquism—but this again was rejected as impossible. The idea of hypnotism occurred to the doctor, who thought it was probable that the sitters had been hypnotized by Mrs. Corner in the manner that the Indian Fakir hypnotizes his audience in the Rope Ladder phenomena.

Sir Ernest Bennett declared this to be impracticable, as no collective hypnosis of a number of people has ever been known to scientists : no case of hypnotic suggestion is ever effective the first time, especially in default of consent, and a dozen or more normal individuals could certainly not be hypnotized by an "invisible" stranger.

Marie remains an unsolved mystery, and it is strange that although Mrs. Corner objected so strongly to anyone touching a materialized figure, Marie had no objection to shaking hands of her own free will, or of displaying a foot which certainly appeared solid. Sir Ernest Bennett regards Marie in the light of the strangest experience of an eventful life, and he always regrets that he missed the chance of following her directly she disappeared behind the curtains for the last time.

The problem becomes the more intriguing by reason of Marie's vitality and crudeness : repellent, sordid and un-refined, she was a Zolaesque creature of her own world—but what brought her to Gloucestershire, and where did she go to afterwards ?

THE MAN IN THE IRON CAGE

Lady Pennyman's Experience at Lille

MANY years ago a house in Lille was the scene of ghostly phenomena corroborated at the time by reliable witnesses, which places Lady Pennyman's experience well within the category of authentic ghost stories, under the title of "The Man—*not* in the Iron Mask, but in the Iron *Cage*".

I am unable to give the reasons which induced Lady Pennyman and her two daughters to leave England, and make their temporary home in Lille. This they did, and they were lucky enough to find a large furnished house at a very low rental. The first hint that anything was wrong occurred when Lady Pennyman went to cash a draft from her husband, Sir John Pennyman, and Lady Pennyman, who wanted a bank messenger to take some private papers back to her house, asked the man whether he was quite sure of the direction.

"*Parfaitement*, Miladi, since Miladi resides at the Haunted House," he replied, and Lady Pennyman, surprised at hearing her new home described as the Haunted House, supposed that, as it was an old place, there might possibly be some legend connected with it.

One morning, Mrs. Carter, the Pennyman housekeeper, who had come from England with the family, told Lady Pennyman that two of the English housemaids had given in their notices. . . . "And," said Mrs. Carter, "I'm afraid they mean it."

"Why won't they stay?" asked Lady Pennyman. "What a pity, they seemed such nice girls."

Mrs. Carter pursed her lips. "The reason for their notices, your ladyship, is beneath contempt—a parcel of silly ignorant young women, who say they can't stay because of the 'noises'. Noises indeed! Servants haven't

223

no business to pay attention to noises in a gentleman's house." Mrs. Carter then proceeded to give her mistress a lengthy explanation that, according to the maids, the noises were due to ghosts.

On hearing this Lady Pennyman remembered—the "haunted house".

"I know how sensible you are, Carter," said she ; "try to persuade the maids to stop—none of us are in the least superstitious, and no doubt the noises are only a mixture of wind—and rats."

Unfortunately Mrs. Carter's sound common sense was not strong enough to overcome the "silly" sensibility of the housemaids, who refused to stay the month out, and returned to England within the next twenty-four hours ! Here was a pretty state of affairs, and Lady Pennyman, angry and worried, called in Mrs. Carter's assistance to find out of what the noises consisted, and where they were located.

It appeared the mysterious sounds were supposed to come from a room formerly shared by the two servants, well distant from Lady Pennyman's part of the house, and, accompanied by Mrs. Carter, she made a thorough inspection of every nook and corner of the building.

The "haunted" room immediately below the *grenier* (always an important feature in French houses) was long and spacious : at a first glance, except for feeling that it hadn't been lived in for years, there was nothing out of the ordinary. All at once, Lady Pennyman noticed *something* in a corner—the last thing one would expect to find as a fixture in any desirable residence.

This was a large iron cage.

"Look, Carter, whatever is this cage doing here ?" cried Lady Pennyman.

"Seems to me as if someone had been keeping a monkey in it," said the unperturbed Mrs. Carter. "Naturally I saw it when we first came, but—what's a cage, your ladyship ? A cage doesn't give girls an excuse to tear back home like two mad things."

Lady Pennyman took a good look at the strange circular

cage—large and high enough to contain a man, and it crossed her mind that the former occupant must have been a gorilla !

She was a woman of quick decisions, accustomed to a well regulated household running on oiled wheels—she was annoyed by this sudden domestic upheaval, and she felt she must put an end to it.

"Listen, Carter," she said, "are there any stories about this room ?"

Mrs. Carter was non-committal. "There may be, and there may *not* be . . . but as I don't understand the language, I don't listen to a lot of foreign gabble."

"Well, I've made up my mind," said her mistress. "I shall sleep here myself, and then we shall not hear anything more about noises !"

Shaken out of her usual genteel composure, Mrs. Carter so far unbent as to try to make Lady Pennyman change her mind, but to no purpose, and the next night saw her settled in the long room with the empty cage standing in the corner.

For a week all went well : Lady Pennyman's rest was not even disturbed by a wandering mouse, and Mrs. Carter surveyed the servants with triumphant scorn. But there was no lasting peace. One night Lady Pennyman was awakened by hearing a slow, heavy step, pacing the *grenier* overhead. This monotonous "pacing" moved backwards and forwards, with the same regular motion, for nearly an hour, but perhaps Lady Pennyman's nerves may have deceived her, and she thought the time longer than it actually was. At last the steps ceased, and when morning came, Lady Pennyman's common sense having enabled her to argue out whys and wherefores, she came to the conclusion that there must be a way of getting into the *grenier* known to someone outside. She decided to talk it over with Mrs. Carter, dismissed the occurrence from her mind, and went to breakfast.

The sight of the essentially English breakfast-table restored her poise—the two Pennyman girls, pretty and vivacious, were already waiting for their mother . . . but

Lady Pennyman noticed that her son Charles, then on leave from his ship, had not come down ; in fact breakfast was nearly over when he put in an appearance, looking for all the world as if sleep had given him the go-by.

Those were the days when parents were allowed to comment unafraid on the habits of their children. Lady Pennyman, who detested unpunctuality, did so. "I wonder you are not ashamed of yourself," she said.

"Well, Mother, it's not my fault if I am late," replied the sailor. "I haven't had any sleep all night. There have been people knocking at my door every half-hour since I went to bed—some interfering servant, who wasn't certain that I had put out my candle. And," continued Charles, now thoroughly bad-tempered, "if you imagine I'm likely to drop off and set the place on fire, at any rate you needn't say so to the servants."

"Why, Charles," exclaimed his mother, in genuine surprise, "of course I *know* you are capable of taking every precaution against fire, and I should never give orders to anyone to worry you ; but are you *quite* sure that you have really been disturbed—perhaps you've dreamt it."

This was the last straw, and Charles, flinging his habitual politeness to the winds, tersely told his mother that he had not made any mistake. "Damn it all, I wish I had," said he, "I shouldn't be so tired now."

After breakfast Lady Pennyman talked to Mrs. Carter, and Mrs. Carter talked to Lady Pennyman. The household was completely disorganized, the servants, one and all, declared they would not stop—everyone, so it seemed, had something fresh to say. What was to be done ?

Then Mrs. Carter had a brain wave. "Your ladyship had better ask Mrs. Atkins to come over—if she can't settle things, why, *no one can.*"

The name of Mrs. Atkins stood for friendship, affection, and reliability with the Pennymans. She was one of those people created to cope with any kind of situation ; to whom the worst emergencies were child's play. She was everybody's friend, and Lady Pennyman promptly wrote, telling Mrs. Atkins a little of the supernatural troubles which had beset her since her arrival in Lille. As might have been expected, Mrs. Atkins replied in person, bringing with her an energetic fox-terrier with a great reputation for being dead on rats.

Mrs. Atkins was destined to play an important part in this true ghost story, but, as she had not a particle of superstition in her make-up, she laughed at the supernatural side of the disturbances.

"I'll soon silence this silly talk," she cried, "but there must be no half measures! I intend to sleep in the Cage Room; I shouldn't mind sleeping inside the cage. You were very foolish, my dear, not to go on sleeping there." (By this time Lady Pennyman had gone back to her bedroom.) "After all, you *saw* nothing, and you have played into your servants' hands by acknowledging that you were frightened of *Something*."

So the Cage Room was once more made habitable, and before Mrs. Atkins went upstairs to bed she said in a voice intended to reach the ears of the butler and others listening behind the door : "I and Bob are equal to anything or anybody, and I'm certain that, in 'chasing' rats, he'll save me the trouble of 'laying' the ghost. *Good night, everybody.*"

Alone in the Cage Room, Mrs. Atkins examined it thoroughly : she tapped the panelling to discover the possibility of a hidden passage, she bolted and locked her door, dismissed the existence of the cage as entirely uninteresting, and got into bed, secure in the knowledge of her moral strength. She was absolutely convinced of the non-existence of ghostly returns.

Her self-confidence was short-lived . . . she was suddenly awakened by a loud howl from Bob, the terror of all created rats, who sprang upon the bed and crouched down beside her.

The bedroom door slowly opened, and a pale, thin, sickly youth came in, glanced at Mrs. Atkins, and walked to the iron cage. Here he stood for a few moments in an attitude registering extreme unhappiness, and, retracing his steps, went out of the room.

More than ever convinced that the noises and visitations represented some plan to drive the Pennymans out of the house, Mrs. Atkins determined to follow the mysterious individual, and, taking her lamp, she hastened after him, when, to her amazement, she found the door was fastened as she had left it. However, when she opened the door, she was just in time to see the back of the youth descending the staircase.

As I have said, Mrs. Atkins was equal to cope with any emergency, so she followed on, until, at the foot of the stairs, the form dissolved into nothingness—and Mrs. Atkins, alone in the gloomy hall, promptly fainted.

Doors opened, and the Pennyman family descended *en masse*, awakened by the hideous noise which Bob now considered necessary to advertise the night's work.

When at last Mrs. Atkins came to herself, and was able to relate what had happened, she insisted that her friends ought not to remain in such nerve-racking surroundings.

"I cannot deny the evidence of my own eyes," she said ; and the very next day Lady Pennyman asked her landlord to release her from her tenancy.

As landlords, past and present, are not humanitarians or philanthropists, her application was unsuccessful ; in fact, the excitable Latin temperament of the landlord of Lille made him, to say the least of it, extremely aggressive, and the Entente Cordiale being at that time non-existent, he went so far as to threaten the English lady with all kinds of sanctions, and reprisals, if she dared drop a word which might injure his property.

Truth will out, and before Lady Pennyman left Lille she heard the tragic story associated with the house, where a former owner had imprisoned his nephew in the Cage Room, and hastened his death by cruelty and privations. The boy was heir to great wealth, and his uncle, who acted as his guardian during his minority, determined to "remove" him. The removal was not easy, probably because the unfortunate and unwanted possess some unexpected hold on life, so at last the "moral" murderer thought out the final torture of the iron cage.

At first the cage only represented an object of terror to his nephew, much in the same way that the sight of the Iron Maiden of Nuremburg still makes people shudder, although she has been out of action for centuries ; but the boy was warned that the next time he offended his uncle he would be shut in this narrow circle without the possibility of rest—and certainly without food.

Twice the punishment of the cage was threatened and remitted—but the respite was not for long, and when at last lack of nourishment and rest told on the enfeebled body, the broken spirit was mercifully released by death from any further torture.

Ill-gotten wealth is usually dearly purchased . . . and the murderer became haunted, not only with the memory of the dead boy, but also with his ghostly presence. It was rumoured that whenever he went into the room of death, he saw his unfortunate nephew lying in a crumpled heap at the bottom of the cage, with glazed and staring eyes, half-open mouth, and hands tightly clenched on the iron bars.

Finally, driven frantic by terror and remorse, as well as being perpetually haunted by the spirit of the unrestful dead, he sold the property for a song, and left Lille. It is not known what became of him, and he probably died in his self-imposed exile. The house remained definitely haunted, and for this reason the owner was glad to let it at the low rent which induced Lady Pennyman to become his tenant.

This strange experience, now told in narrative form, is correct in every detail ; even the names remain "as they were". Thus, it constitutes a statement of facts, vouched for at the time by the responsible persons possessing first-hand knowledge of them.

TRUE STORIES OF ANIMAL GHOSTS

Introduced by Maude M. C. ffoulkes.

Though I am far from denying that to this day the counsels of Divine Goodness regarding dumb creatures are, for us, involved in deep obscurity, yet we see, nevertheless, that Scripture foretells for them a "glorious liberty", and we are assured that the compassion of Heaven, to which we owe so much, will not be wanting to them.— Lecture 19, Bishop Keble (1792-1866).

THE question as to the existence of animal ghosts creates a wide field of speculative argument, but the belief that faithful and loving dumb friends do not meet with total extinction in death is very consoling to animal lovers, who find this aspect of companionship more satisfactory than the possession of uncongenial friends and relations.

I do not include in this category dog- and cat-owners who spoil unfortunate creatures by that false kindness which "destroys all vigour of both mind and body", or the hysterical women who kiss the "sweet little noses" of their pets, regardless of what that inquisitive little nose may have previously sampled during its walks abroad. These people do not, and never will, understand animal mentality.

Individuals who welcome "returns" treat animals sanely and humanely, and the idea of future compensation to animals worn out in the service of man is very comforting. In connection with the belief in "returns", I always remember the words of a small child when he saw a pitiful little "stray" lying dead in the gutter. "Never mind, pussy," he said, as he bent down and smoothed the draggled fur, "in Heaven *all* the cats have golden tails."

Some of our greatest poets have believed in animal survival, and which of us does not know Pope's beautiful lines?

Lo, the poor Indian, whose untutored mind
Sees God in clouds, or hears Him in the wind.
His soul proud science never taught to stray
Far as the solar walk, or Milky Way.
Yet, simpler nature to his hope has given,
Behind the cloud-topped hill, a humbler heaven.
But thinks, admitted to that equal sky,
His faithful dog shall bear him company.

Unfortunately the majority who have received proofs of animal survivals usually hesitate, for fear of ridicule, to discuss them. There are, however, well known and well authenticated hauntings—notably the strange case of Ballechin House, Perthshire, a record of which was published in 1900, when the wealthy family who rented it left precipitately, after a tenancy of barely seven weeks.

The late Marquis of Bute, a member of the Psychical Research Society, who was keenly interested in psychic phenomena, rented Ballechin House, with the owner's consent, in order to investigate the hauntings in collaboration with Major le Mesurier Taylor, and some other members of the Society.

The manifestations first began in 1876; and shortly before his death, Major Stewart, the then owner of the property, a great dog-lover, insisted that he would return to Ballechin in the body of his favourite black spaniel. Evidently his heirs did not wish to renew his acquaintance in "doggy" form, so the spaniel, and fourteen other dogs, were shot immediately after the Major's funeral.

The "removal" of the dogs resulted in their ghosts invading Ballechin, especially the library, where Major Stewart's niece felt herself pushed aside by them, and a visitor saw a black spaniel run across the room, greeted with evident pleasure by his own dog. Sounds of dogs' feet, and the noise of tail "wagging" on doors and woodwork were common occurrences; real dogs would often be seen watching the movements of other dogs invisible to humans; and one night a lady, awakened by the uneasiness of a pet dog who slept on her bed, actually saw two black paws on the table beside her.

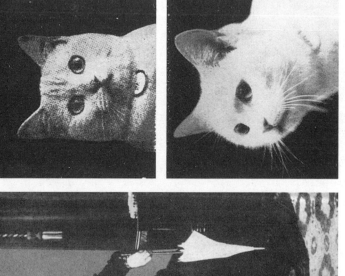

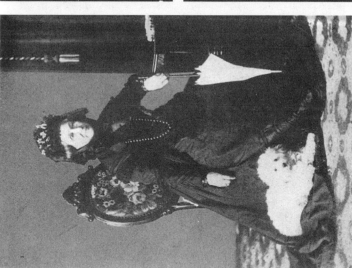

VILLISH MONA VEEN
(*Above*) FAIRY FLAX

THE LATE MRS. BROWNLOW AND THE
MALTESE DOG WHO "RETURNED"

True Stories of Animal Ghosts

THE LATE ALFRED LOUIS
(See p. 271)
My two meetings with the ghost of the late Alfred Louis

The story of Ballechin House became common property in 1897, when *The Times* published a lengthy correspondence concerning the hauntings, corroborated by independent and reliable witnesses.

. . . . .

There are many other stories of ghostly dogs. In Ireland, the belief in the Black Dog is widespread, and one particular bedroom at a farm in Co. Tyrone is haunted by a huge black dog seen by people who have slept there; and at Rathfarnham the ghost of a dog, who tried to rescue his master from drowning, is said to haunt the road between Rathfarnham Castle and a bridge lower down.

Incidentally, a monument was erected in 1841 to commemorate the dog's devotion, but like sentimentalities of this description it has gone the way of most pretty things, and only a fragment of the pedestal remains.

. . . . .

True ghost stories of cats are few and far between, so cat-lovers in general, and those who remember seeing "Villish Mona Veen" and "Fairy Flax" at important cat shows will welcome the description of their after-death returns, contributed by their owner—Miss Thessel Cochrane.

Miss Cochrane, a daughter of the late Colonel Cochrane, lived for some years with her mother, brother, and sister, in a delightful old house at Whitehead's Grove, Chelsea, now, alas! swept away by the invasion of flats, and "No. 29" was run by Miss Cochrane as a Nursing-home for Animals in conjunction with the late Mr. Alfred Sewell, Veterinary Surgeon to King Edward VII and His late Majesty King George V.

Mr. Sewell's clientèle included royal, aristocratic, and distinguished names, so the nursing-home in Chelsea represented the class of patients in the animal world that

Almina Countess of Carnarvon's Nursing-home represents in Mayfair ; in fact a new arrival might easily have
been challenged by the other canine patients as to his
owner's social position, in the words described on the collar
of a dog belonging to Frederick, Prince of Wales :

> I am His Highness's dog at Kew,
> Pray tell me, Sir, whose dog are *you* ?

It was a charming place : the wards were airy, clean,
and flower-filled like those of a hospital. There was also
accommodation for "private" cases, and, as Prince of
Wales, His Majesty's Cairn, Cora, was one of them. How well
Miss Cochrane remembers the Prince's charming informal
visits, and his appreciation of her attention and care of the
proud mother and her puppies, in a personal letter written
after he left London for Sandringham.

It is sad to think that not a vestige of the old house
(which I always looked on as my real home) remains. In
the garden an ancient mulberry tree was laden in summer
with purple-red fruit and a vine luxuriated over the
windows along the balcony at the back of the house. How
excited we were when the little bunches of green grapes
ripened, and how pretty the vine became in early autumn
when its leaves blazed with crimson and orange. Massed
lilac trees in the front garden hid the exterior of the house
from those who passed by . . . and the dear mother,
even when she was slowly and painfully dying, never
allowed any gloom or sadness to spoil the "happy" atmosphere in the shady rooms, full of associations with the
family's distinguished military and naval record, where old
china, miniatures, and pictures featured the colourful
past.

Both Thessel Cochrane and her sister Barbara are great
cat-lovers, and the former would not allow these stories to
appear under her name unless she were convinced that they
were absolutely true.

The following is Miss Cochrane's contribution :

THE RETURN OF VILLISH MONA VEEN AND THE FAIRY FLAX

Contributed by Miss Thessel Cochrane

VILLISH MONA VEEN, the first of my two "returns", was brought from the Isle of Man as a tiny snowflake of a kitten. Even then we recognized that the "snowflake" possessed remarkable points, but she did not appeal to me as a possible winning investment. I loved her for her helpless, adorable, tail-less self, and I had no idea of her future sensational show career, when she won eleven championships, innumerable firsts, and a plethora of silver cups during her short life.

Whenever Mona appeared at shows, her "pen" was surrounded by admirers, and, always delightfully self-possessed, she accepted the adulation she received as her due, although in "private life" she was just a very simple affectionate cat without a vestige of side in her make-up. She shared our lives for six years; then, one day in April, she was taken suddenly ill.

I nursed Mona, sitting up for three nights in a little room set apart, and anyone who has watched an animal suffer will understand my feelings in the long hours when I fought Death, and at last realized I couldn't save her.

With sick babies, very young children, and animals, what most stabs the heart is their inability to *tell* you *how* they feel—they can only *look* or "cry", and at last you dare not read the muted suffering that finds an outlet in their eyes. Strange that the physical ailments of old age do not usually meet with the sympathetic response given to those of the young; but perhaps old people protest too much?

As I watched Mona, and stroked the tormented little body, I thought of her, only a week ago, serene and beautiful, and I wept for the pity of it all—the waste of a happy life and the loss of her "friendliness"—as I am sure she felt genuine pleasure whenever she won prizes for "dear aunts" (we were always "aunts" to our animals).

Tomorrow there would be no Mona, and I should repeat the same untruth, "I'll *never* have another cat", only to fall for some cuddlesome bundle of fluff, rose-thorn claws, and what a dear old lady used to call "velvret" paws.

Then Mona died. Afterwards habit, such a factor in my workaday life, asserted itself. I looked at my watch. Past midnight! At six o'clock our daily round would re-commence.

Almost mechanically I began to "tidy up", I shouldn't have time later. I left the snowdrift that had once been the kitten-snowflake lying peacefully in her basket—I put medicine and dressings back in their places, and rearranged the sickening paraphernalia of illness.

I sat down by the open window. The little wind that runs before the dawn was early astir—the garden was fast asleep, and I wondered whether, as the Scriptures say, God gives His dumb creatures "a glorious liberty". If only poor little Mona were happy in This Freedom!

As if in answer to my question, I heard her familiar purr—close beside me. I couldn't possibly mistake her song, with its throaty cadences, its joyous "gurgles", and I knew she wanted to say :

"Dear Aunt—it's all right—don't worry."

Afterwards the room was quiet again. *This actually happened.* It was no question of imagination, and I am convinced that a compassionate God allowed Mona to return and heal a little of the pain which results in loving humans or animals over-much.

Directly it became known that Villish Mona Veen was dead, the authorities at the South Kensington Museum asked me to allow them to have her body stuffed, in order to exhibit it in the Natural History Section as a specimen of the perfect tail-less Manx cat ; so today Mona looks at life from a museum angle !

For some time I was strong in my determination not to own another cat, but one afternoon my good intentions added other paving-stones to a well-known road, when I saw a white kitten in the animal department at Selfridge's pleading to be bought. I could not resist the appeal of the bluest eyes imaginable, so I brought her back to "29", and, remembering the lines "Blue were her eyes like the Fairy Flax", I christened her Fairy Flax.

Fairy Flax was the sweetest kitten, and the mantle of Mona's past triumphs fell on her. She swept the board at her début in the show world with ten "firsts" and many "specials", but—Fairy Flax died of an epidemic of gastric influenza which devastated the cat world, and during her illness I nursed her in my bedroom, where she lived and slept with me.

We loved Mona, but this blue-eyed creature was in many ways more human than the "Champion". Fairy Flax loved to frolic; she jumped through an invisible hoop like a circus star ; it was impossible to feel lonely where she was. Thus, the "miss" of her at times was unspeakable, although during the day, every hour had its appointed tasks.

The third night after her death, Fairy Flax returned. I state this quite seriously, *not* as a morbid hallucination, and the conviction that this *really* happened enables me to face possible ridicule or adverse criticism with complete indifference.

I was lying awake ; a night-light burned on a nearby table—when suddenly there was a rushing gleam of white. *Something* sprang on the bed and nestled down in the usual place. It was Fairy Flax! For one moment she was *real*—then she was gone ! She never came again, but I think, like Mona, she was anxious to let "dear Aunt" know that all was well with her !

A MALTESE DOG FROM THE OTHER WORLD
THE CURSE OF PASHT

Contributed by Miss Thessel Cochrane

MAUDE FFOUKES' account of "29" has recalled two strange occurrences, one connected with our mother, the

other with the revenge of Pasht, the Cat Goddess, which
are not without interest, although, strictly speaking, they
cannot be classed as ghost stories.

Some time after our mother's passing, my sister Barbara
went to a private seance where the well-known Mr. Vango
was the medium, and Barbara's astonishment may be
imagined when he described Mamma exactly as she had been
during her last illness, and, more extraordinary still,
he was correct in quite trivial details.

We had always insisted upon Mamma looking what we
called "beautiful", it helped us in those sad days to go into
her bedroom and admire her embodied daintiness, and one
of our especial duties was to arrange her still lovely hair in
two plaits, and tie it with little ribbon bows. This was
especially commented on by Mr. Vango, who also said
that Mamma was holding a white Maltese poodle in her
arms.

The curious part of this statement, the truth of which
could not have been known by the medium, is that Mamma's
one-time inseparable companion was this identical little
dog, "Zoe", given to her when she was staying in Malta
by the Aunt Selina (Mrs. Brownlow), who is shown *with*
the dog in the illustration.

We have never been able to explain this, but I give it
as another instance of animal "returns".

The story of Pasht, the Egyptian Cat Goddess, concerns
a small faïence figure discovered in a mummy case, brought
to England by Algernon Blackwood for the friend we call
"The Third Sister", who, thinking an animal's nursing-
home was a sympathetic environment, presented Pasht
to "29" as a luck-bringer.

We put the Cat Goddess inside a cabinet, and it never
occurred to us to attribute the subsequent disasters
to her influence. But inexplicable things happened:
patients hitherto well on the road to recovery died, and
nearly every morning saw another vacant cubicle. Mr.
Sewell was as puzzled and worried as ourselves, but the
climax came when a perfectly good sash-cord broke just as
I was opening the window, which promptly descended on

my head and hurt me more than considerably! The same afternoon, Miss Withers, an old friend, came to tea, and my damaged condition led to mentioning the sudden deaths which would soon destroy "29's" reputation as a place of healing!

"You must have something unlucky in the house to account for this," decided Miss Withers.

We assured her that it was not so, and then Barbara remembered the Cat Goddess. "But she is *connected* with animals, so surely she wouldn't hurt them?" said Barbara.

Miss Withers listened, and asked us for the loan of Pasht. . . . A day or two later she came back, all excitement.

"My dears, I'm convinced the troubles are due to this horrible figure—for goodness' sake do away with it!"

She went on to explain that she had taken Pasht to the British Museum, where she happened to know someone in high places. Referred by him to a learned member of the Egyptian Section, to whom she related the story of "29", Miss Withers was informed that although Pasht was an animal deity, her image was never placed anywhere in direct contact with them in the past—as, if so, the Goddess destroyed life at once.

After hearing this we were weak enough to have "Pasht, who has green beryls for her eyes", buried secretly at night "somewhere in Chelsea", and—call it coincidence if you like—next morning we resumed our nursing with no "outside" interference.*

---

* Miss Ivy Bright tells me she has experienced two animal "returns". Her favourite cat could not bear the sound of whistling, and whenever he heard his owner transgressing, he jumped on her lap, stood up, and placed two paws on her shoulders. One day, after his death, when Miss Bright began to whistle to a radio dance tune, she distinctly felt the familiar paws on her shoulder, although nothing else was visible.

The second return was that of an Alsatian, who, owing to highly strung nerves, had to be put to sleep. On two occasions since then Miss Bright and her mother have seen him curled up in his accustomed corner.—M. M. C. FF.

THE ELEMENTAL ON THE CHURCH STEPS AT FIESOLE

Contributed by Maude M. C. ffoulkes

STUDENTS of psychic phenomena place certain manifestations, usually to be met with in localities possessing remains of an ancient civilization, as elemental, and I am inclined to believe this theory, as I once saw a most extraordinary elemental when I was staying at Fiesole as the guest of the ex-Crown Princess of Saxony.

Fiesole, one of the loveliest gems in the Nature-Crown of Italy, was originally the Etruscan town of Faczula, and the ancient houses and *palazzos* are built above the foundations of buildings destroyed by Sulla in 82 B.C. I had been told that weird happenings were frequent in the neighbourhood, and if my bedroom in the little Hôtel Aurora could have spoken, it would have yielded copy for another true ghost story. But I only heard occasional sobbing near the window ; nothing ever materialized, so it was evidently decreed that I was to encounter my ghost, or, rather, elemental, *outside*.

The ex-Crown Princess's villa was barely ten minutes' walk from the hotel, but we thought it better for both of us, as "collaborators", if I went back to the hotel every evening and came to the villa in the morning, ready to work, after the mental rest represented by a complete change of environment.

We usually finished our collaboration for the day about six o'clock, and I dined in my room at the "Aurora", afterwards reading or writing letters until it was time for bed. Sometimes I stayed to dinner at the villa, and one night the Princess declared that I must take a walk with her husband, Enrico Toselli, and see Fiesole by moonlight.

"It's quite wonderful," she said ; "you've no idea of the glamour of moonlight until you look down on Florence ; the cypresses are like black plumes against a night-blue velvet background, and I'm sure you've never seen such stars in England."

She was right. Even the Villa Paganucci, by day the ugly conception of an "Art Nouveau" architect, became romantic, and the steep rough road leading to it looked like a silver stream, as Enrico Toselli and I walked down towards the Piazza. Not a soul was stirring. Fiesole might well have been uninhabited, so we planned to walk up the Via San Francesco to the top of the West Hill from where one is able to look across the valley towards Florence, bounded by ranges of hills and Monte Albano.

At the Church of Santa Maria Primerano I noticed a large dark object lying half-way up the steps.

"Whatever can that be ?" I said.

"Most probably it's a sheep-dog from the hills," replied Enrico Toselli.

"But it doesn't *look* like a dog," I persisted. "It's much too large."

"The effect of Luisa's glamorous moon; perhaps it's a calf. How does *that* fit in, Signora ?"

At that moment the Thing moved, and stretched itself like a spreading ink-stain on the moon-bathed steps. I have never seen such a sight before or since. The Thing was black—much bigger than a calf, with an enormous head ; its eyes shone like twin emeralds, its jaws slavered ; one felt instinctively that it did not belong to this earth.

We watched the Thing amble leisurely down the steps until it reached the level of the ground, when its pace changed into a stiff gallop, until it finally "slooped" up the hill . . . and I remember how its long whip-like tail lashed the air from side to side.

"I don't think we'll go any farther," I said . . . for, to be perfectly honest, I was well and truly frightened, and I had not the slightest wish to become better acquainted with the Thing.

Enrico Toselli agreed with me.

Once inside the hotel, I ran up to my bedroom, but I was too nervous to go on the balcony and gaze at stars which, according to the Princess, didn't exist in England. I dreaded lest I should see something streaking silently across the sleeping landscape, so, closing the jalousies, and shutting out the night, I undressed and got into bed.

Next morning I made tentative inquiries, and my reputation of being *simpatica* helped me to find out that Shapes—or *Things*—*animals*—yet not animals—were often seen by people returning late at night from some distant village, or by shepherds moving their flocks from pasture to pasture in the summer-time. "These creatures are certainly from purgatory," said my informant.

In after years I learnt that animal elementals are common on the Roman Campagna, and certain localities in Rome are definitely haunted by the "returns" of dogs and cats, notably outside the Church of San Giovanni Decollato, and the famous Bocca della Verità. But the accounts of what is seen inside the Coliseum at the fall of the year are best left hidden in the mists which rise from the blood-saturated soil. According to reliable witnesses, the ghosts of the wild beasts, especially in the underground passages where they were once caged, are horrors which should remain unsought and undisturbed by even the most fearless ghost-seers.

So much for Italian elementals ! And I will conclude my stories of "returns" with an account of the psychic phenomena of "The Ape Man".

THE APE MAN WHO HAUNTS AN IRISH CASTLE

By courtesy of the Rev. Archdeacon St. John D. Seymour, B.D., Litt.D.

THE truth of this story was vouched for to Mr. Reginald Span by the Vicar of the Anglican Church, Arizona, as it "happened" to some friends of his when they once rented a picturesque castle in the South of Ireland.

The visitors from the U.S.A. were delighted with the castle and its beautiful grounds. There *were* certainly rumours not calculated to make the nervous *less* nervous, but the enthusiastic tenants put down everything out of the ordinary to the imagination of the villagers, and perhaps they were secretly pleased to find they were living in a house of traditions.

One night Mrs. A. was sitting by her bedroom fire expecting her husband's return from Dublin, when the stillness was shattered by the loud banging of a door in the corridor, followed by stealthy footsteps creeping and crawling about in a very peculiar manner. Mrs. A., neither nervous nor imaginative, opened her bedroom door and hurried outside.

At first she saw nothing ; afterwards, as she stood holding her lighted candle above her head to get a better view, she noticed an extraordinary figure shambling in the direction of the staircase. Before she had time to wonder who on all the earth was roaming around, the creature turned and looked at her, and Mrs. A. saw what appeared to be a hideous human face on the body of a huge ape. The revolting creature stared at the frightened woman for a few seconds—and then vanished.

Mrs. A. ran back to her bedroom, shrieking as she ran, and one of her daughters, awakened by the noise, tried to calm her mother by assuring her that the ape was nothing but a waking nightmare. Knowing how futile it is to argue with certain mentalities, Mrs. A. did not enter into a discussion on nightmares, neither did she confide in her husband, and a few nights later Mr. A. experienced the supernatural without any suspicion of undue influence, when he was coming upstairs from the entrance-hall, where he had been smoking and reading long after everyone else had gone to bed.

All at once he heard a queer kind of laugh, and, looking up at the landing, he saw an ungainly figure leaning over the banisters. The obscene face, of a leprous whiteness, was that of a clean-shaven, youngish man, and its expression was not only evil—but horrible. As the creature looked at

Mr. A., its body positively shook with laughter—and Mr. A. noticed that the hands and arms resting on the banister rails, covered with thick reddish-brown hair, were those of an *ape*.

Mr. A. rushed up the stairs, a proceeding which seemed to appeal to the ape's sense of humour, as it laughed so loudly and continuously that the rest of the family hurried out of their bedrooms to see what on earth was happening.

After their father had described his meeting with the Ape Man, Mrs. A. told him exactly what she had seen a few nights previously, adding, presumably for her daughter's benefit, "So, as your father has seen what *I* did, it *couldn't* have been a nightmare."

Next morning the A.s made a thorough search of all the rooms in the castle. The servants who occupied the kitchen wing had heard and seen nothing, so the A.s kept them in ignorance, and, although the search yielded no result, they decided not to relinquish their tenancy, but to keep a sharp look-out and, if the Ape Man appeared again, to shoot at sight.

Nothing further happened beyond queer sounds in the small hours, stealthy footsteps, stifled cries, and door-banging—unaccountable, but not tremendously hair-raising. However, the A.s had not long to wait for the inevitable climax, which caused them to leave the castle and return hot-foot to the U.S.A.

One afternoon, Miss A. was in the drawing-room arranging the flowers, certainly not giving a moment's thought to noises or apparitions, when all at once she heard a rustle behind her, and felt two hands on her shoulders. Thinking the hands were those of a girl staying at the castle, Miss A. turned, and found herself face to face with a loathsome object, chuckling at her discomfiture.

The daylight showed the creature to be neither human nor animal—it was covered with hair like a gorilla, it stood over six feet high, and its appearance was so repulsive that Miss A., overcome with disgust, called loudly for help. But just as her friend came to the rescue, the

Ape Man vanished, although not before the other girl had caught a glimpse of the horror it represented.

After this the A.s thought it better not to risk any further manifestations, and they returned to America, leaving the picturesque castle once more "To be let furnished".

THE SWEET SPIRIT OF GORDON KNIGHT—POET —AND HIS RETURN TO HIS FORMER HOME IN SMITH SQUARE, WESTMINSTER

Contributed by Miss Estelle Stead

ANY story of the supernatural associated with the names of the late W. T. Stead or his equally psychically gifted daughter, Miss Estelle Stead, must of necessity carry with it a guarantee of truth, and the "return" of Gordon Knight, the forgotten poet of the seventeenth century, will interest those who believe in ghosts, more especially as it represents one of Miss Stead's unpublished personal experiences.

This is a true ghost story [wrote Miss Stead], if so be you can call such a sweet little spirit a *ghost*, and I will tell you how I made his acquaintance.

During my absence from England, on a visit to South Africa, my family removed to a house in the S.W. district of London. The bedroom allotted to me after my return home was on the top floor—a large room under the roof, with a sloping ceiling and dormer windows. From the landing beneath, a flight of stairs led to a little passage, at the end of which was the door of my room.

For the first few nights I slept not only "doubtless and secure", but also soundly, and it must have been quite a fortnight later when I was awakened, after about a couple of hours' sleep, by the sound of footsteps coming quickly upstairs and along the passage leading to my room. The door was thrown wide open, and a little man wearing a long cloak black and a large black hat walked in !

As he entered, the character of the whole room changed, much in the same way that a scene changes in a theatre. My bedroom was no longer the comfortable

modern dedication to Sleep. . . . Except for two wooden
chairs and a large table littered with papers, it was now
entirely destitute of furniture and furnishings.

The little man flung his hat on the table, and seating
himself on one of the chairs he began to write, ignoring
me completely. I sat up in bed, entirely fearless, wondering what on earth would happen next. Then . . . I must
have fallen suddenly asleep, as when I woke the room
was its own familiar self, but the door, tightly closed when
I went to bed, now stood open ! However, as I thought my
experience was a dream, and nothing more, it occurred to
me that I *hadn't* fastened the door securely !

The next night, and the following nights, I was always
most careful to make sure that the door was properly
closed, and I was beginning to convince myself that what I
had seen must have been a dream, when once again I heard
the footsteps coming up the stairs and along the passage
—the door was flung open, and the little man entered. . . .
With his entrance, the conditions of the room changed ;
once more he became intent on his writing ; and I fell
asleep, to awaken in familiar surroundings.

But—the door was wide open, and I distinctly remembered having closed it the night before.

I decided to tell my experiences to certain members
of the family, but they were neither "amused" nor impressed, and they suggested that my too vivid imagination
had run away with me.

My father was absent from home, but when he came
back I knew I should find a sympathetic listener, who
would try to get at the root of things. So when we
met, I explained all that had happened, and he suggested
we should use a board called the Spirit Indicator, with
letters and a pointer, and see whether it would work for
us.

"If your visitor be really a little poet," said my father
(for I had definitely made up my mind that the collection
of papers were poetic outpourings), "no doubt he will tell
you something about himself."

I put my hands on the Indicator, and asked the Unknown,

if present with us, to try and use it. For a little while nothing occurred ; then the pointer began to move slowly —gradually gaining in strength. At last it moved quickly, and it spelt out :

I am here. I lived in this house many years ago. My name is Gordon Knight.

Father and I were sitting in the drawing-room, but he insisted on going to the library to look up the *Dictionary of Poets of the Centuries* and find out if there was a Gordon Knight amongst them. Whilst he was away, the unseen visitor continued to spell out a pathetic message which informed me :

He will not find me. I was only a little scribbler of verses, not too well known.

At that moment Father returned. "I've found it !" he announced. "There *was* a Gordon Knight in existence two hundred years ago, but *he* specialized in *hymns* !"

Upon hearing this, the pointer displayed symptoms which, in a human being, might be described as "apoplectic" and it wrote rapidly, disclaiming all connection with Gordon Knight, the Maker of Hymns.

I never wrote a hymn in my life, it spelt out.

"What *did* you write ?" I asked, hoping that the answer would be "Love lyrics". Judge of our amazement when the answer came with unhesitating plainness :

Rollicking songs of the sea.

Anyone more unlike a Poet of the Sea cannot be imagined, and—*par parenthèse*—we were never able to discover any of his "rollicking" compositions. But, after this introduction, Gordon and I became great friends, and although I often heard him run upstairs, and along the passage, he never again opened the door with a "bang", merely clicking the handle—not a bit like turning it. He would then open it a little way and, as soon as I said, "Come in", the door would open widely. Sometimes I was only able to "sense" his presence, at others I saw him quite clearly, at others faintly, but the conditions of the room remained unchanged. . . . I never saw it again as I had done on the first two occasions.

Sometimes Gordon Knight would be absent for months, "working", so he told me. He always heralded his return by clicking the handle of my door, and after my dear father's passing in 1912, Gordon showed him how to "click" the handle and open my door. I still feel him about the house ; sometimes I see him, and get messages from him, but for some years he has not clicked the handle and opened my bedroom door.

We have never been able to find out if Gordon Knight actually lived in this house. He certainly told us so, but perhaps this house, like many old houses in Westminster, was once let out in rooms, and my spirit friend may have rented the bedroom underneath the roof. I wonder whither he went to seek inspiration ? His mode of dress suggested the end of the seventeenth century, when events moved quickly on land and sea. Did he listen to many adventures at Wapping Old Stairs, or did he get copy from the seamen on the great ships anchored in the Pool of London ? And I like to think that he listened to his compositions sung in some "rollicking" waterside tavern and was suitably applauded !

There is no doubt in my mind, and in the minds of others, that we are indeed in touch with one who has a charming and beautiful personality, and who really *exists*, since as my dear father wrote in his prefatory word to his collection of Real Ghost Stories :

The time has surely come when the fair claim of ghosts to the impartial attention and careful observation of mankind should no longer be ignored.   In earlier times, people believed in them so much that they cut their acquaintance ; in later times, people believe in them so little that they will not even admit their existence.   Thus, these mysterious visitants have hitherto failed to enter into that friendly rela-tion with mankind which many of them seem sincerely to desire . . . but your ghost should no longer be ignored as a phenomenon of Nature. He has a definite right to be examined and observed, studied and defined.

These precepts were put into practice in the case of Gordon Knight, and, once more to quote my father :

The subject (occult phenomena) is one which every common man and woman can understand. It is one which comes home to every human being, it adds a new interest to life, and it vivifies the sombre but all-pervading problem of Death.

TWO GHOST STORIES OF ST. ALBANS

Contributed by Mrs. Butt, of Sholdean Hall, Deal

THE DOCTOR'S GHOST

MRS. BUTT, of Sholdean Hall, Deal, who contributes these first-hand psychic experiences, lives in a haunted house, the ghostly "return" being that of an old admiral who lived at Sholdean in the eighteenth century, and amassed a large collection of Buddhas of various sizes and materials.

When Mrs. Butt bought the property, she heard that it was haunted, and although she has often heard the knockings inseparable from certain psychic phenomena, and at times felt a cold wind suddenly rushing through one particular bedroom, she has never *seen* the ghost. This being so, she prefers to rely on the evidence of her own eyes, and describe what she once saw for herself in an old house at St. Albans.

Mrs. Butt's father was a native of the quaint, sleepy, historical town, famous during the Wars of the Roses on account of the battle associated with its name. Like most young men, he fell in love, but with him it was a case of worshipping from afar, and as the only girl in the world was a boarder at a small finishing school, it was difficult to arrange any kind of personal meetings.

The would-be suitor was a super-romanticist, and as man's habit is to pursue distant things, he gradually built up a palace of imagination, where he enshrined the object of his love, until the day when Fate took a hand in the game and made their acquaintance possible.

Afterwards everything happened on the accepted lines of a fairy-tale—the lovers married, and lived happily until death parted them.

As Mrs. Butt's father was a super-romanticist, it is not

surprising that anyone of this type should wish to purchase the house where his wife had passed her school days and where he had first seen her. This is what he did when the property which represented the romance of his life came into the market.

His wife predeceased him, and when he, too, passed, he left certain property at St. Albans to his daughters, who decided to go there with the object of seeing what to retain and what to sell.

The sisters thought they would first inspect the house associated with their parents' romance, and, getting the keys from the solicitor acting for them, they proceeded to "look over" the house.

There is nothing so pathetic as an empty house, especially when it has been vacant for some time. This tribute to sentiment had been unoccupied for years, and, as the merciless sunlight pierced the coating of dirt on the windows and showed up many other defects, the sisters realized that a great deal of money would have to be spent in order to make the place attractive and habitable. They decided, romance or no romance, to dispose of it.

Mrs. Butt, who wanted to explore the rooms on the first floor, left her sister in the one-time library, and went upstairs. As she opened the drawing-room door she saw a gentleman standing by one of the tall windows. The stranger was youngish and good-looking, dressed in country clothes, and he gave Mrs. Butt the impression of being a professional man. Naturally, she wondered what had brought him there, then, remembering that an agent was interested in the property, she concluded it must be him. Advancing, she held out her hand.

"You've stolen a march on us," she said, "but I'm glad to see you, as now we can go thoroughly into the question of selling the house."

To her amazement there was no reply—the next moment the figure disappeared, and the tall window space was vacant!

At first, Mrs. Butt was too surprised to move ; then, realizing she had seen a return from another world, she ran quickly downstairs, to find her sister in a state bordering on hysteria.

"Let's get out of this dreadful house at once," she sobbed—"it's *haunted* ! I've seen the ghost !"

Mrs. Butt endeavoured to calm and console the frightened woman, who, gradually regaining her self-control, told her sister that a man had walked through the "library" and *disappeared in the opposite wall*.

"I couldn't have been mistaken," said she ; "he was so natural-looking that I really thought it was someone who had come to see us on business. It was only after he vanished that I knew it was a ghost."

When the sisters compared notes, they found that they had both seen the same figure.

The story had a curious sequel. Some months later, when Mrs. Butt and her sister were looking over some of their mother's possessions, they found the usual collection of old letters tied with faded ribbon, pressed flowers, family photographs, and fanciful knick-knacks belonging to the past, and Mrs. Butt casually picked up a packet of a dozen letters sheltering a photograph in their midst. These letters were docketed, and the label, in their mother's handwriting, bore the inscription :

Love-letters from Dr. T—— when I was at school.

Mrs. Butt untied the protecting ribbon, and as the photograph fell out she recognized it as the original of the ghost in the Empty House ! Without saying a word, she handed the photograph to her sister, who exclaimed :

"Why, that is the same man I saw at Mother's old school !"

The letters disclosed another romance. Mrs. Butt's father had not been the pretty schoolgirl's only admirer. The writer, a well-known doctor at St. Albans, had likewise fallen in love with her, and Mrs. Butt found out afterwards he had died unmarried.

This perfectly true story possesses a certain pathos, as featuring the truest form of fidelity which refuses to yield to time and triumphs over mortality and the grave.

Mrs. Butt was never able to find out whether, prior to her visit, the house had the reputation of being haunted, or whether the manifestation had some special significance for herself and her sister.

Perhaps the "return" may have been permitted to prove to these charming "moderns" that "he is no lover, who doth not love for ever".

"BATTLEFIELD"

AFTER the death of Mrs. Butt's father she inherited, certain properties in St. Albans, amongst which was another old house called "Battlefield", and although it has been demolished to give place to a row of shops, I believe the original name has been retained.

According to Mrs. Butt, "Battlefield" comprised part of the original battlefield, and it was well known that at times the sounds of galloping horses and the clash of swords and mail were plainly to be heard, although the ghostly soldiers never materialized. An extraordinary discovery was made in the kitchen of the house when a new floor was being laid down, as the ground suddenly subsided, and disclosed a tunnel-like passage, with a small chapel half-way down it, in which were found various church vessels in good preservation, probably removed there for safety during the Wars of the Roses.

Until the subsidence in the kitchen, the existence of the passage was unsuspected, and it was afterwards closed, and not re-opened when the house was finally pulled down. However, it is difficult to efface the power of the supernatural, and it is said that occasional "hauntings" persist, even on the modern "Battlefield" which covers the site of one of the landmarks of history in the days when "every chance brought out a noble knight", those "who battled for the true—the just", and who have handed on the torch of Patriotism throughout the centuries.

QUAKER'S BURYING-GROUND

Contributed by Miss Grace Weh

THE period of these strange happenings was somewhere about 1863-4, when my father, a lad of fifteen, was living with his father in the village of Sparleford on the borders of Dorset and Somerset. Two of his cousins, young men of nineteen and twenty, and a friend, Larry by name, were then staying at the house, and Larry, a fine judge of horse-flesh, had just broken in a mettlesome young mare that he proposed to sell at the local cattle and horse fair.

On the evening of the horse fair one of the cousins had promised to meet his sweetheart (I don't remember what the other one was doing on this particular night), but my father was asked to sit up and let in the horse-dealer, and the young man in love, who in all probability would be "homing" late.

The two friends planned to return by the main road, and to meet where three roads converged at a little triangular enclosure known in the countryside as "Quaker's Burying-ground".

Many years previously a temperamental Quaker who had committed suicide was buried here with a pointed stake driven through his heart, and it was firmly believed that at certain times of the year the ghost walked, and super-stitious pedestrians were careful to avoid Quaker's Burying-ground after nightfall, whilst those on horseback or awheel invariably put on speed until they had left it far behind!

My father's cousin had not given a thought to the Quaker when he suggested the rendezvous, where he was due to arrive about half past ten. It was a cloudless moon-light night, and as he walked briskly up the white ribbon of the road he noticed someone apparently coming towards him who made no appreciable progress. When he got nearer, he saw that the "someone" was a tall man in black, wearing a shovel hat, who disappeared into the hedge, groaning in rather an alarming manner.

Youth is invariably suspicious, and Sam, rudely disturbed in love's young dream, at once put down the groans and the figure as a practical joke staged by some would-be-humorous friends.

He leaped the hedge and promptly laid about him with his thick ash stick, but as the groans still continued, he proceeded to examine the length of the ditch for a possibly "bogged" sheep. Finding nothing, and still angry with the "jokers" who had disturbed his arrangements with Larry, he did not remember the story of the ghost until he had almost reached home, when it gradually dawned on him that he had met an uneasy "return" from another world.

As soon as he saw my father he announced impressively : "Bill, I've seen the Quaker."

The sleepy lad did not attach much importance to Sam's further colourful revelations, inspired by cold beef, cheese, and good cider, until an hour later, when loud shouts proceeded from outside, and Larry, leading his once mettlesome mare, now a trembling sweat-drenched creature, stumbled into the kitchen, exclaiming :

"By God, Bill and Sam, I've seen the Quaker ! *And so has the mare !*"

After comforting the trembling mare, and settling her for the night in a roomy loose-box, Sam returned to the house to find Larry in a state of collapse, from which he did not recover until given a stiff dose of brandy. He then explained what had happened.

Close to the place where the figure had previously appeared to Sam, he had seen a man in black, wearing a shovel hat, walking towards him, who suddenly vanished with a loud groan behind a heap of stones at the side of the road. The mare, who had evidently seen the figure, shied violently, snorted with fear, and absolutely refused to pass the heap of stones.

For quite half an hour neither spur nor coaxing had had

any effect on the mare, and Larry was forced to dismount and lead her all the way back. He told Bill and Sam that not for all the world's minted money would he go through another such experience.

"There I was, trying to quiet the mare," he said, "hearing, on and off, horrible groans which turned my blood to water, wondering what I should see next—and not a soul in sight. The next time they bury one of those kind of friends, I hope they'll plant him in some place where he can't upset people."

Both my father and his cousin were able to testify to the condition of the mare and her rider, and, as barely an hour before Sam had seen the Quaker's ghost, it can be assumed with some degree of certainty that neither had been mistaken, nor acted in collusion. Sam and Larry were healthy, normal youths, unblest with imagination, as well as being eminently practical, the horse-dealer being especially distinguished for shrewdness and common sense.

For what reason was this psychic phenomena made manifest? It would be interesting to know whether it produced any lasting impression on those who witnessed it, and, if so, of what nature? The young men always declared that they had seen the Quaker's ghost, and although my father never saw it, he followed the example of his elders and betters, and believed in it as thoroughly as George IV believed he had been present at the Battle of Waterloo, and made "such a sinner of his memory, to credit his own lie".

THREE GHOST STORIES

Contributed by The Hon. Mrs. Greville Nugent

THE LATE LADY VANE'S STORY OF THE GHOST IN THE UPPER ROOM

SOME years ago, when the late Lady Vane and I were discussing the case for, and against, the supernatural, she suddenly said, "You see, Ermengarda, I *must* believe in the possibility of 'returns', as I actually came in contact with the earth-bound spirit of a suicide, when Sir Henry and I were staying at Ems."

"A suicide ?"

"Yes, and an Englishman—more's the pity."

Interested and intrigued, I begged Lady Vane to relate her experience, and here is the story, which she assured me was true in every detail.

"At one time," said Lady Vane, "my husband and I occasionally went to Ems to take the waters, in the far-off days when gambling was allowed at the various *Bads*. This particular summer we had engaged our rooms beforehand at the best hotel, but, strange to say, although it was the height of the season, the bedroom over ours remained unoccupied when chance visitors unable to find any accommodation were being turned away. However, I thought no more about the empty room until one night, when we were disturbed by the heavy footsteps of someone walking backwards and forwards overhead.

" 'H'm, I suppose the room has been let,' said Sir Henry, 'but I hope whoever is walking about will soon go to bed.'

"The restless visitor had not the slightest wish or intention of going to bed, and the ceaseless *va et vient*

263

continued for quite an hour till we were nearly driven mad. Then the footsteps ceased.

" 'Thank heaven for small mercies !' ejaculated (by this time) my thoroughly bad-tempered husband.

"All at once we heard the window thrown open with a bang, as if the occupant of the room was in a great hurry to let the cool fresh air into the room.

"Afterwards silence, deep and undisturbed, descended on us for the remainder of the night."

"I hope you were not troubled again by the footsteps ?" I asked.

"My dear, we suffered three nights' repetition of what we thought to be selfishness on the part of this sleep-preventing individual, until our nerves were worn thin, and on the fourth morning I questioned the floor waiter.

" 'Who occupies the room above ours, and makes so much noise at night ?'

" '*Gnädige Frau*,' said the man in an expressionless voice, 'the room above you is empty—the *gnädige Frau* must have been mistaken.'

" 'Mistaken ?' I cried. 'How *could* I possibly mistake such ordinary sounds ?'

"The man shrugged, made no answer, snatched up our breakfast tray and hurried off.

" 'I expect he's been well tipped by the person upstairs to say nothing,' I sighed. 'However, I'll try Amalia (our chamber-maid). Perhaps she will be more communicative.'

"Amalia, of the lint-white locks and speedwell-blue eyes, with the smile which invariably refused to 'come off', was more talkative than the floor waiter, and not only did she take her solemn oath that the room was empty, but she volunteered the information that it was also locked up.

" 'So, *gnädige Frau*, it's clearly impossible for anyone to get inside, much less to walk about in it.'

"Realizing that our 'cure' was in danger of coming to an abrupt conclusion, and visualizing our precipitate return to England, I decided to have a heart-to-heart talk with the proprietor, and when this came off I told him bluntly that we must change our rooms, or leave the hotel.

" 'It's no good putting us off with any more lies,' roared Sir Henry, now all-British in this just quarrel. 'It's a pretty state of things when English people abroad are treated like a lot of fools. If you have any reasonable explanation to offer for this secrecy and prevarication, I'm prepared to listen, but don't dare to say that Lady Vane and myself have dreamt we heard footsteps when we've scarcely been able to get a wink of sleep.'

"I began to feel sorry for the apologetic, agitated proprietor, who, knowing by this time that frankness was the better part of discretion, begged us to come into his private office, 'as I cannot run the risk of what I shall tell you being overheard', he said.

"Once in his office, with the door securely shut on possible eavesdroppers, the bespectacled proprietor, who looked something like an angry owl, said :

" 'The room is haunted.'

" 'Tosh !' ejaculated Sir Henry.

" 'It is the truth. Once I, too, should have Tosh said, but I understand I must now cease to let the room underneath the so noisy one upstairs.'

"I asked the worried little German to explain himself, and, after a long prelude, he eventually told us that five years previously an Englishman, 'young, rich, and well-born', had occupied the upstairs room for several weeks. His reason for coming to Ems was not to be cured of any bodily ailment—the cure for his particular complaint being an impossibility. He was a born gambler, who played for high stakes, and he alternately won and lost (afterwards he lost—all day and every day), until one night he returned from the Casino a ruined man.

" 'We were sorry for the disaster to this never-to-be-forgotten so charming young man, but when I went upstairs to offer my respectful sympathy he had locked his door. I heard him pacing to and fro, so I did not disturb him. But—*Gott in Himmel !*—hardly had I gone to bed than people began to shout in the street. . . . Then we were called by the police, and when I came down to see what was the matter, imagine my horror to hear that the Englishman had thrown himself out of the bedroom window and had been killed instantly.

" 'Afterwards there were complaints from visitors who slept in the room, who insisted that someone walked to and fro in the darkness. So I closed it and I have never let it again. It seems, however, that the spirit of this suicide cannot rest, especially at the time of the year when he put an end to his life. It is almost the month. . . . So I will offer the *hochgeboren* Sir, and Lady, better rooms in another part of my hotel, whilst praying them not to mention this disastrous affair to their friends.'

"We promised to say nothing—changed our room for the better, and completed our cure. But there is no doubt whatever in my mind as to the reality of my ghostly experience."

THE LATE LADY STRICKLAND'S EXPERIENCE AT "PLAS-YU-RHIW"

So much for Lady Vane's story, and as supernatural history often repeats itself, my *own* ghost story is also connected with footsteps !

In the summer of 1892 I was staying with my friend the late Lady Strickland, at an old manor house called "Plas-yu-Rhiw", near Pwllheli. I was the only visitor, and one night Lady Strickland and I sat up so late playing cards that it was long past midnight when we prepared to go to bed. In view of what happened, I should mention that the servants at "Plas-yu-Rhiw" (who had all gone to bed long before) slept in another wing, and as they used the back staircase to go to their rooms, *no one but ourselves could possibly be using the front staircase at that hour*.

The old house was in absolute stillness, and the moonlight lay in pools of silver on the oak staircase. My bedroom, on the first floor, faced the landing, and Lady

Strickland, who slept on the floor above me, was just in the act of lighting her candle from mine, when we heard heavy footsteps coming upstairs from the hall. The steps were slow and hesitating, apparently those of an old man, and they were accompanied by the sound of laboured breathing, punctuated by various degrees of coughing. We exclaimed simultaneously :

"*Who's that coming upstairs ?*"

There was no reply—we looked over the balusters, but although the coughing and wheezing came nearer and nearer, we saw *no one*. By this time we were too scared to move, our candlesticks fell to the ground, and we clung to each other in fear of the unknown.

The steps paused for a moment beside us, as if the unseen owner of the feet had stopped to take breath. He then continued his upward progress, until the coughing gradually died away and we heard no more.

I implored my hostess not to go up to her bedroom, but to share mine, or any other on the first floor, but she refused, saying :

"I have some Holy Water in my room, and with spiritual protection I fear nothing."

Next morning when we compared notes we found that neither of us had heard any more footsteps, and had not been disturbed in any way.

So ended my ghost story, but some weeks later, after my return to England, I received a letter from Lady Strickland :

"After you left 'Plas-yu-Rhiw'," she wrote, "I made cautious inquiries in the neighbourhood, and imagine what I've discovered! It appears that, at the end of the last century, the manor house was occupied by an old reprobate squire, who drank himself to death, and whose death-bed 'horrors' seem to have been something unthinkable. It is said that his earth-bound spirit occasionally revisits his home, vainly trying to obtain some gratification for his ceaseless thirst, so we were evidently favoured with one of his periodical returns."

This explanation interested me greatly, but, let me admit, I am thankful I never saw, but only *heard*, what would doubtless have been a very dreadful psychic phenomena had it been permitted to materialize.

THE DUN COW OF WARWICK

MY last authentic ghost story is about the famous Dun Cow of Warwick. The legend is well known, and can be found in any topographical history of Warwick dealing with the days of the semi-legendary hero, Sir Guy of Warwick.

This ghost story was told me, and vouched for, by the late Dowager Marchioness of Downshire (a relation of the Greville family) when I was staying at Easthampstead Park in 1889.

Lady Downshire said that when she and Lord Downshire were on a visit to Warwick Castle (I forget in what year), the then Lady Warwick mentioned casually that fresh turf had been laid down on a grass plot under the windows of the rooms allotted to the Downshires. "And," she added, "I hope no one will walk on it till it has taken good root."

It was glorious summer weather, and when Lady Downshire, who was feeling the heat oppressive, got up at dawn to open the window, she saw, to her astonishment, a dun-coloured cow trampling over the newly laid turf. She roused Lord Downshire, and they both leant out and tried to shoo away the heavy-hoofed intruder, who took not the slightest notice of their united commands to "keep off the grass".

"Must have escaped from a herd in the park," said Lord Downshire, preparatory to resuming his interrupted slumbers. "But won't Lady Warwick be furious when she finds the turf ruined, as it's bound to be after that uprooting. Damned carelessness, I call it."

Judge for yourself Lady Downshire's feelings when next morning *no hoof-marks were visible*, and the lovely turf, sparkling with dew, was unspoilt!

At breakfast, which represents the one meal of the day relegated to bills and general unpleasantness, which, in my opinion, should always be partaken alone, Lady Downshire, knowing nothing of the legend that the Dun Cow always appeared before a death in the Warwick family, innocently related her experience, backed up by her husband's evidence. Lord Downshire, who was still "difficult" from loss of sleep, enlarged rather forcibly on the occurrence, due to the carelessness of those who allowed dun cows to go astray, regardless of Lady Warwick's frantic pantomime signifying : "Stop—*at once* !" And he could not understand why unrelieved gloom fell on the breakfast-table.

Afterwards Lady Warwick confided to Lady Downshire that she had seen the spectral cow. "And you will hear very shortly that one or another of us has passed away," said her tearful hostess.

Her words proved only too true. A few weeks later Lord Warwick died.

MY TWO MEETINGS WITH THE GHOST OF A DEAD MAN ON THE FOLKESTONE ROAD

By Maude M. C. ffoulkes

THESE supernatural experiences happened to me in the summer of 1925 and the New Year of 1928, and they are corroborated by reliable witnesses who, if they do not believe in the reality of "returns", are sufficiently fair-minded not to dispute facts, which even their unimaginative common sense still puts down as "very odd".

As for myself, I offer no explanation beyond stating what actually occurred, and I shall always believe that on two occasions I met the ghost of the late Mr. Alfred Louis on the Folkestone road.

Alfred Louis, the original of "Daniel Deronda" and "The Old Man of Visions", was one of the most extraordinary personalities I have ever met, and as such merits an introduction in this true ghost story. I owed my friendship with him to Algernon Blackwood, who brought him to see me in 1908, and not only was I impressed by the atmosphere of tragedy which enveloped the frail old man, but I had never heard beautiful thoughts so beautifully expressed as by this dreamer of dreams, who was so far above the sordid happenings of life.

At one time Alfred Louis was well known in political and literary circles; it is said that his family (Jewish, and proud of it) came from the Midlands. He had a distinguished career at Cambridge, and was called to the Bar. His intense desire to enter Parliament being thwarted by Gladstone, he shook the dust of England off his feet, and went to New Zealand, afterwards to India. Returning to England he hid himself from public life.

Algernon Blackwood first met Alfred Louis in New York. He was then living in an attic, producing occasional

271

poems of singular beauty. To money, and the rewards of this world, he was divinely indifferent, and Algernon Blackwood remembers him rising at dawn, walking the streets in his shabby frock coat, tie-less, wearing the oldest boots, conscious only of the eternal verities. His conversation was marvellous, his memory never at fault, his power of quotation superb. According to Algernon Blackwood, here was the wreck of a big intellect, and it was intensely sad. He spoke little of his past, but the passion, the sacrifice, the resignation of his poetry betrayed him.

Algernon Blackwood can testify to Alfred Louis' exquisite speaking voice, which I heard during his life, and later *outre tombe*. In writing of him, the famous author says : "When I knew him, his aloofness from the sordid side of human life, his loftiness of outlook, his stern and icy morality, his intense and acute tenderness for others, all amounted very nearly to that state of being out of relationship to environment. But everybody loved him, and he loved everybody. He had been intimate with George Eliot—a frequent visitor to her house, where Lewes, Spencer, and Huxley were of the party. Manning was also his friend—Longfellow more than a friend."

He came back to England from New York through a friend of Algernon Blackwood's, who had decided to settle in England, and who had been instructed in English law by Alfred Louis, who remained in England until his "passing".

Mr. Louis once sent me some stanzas with a little memo —"A. H. L. feels deeply the appreciation of Mrs. F. F." And, before me as I write, is a faded sheet of paper covered with tremulous fine characters—his heart-rending sonnet— "Hereafter".

I heard that Mr. Louis had "passed over" from Algernon Blackwood, and how the last "clouded" years had been made free from material anxieties by the kindness of the American friend of his New York days. We had not met for some time, and I had certainly not been thinking of him on the day when I overtook him on the Folkestone road,

One afternoon in July 1925, I was motoring from London to Sandgate with my friend Elizabeth Broad. I had hired the car from William Ludlow, of Sandgate, who at that time often took me backwards and forwards to town. I mention this to show there was nothing out of the ordinary, either in connection with those who shared the experience, or the reason for the journey.

On this afternoon of afternoons there were few pedestrians and not much traffic on the road. I was comfortably tired, not paying much attention to things around me, and we were well out of London when the car gradually overtook a solitary individual dressed in black, walking slowly on the footpath on the near side of the car.

All at once the incoming tide from the sea of distant memories flowed over my soul : there was something familiar about this figure in black. Where had I seen it before ? As we approached nearer, I saw an old man, wearing a frock coat of an antiquated cut, black trousers, a silk hat—and most incongruously—evening pumps. For the moment my heart stood still. In this individual I recognized *Alfred Louis* ! Yet—*it couldn't be*. My friend was dead. But it was impossible to mistake the eccentric ensemble, which during his lifetime had made him noticeable alike in the Reading-room of the British Museum and the streets of London. I looked, and looked again, until common sense urged me to pass by on "the other side". This I did, saying to myself—moral coward that I was—"*It couldn't have been Mr. Louis.*"

No sooner had I left the figure behind than a belated sense of self-respect made me return. I said to Ludlow, "Go back and tell the person we passed a few minutes ago that I should like to speak to him."

Ludlow, accustomed to my impulsive ways, stopped the car, and returned with—*Mr. Louis*. . . . It was surely none other than Mr. Louis, and my last doubts were swept away when I heard the magic of his unforgettable voice.

I don't know how I contrived to speak in an ordinary manner.

"You look very tired," I said. "Will you let me offer you a lift ?"

The familiar, kind eyes looked at me. "Willingly —I am going a little way beyond Maidstone," replied "Mr. Louis".

We were then about thirty miles distant from Maidstone.

"Why, you cannot possibly *walk* all that way !" I cried.

"Oh yes," he said gently.

There was no mutual recognition, no explanations— after all, how could there be ?—it seemed quite natural for us to meet again.

Inside the car "Mr. Louis" sat next to Ludlow. He carried a small attaché-case—nothing else—and we continued our way under the spell of a peculiar stillness, representing something of the peace of an immortal hour.

At last, "Have you come far ?" I asked.

He smiled. "A long distance—I've brought the key of my home with me"—and opening the attaché-case "Mr. Louis" took out a large rusty key, that didn't look as if it had been made for a door, it was more suitable for an entrance gate.

We talked little and casually. At the time I was so astonished that I cannot remember much of our conversation, but I gathered he had come for some special reason. I knew, subconsciously, that I was expected to "understand", to make no comments, and to accept this fantastic happening for a wise purpose.

It is impossible to describe the psychical impression of this amazing journey. As I sat immediately behind "Mr. Louis", I could see every detail of the familiar personality— the "shiningness" of his tightly buttoned frock coat, the seams showing rusty green, the wide elastic bands which kept the patent leather pumps on his small feet, the way his beard "rippled"—the curious resemblance to the prophets of old depicted in the Sistine Chapel by Michelangelo.

I longed to say, "I know *you*—you know *me*—tell me something of yourself." But how on earth could I do so ?

We reached Maidstone about five. I said : "Let me know where I can put you down."

He replied with that old-world courtesy so peculiarly his own, that as his destination lay some miles on the other side of Maidstone he would not take me out of my way. He would leave us here.

I refused to listen. "I'll not let you walk another step."

We skirted Maidstone, and were soon lost in tree-bordered roads and the dreaming silence of the countryside. The sun was firing the western skies ; the hour was incredibly lonely—it seemed a little cold.

When the car reached a spot where a weather-worn signpost showed four roads diverging from its ancient arms, "Mr. Louis" told Ludlow to stop.

"My way lies here," he said, pointing to a stretch of meadow land. To me he said : "Do not forget our meeting."

"Then—you *know* !" I cried.

He smiled, crossed the road, opened the meadow gate, and the sunlight took him to itself : he became unreal, a golden figure lapped by waves of dying fire—then he was lost to sight. Whither—oh, whither goest thou ?

"Bill" Ludlow, the sailor man who had laughed at danger in the North Sea during the War, was the first to speak.

"Well—I'm blest," said he. "*Whoever was that gentleman ?*"

·   ·   ·   ·   ·

A few evenings later I dined with the Ralph Philipsons at Encombe. Algernon Blackwood was staying there. Encombe was the only English environment, save one, in which I have not felt an outsize, and an outsider (perhaps not an outsider in the usually accepted sense, but someone who always stood outside the social whirl). I knew I should not be laughed at, or howled politely down, when I described my meeting with old Mr. Louis—my story was accepted quite naturally . . . with a proviso from Ralph Philipson that it would be interesting to know whether anyone answering the description of Mr. Louis had gone to the hop gardens as a lay preacher.

"It's difficult to explain the resemblance, but it *may* have been someone well known by the hop-pickers," said Ralph.

We made inquiries—discovered nothing—and, save for its memory, the incident was closed.

An anti-climax in fiction is a daring experiment. This story is *not* fiction—and an anti-climax is necessary. One morning in the New Year of 1928 I was motoring towards London when I suddenly came on Mr. Louis in almost the identical place where I had first seen him.

At this period I was storm-tossed, entirely *desenchanée*. To me, the sight of this serene figure meant spiritual safety. I think he was waiting for me. I stopped the car and walked up to him.

I said : "I knew all the time who you were. Oh, Mr. Louis, tell me, where are you going ?"

He indicated the high road. "My mission lies in many places."

"Oh, let me come with you," I begged. "I'm so unhappy."

"Not yet," he answered ; "at present you must take your road alone"—and raising his right hand in blessing, he left me. I have never seen Mr. Louis again, and I have described what actually happened as dispassionately as possible.

I can never forget Alfred Louis, and his memory is one of the tender thoughts which serve to soften my heart when it hardens towards life, for it is impossible to recall him without feeling that he suffered many things uncomplainingly, and his patience and tenderness under affliction were in the nature of a martyrdom.

There is no doubt that some kind of a tragedy had darkened his life ; the late Canon Harford and Archbishop Benson, who knew the whole story, never betrayed it.

All that I have written concerning these strange meetings on the highway is true. Explain it, or deny it, as you will.

THE FARRIER OF SABLON

(A true ghost story of the reign of Louis XIV. Vouched for by the Duc de St. Simon in his reminiscences)

SOMEWHERE in the August of 1698-99, a wonderful instance of supernatural guidance set Versailles agog, and as it concerned no less a person than Louis XIV, it deserves to be included in true ghost stories from France.

One day, a man wearing the coarse clothes and leather apron of a farrier, hailing from the little town of Sablon in Provence, arrived at Versailles, and demanded to see the king in private. It is easy to understand the amusement which this "modest" request created—but, heedless of the laughter and rebuffs which met him on every side, the farrier persisted in his pressing request to speak to His Majesty.

Louis had means of his own of knowing all that transpired around him, so it was not long before the farrier of Sablon was told that the King was not accustomed to grant audiences to whomsoever chose to ask for them.

This personal message would have made the majority of people "fade out" as soon as possible. Not so the farrier— who declared that if he were to see His Majesty he would tell him things so secret, and so unknown to everyone, that the King would be absolutely convinced of their importance.

"If His Majesty still refuses to speak with me, let me be sent to a Minister of State," said the obstinate peasant.

Upon hearing this, the King, who invariably preserved an open mind, arranged for the farrier to interview Barbezieux, one of his private secretaries, not dreaming that the visitor's psychic intuition would enable him to know that Barbezieux was no minister, but a mere secretary, and, as such, of no value whatever. This proof that the farrier was indeed someone out of the common made Louis hand him over to M. Pomponne, who certainly filled the bill in a ministerial capacity.

This is the story which the farrier told the Minister of State at Versailles, after every precaution had been taken to prevent the possibility of palace walls possessing ears.

"I was returning home late one evening," said the man ; "my way lay through a wood, and I suddenly found myself surrounded by a great light. In the midst of this, monsieur, stood a lady, whom I knew to be even higher in rank than an aristocrat. This lady called me by my name, and spoke to me for more than half an hour.

"Proceed," said M. Pomponne, with hardly concealed, lazy indifference.

"The lady told me that she was the Queen who had been the wife of His Majesty, and who died in 1683."

M. Pomponne lifted his eyebrows. This fellow possessed audacity ! To dare to look at a Queen's ghost, much less talk to it, was unheard of !

The farrier appreciated M. Pomponne's hostile attitude, but, entirely unaffected, he continued : "The Queen ordered me to go to Versailles, and report to His Majesty all she had communicated to me, especially one secret thing, known only to the King, which would convince him of the truth of what I had to say. The Queen added, that if I could not see the King in person, I was to speak to a Minister of State, telling him certain important things, reserving others for His Majesty alone.

" 'If you do not set out at once,' she added, 'you will most assuredly be punished with death'."

"Well spoken, my good fellow," said the Minister, "but it savours not of the late Queen's disposition. She was, —God rest her soul—never in favour of extreme measures."

"I promised to obey her in everything," replied the farrier, "and the next moment I found myself in complete darkness near a large tree. I wanted to think over what had happened, so I spent the night in the wood, but I did not know whether I was awake or asleep. In the morning I went to work, convinced that what I had seen was a delusion . . .

and you may be sure I kept my tongue well between my teeth at Sablon."

"Why not equally so at Versailles ?" yawned M. Pomponne.

"Because, monsieur, two days later I saw her late Majesty again. She addressed me in the same terms, and told me to go at once to the Intendant of the Province, who would furnish me with money, after I had told him with whom I had spoken."

"A little improbable, eh ?"

"If you had been in my place, monsieur, you would not have known *what* to do for the best. I did not dare confide in anyone, so I left things alone for eight days, and then I decided to do nothing more. But her late Majesty thought otherwise. You say that she was not in favour of punishment. Well, she must have changed greatly since she died— she was so angry, that my one idea was to get to Versailles as quickly as possible. I left the forge to take care of itself, and two days afterwards I saw our Intendant at Aix, who listened to me, and gave me sufficient money to travel by a public conveyance."

The Intendant's attitude in carrying out the dead Queen's wishes carried weight, and the unbelieving Minister began to take things more seriously. The farrier had three interviews with M. Pomponne, each of two hours' duration, and an account of these was rendered privately to the King, who ordered M. Pomponne to discuss the question in a special council, composed of the Dukes of Beauvilliers, Pontchartrain, and Torcy—Monseigneur alone was excluded.

After a lengthy sitting, the council dispersed, and the farrier of Sablon was sent for to converse with the Sun King in the privacy of his cabinet. Two days later Louis saw the man again, and each time the King spent more than an hour with him—moreover, special precautions were taken to make sure that no one was within hearing.

The morning after the first interview, the King, dressed for hunting, was descending the great staircase, when Monsieur Duras, one of his few intimates (whose relations with royalty were evidently something like those of the Prince Regent and Beau Brummel), began to speak contemptuously of the farrier, and he went so far as to quote the proverb that, "The man was mad, or the King was not noble."

Louis XIV stopped on the staircase, looked M. Duras up and down, and said coldly :

"If that be so, then *I* am not noble, for I have discoursed with him long, and he has spoken to me with much good sense. *I assure you, he is far from being mad.*"

These words were pronounced so gravely, and with so much emphasis, that silence fell on the King's entourage . . . and it was afterwards agreed that here indeed was a whole-time mystery to intrigue the Court.

Louis XIV allowed his world to know that his second interview with the farrier had absolutely convinced him that the man's uncanny knowledge could only have been derived from personal communication with the spirit of the Queen, as he knew of an occurrence which had happened in the Forest of St. Germain twenty years previously, about which the King had never breathed a word to anyone.

The King invariably spoke highly of this particular village blacksmith, and, not only did he pay all the expenses which he had incurred, but he gave him a gratuity, and desired the Intendant of Aix to take particular care of his protégé, and never to let him want for anything during his lifetime.

The surprising thing about this surprising story is that none of the Ministers in Council could be induced to speak a word about the important revelations of the farrier. Their friends questioned them in vain ; the farrier was as silent as the grave ; all that could be extracted from him was that he was not *allowed* to speak. He was about fifty years of age, somewhat of a rough diamond, a typical provincial, an excellent blacksmith, and when he returned to Sablon he never boasted of his interviews with the *Grand Monarque* . . . slipping back to his work as if nothing out of the way had happened, and the ghost of Marie Thérèse never appeared to him again.

Such is the true story which filled the French Court with astonishment, and which nobody has ever understood. Some people persuaded themselves that the farrier had been the dupe of a certain Madame Arnoul, but as the honest man knew nobody outside his own village this idea was dismissed as absurd and impracticable.

Why, then, did the phantom of a Queen of France choose such a humble mouthpiece? It may be argued that, if she had fixed on any person at Court, or anyone moving in Parisian Society, their disclosures would have been somewhat in the nature of tainted evidence. Hence her selection of a simple man whose life was above suspicion of any intrigues.

The truth of the story has never been arrived at. The Duc de St. Simon gives it in detail, and in all sincerity ; Louis XIV confirmed the farrier's knowledge of a secret known only to himself—the Ministers of State received the farrier's messages with conviction, and allowed no details to pass beyond the Council Chamber. But—after the lapse of nearly two hundred and fifty years, one cannot help wondering what it was that the Queen of France told the farrier of Sablon.

•   •   •   •   •

The mere mention of Versailles opens up tremendous ghostly possibilities, especially as most parts of it are well known to be haunted. The great echoing palace has seen more tragedies and more pulsating life stories than most royal residences, and in 1720 Madame ——, the Princess Palatine, Louis XIV's outspoken sister-in-law, relates one of the earliest recorded ghost stories of Versailles.

"Madame," a pleasant-looking, stout little woman, utterly devoid of imagination, German to the last drop of her blood, had no use for, and no belief in, ghosts.

"We people of the Palatinate never see ghosts or dream dreams," she said, and yet, in all seriousness, she gave the world in her famous letters *three true stories* of the supernatural.

On November 14, 1720, Madame wrote to Monsieur de Harling :

"The Queen Mother had a lodging made for herself above the gallery at Fontainebleau, and her chamber-women had to pass the night in the Long Gallery. They say that they have seen King Francis walking about, clad in a green-flowered dressing-gown, but he never did me the honour of showing himself to me. I don't think I can be popular with ghosts, because I slept for ten years in the room in which the late Madame died,* and I was never able to see anything. But the first time that the Dauphin slept there, his aunt (the late Madame) appeared to him. He told me about it himself. One night after he had gone to bed he heard the door leading to the drawing-room open—that evening a great ball had been given in the drawing-room—and he saw a beautifully dressed woman come in, wearing a blue over-dress, a lovely yellow petticoat, and many yellow ribbons in her hair. Her head was turned towards the window, and the Dauphin, who thought it was the young Duchess de Foix, coughed in order to make her glance in his direction. The lady did so, but instead of the Duchesse de Foix, it was the late Madame whom he saw before him, just as he had seen her for the last time before her death. He was so frightened that he awakened the Dauphiness.

" 'What has happened ?' she asked.

" 'I'll tell you tomorrow,' he replied.

"The Dauphin maintained throughout his life that this story was true."

· · · · ·

Another first-hand ghost story was told the Palatine by Comtesse de Furstenburg, after the latter had confessed to her friend that she could not bear to be alone because she was afraid of ghosts.

The matter-of-fact Palatine laughed.

---

* Henriette d'Angleterre, the sister of Charles II, who married "Monsieur" the Duke of Orleans, Louis XIV's brother. "Madame" became Monsieur's second wife.

"Like you, I should probably have thought it funny," said the Comtesse rather sharply, "if I had not *seen* a ghost." She then proceeded to say how, in the days of her youth, a certain Comte de Ruberta, whose people were trying to force him to marry a de Furstenburg, was in love with her, and in order to avoid a distasteful marriage the Count determined to go to the war. Before leaving Germany, he had his horoscope cast, which foretold that, if he saw active service, the first shot fired on the field of battle would be for him, and would kill him.

"He came to me," said the Countess, "and promised if he were killed, he would return to say good-bye. He also asked me if I should be frightened.

" 'I would much rather see you living, than as a ghost,' I replied.

" 'Come,' said he, 'give me your hand, and promise you will *not* be frightened.' And, as I thought he was only teasing me, I gave him my hand.

"Some time later, he joined his regiment. It was summer, and one night I could not sleep, so I got up, and, seated by a table, resting my head on my hands, I dropped into an uneasy doze.

"Suddenly I heard a noise in the corridor, as of someone walking in spurred boots. Who can be coming so early? and, turning my head, I saw a figure in brown, which disappeared immediately. It was impossible to distinguish the face, but its general appearance was that of Ruberta! I started to scream, and, as I did so, an invisible hand gave me a sharp blow!"

The first news that the Countess received from the front was the death of Ruberta, and, when she asked her informant what clothes he was wearing, she was told that he was clad in brown, just as she had seen him. It also transpired that he was killed at the very moment when his ghost appeared to the Countess.

.   .   .   .   .

Now for the third story.

It seems that a certain Princess de Ragotzi (another friend of Madame's) died suddenly after the extraction of a tooth, following the indiscriminate system of bleeding then in vogue ; and, after her death, the Princess' servants told Madame an extraordinary experience which their late mistress had had at Warsaw, previous to her arrival in Paris.

One night the Princess dreamt that a stranger came to speak to her, in a little room that she had never seen before, and offered her a glass of water, telling her to drink. As she was not thirsty, she refused.

"This will be your last drink," said the stranger, and at this moment the Princess awoke !

The dream made a great impression on her, and when she came to Paris, and her friends recommended the King's doctor as her medical man, Dr. Helvetius, who was Dutch, and a clever and charming individual, could not understand his patient's obvious distress when she first saw him. This, after all, had he but known it, was quite understandable, as Dr. Helvetius reproduced, feature by feature, the dream man the Princess had seen at Warsaw !

Then she laughed. "After all," said the Princess, "I shall not die, because this room is not in the least like the one I saw."

At that time it was customary for great ladies to live at aristocratic convents, and, as the convent at Chaillot was "in the fashion", Princess de Ragotzi decided to stay there for a time. On her arrival, when she was shown the bedroom prepared for her, she said very quietly : "I shall *never leave here alive : this is the room I saw*, and here I shall drink for the last time."

In the course of a few weeks the dream was fulfilled, when Dr. Helvetius handed the dying woman a glass of water !

In concluding the account of her friend's death, Madame, worried, and perplexed by something out of the ordinary, demands : "What is the reason of it ?" And with immense philosophy she answers her question by saying quite simply : "God knows."

So much for these scattered stories from Versailles, but there must be others, as King Ferdinand of Bulgaria once described the town as one of the most "haunted" in Europe.

A few years ago two serious-minded ladies published an account of a supernatural adventure which befell them at the Trianon, when yesterday was called back and they saw Time return. . . .

I often wonder whether the wraith of the Dubarri lingers in Louciennes; if so, she may not be alone, and perhaps the Duc de Brissac, that great lover and gallant gentleman (whose severed head is buried in some unknown spot at Louciennes), bears her company. But I hope Jeanne's "return" is not as the poor creature, wild with terror, who begged Monsieur le Bourreau to give her "one minute more"—but rather, as the charming exile from Court, happy in her enchanted retreat, the woman to whom de Brissac wrote, "I love you—and for life."

THE END